HER MAJESTY'S
OTHER CHILDREN

HER MAJESTY'S OTHER CHILDREN

SKETCHES OF RACISM FROM A NEOCOLONIAL AGE

LEWIS R. GORDON

WITH A FOREWORD BY

RENÉE T. WHITE

ROWMAN & LITTLEFIELD PULISHERS, INC.

Lanham • Boulder • New York • Oxford

ROWMAN & LITTLEFIELD PUBLISHERS, INC.

Published in the United States of America
by Rowman & Littlefield Publishers, Inc.
4720 Boston Way, Lanham, Maryland 20706

12 Hid's Copse Road
Cummor Hill, Oxford OX2 9JJ, England

British Library Cataloging in Publication Information Available

Library of Congress Cataloging in Publication Data

Gordon, Lewis R. (Lewis Ricardo), 1962—
    Her Majesty's other children : sketches of racism
from a neocolonial age / Lewis R. Gordon.
        p.   cm.
    Includes bibliographical references and index.
    ISBN 0-8476-8447-4 (cloth : alk. paper). — ISBN 0-8476-8448-2
(paper : alk. paper)
        1. Race relations.   2. Racism.   3. Blacks—Social conditions.
    4. Philosophy, Black.   5. Philosophy, African.   I. Title.
    HT1521.G57   1997
    305.8—dc21   97-7371
                                                                      CIP

ISBN 0–8476–8447–4 (cloth : alk. paper)
ISBN 0–8476–8448–2 (pbk. : alk. paper)

Printed in the United States of America

 ∞ ™ The paper used in this publication meets the minimum requirements of American
National Standard for Information Sciences—Permanence of Paper for Printed Library
Materials, ANSI Z39.48–1984.

Each generation must out of relative obscurity discover its mission, fulfill it, or betray it.

—*Frantz Fanon,* Les damnés de la terre

Some scholars have estimated that in the three centuries that the European slave trade flourished, the African continent lost one hundred million of its people. No one, to my knowledge, has ever paid reparations to the descendants of black men; indeed, they have not yet really acknowledged the fact of the crime against humanity which was the consequence of Africa. But then—history has not been concluded either, has it?

—*Lorraine Hansberry,* "Les Blancs" and Other Plays

. . . survival is not an academic skill.

—*Audre Lorde,* Sister Outsider

To

Sylvia and Gertrude,

Mathieu and Jennifer

––––––––––––––––

Contents

ACKNOWLEDGMENTS

In the words of Fats Waller, "One never knows. . . ." A few years ago, I only *thought* about this book. Through a chance meeting and discussion with Amiri Baraka, with whom I shared a commuter plane from West Lafayette to Chicago, I was encouraged to put this work together. I would like to thank him for that moment of encouragement. He didn't know whether his encouragement fell on deaf or interested ears. Contemplating the project, I later found myself in a kitchen in Santa Cruz, talking to Angela Davis and her mom, both of whom provided similar encouragement with the suggestion of my including some of the more personal essays in the volume. Thanks, Angela and Mrs. Davis. I also would like to thank my friends and colleagues, in alphabetical order, with whom I have shared passages from this work and from whom I have received suggestions on this and other work over the past two years, Lisa Anderson, Nancy Armstrong, Sandra Bartley, Linda Bell, Carmen Benoit, Janet Borgerson, Shawn Copeland, Wendell Dietrich, Anani Dzidzienyo, Nada Elia, Randy Friedman, David Theo Goldberg, Leonard Harris, Floyd Hayes III, Paget Henry, bell hooks, Joy Ann James, Carolyn Johnson, Peniel Joseph, Tommy Lott, William McBride, Cora Monroe, Patricia Morris, Monique Roelofs, Katherine Rudolph, Marilyn Nissim-Sabat, Gary Schwartz, Ato Sekyi-Otu, Renee Schroff, T. Denean Sharpley-Whiting, Gloria Soto, Robert Stone, Sumner Twiss, Elmo Terry-Morgan, Elizabeth Weed, Renée T. White, Sylvia Wynter, and Naomi Zack. Thanks also are due to Karen Baxter for permission to print a copy of Vusi Khumalo's striking untitled painting and thanks to Robert Dillworth for photographing it. To my students at Brown University, especially those in my seminars on poststructuralism in liberation thought, contemporary African philosophy, black existentialism, and blackness in the present age, thanks for the kindness and enthusiasm extended during my premier year at Brown. A special thanks in this regard is due to James Bryant, Renea Henry, Brian Locke, Nelson Maldonado, Angela Mooney, Annisah Umrani, and Sandra Vernet, with whom I have not only discussed portions of this work but also continued a conversation on race and popular culture. To Pam Connolly, Donna Mitchell, Sheila Grant, Kathleen Pappas, and Gail Tetreault, thanks for the clerical help and support. And to Vartan Gregorian, thanks for your support and encouragement over the past two years, and I wish you and Clare all the best on your new venture.

Some of these chapters are revised versions of previously published work, copyrights to which are mine. A version of chapter 1 appeared in *Soulfires: Young Black Men on Love and Violence*, edited by Daniel Wideman and Rohan Preston (New York: Penguin, 1996); chapter 3, in *Social Identities* 1, no. 2 (1995); chapter 4, in *Race/Sex: Their Sameness, Difference, and Interplay*, edited by Naomi Zack (New York and London: Routledge, 1997); chapter 9, in *Postcolonial African Philosophy*, edited by Emmanuel Eze (Oxford: Blackwell, 1997); chapter 7, in *The C.L.R. James Journal* 5, no. 1 (1997); 12, in *Political Affairs* 75, no. 2 (February 1996); and a portion of chapter 14 appeared in *differences* 8, no. 3 (1997). Nearly all were presented in the colloquia series and conferences of the following programs and organizations: Brown University's Afro-American Studies and Religious Studies Programs, the Pembroke Center's Seminar on Psychoanalysis and Gender, Yale University's Afro-American Studies Colloquia, York University's Antiracism Certificate Program, Queens University's Symposia on Philosophy and Racism, Purdue University's Women's Studies Program; the Radical Philosophy Association, the African Studies Association, the Society for Phenomenological and Existential Philosophy, the International Association of Philosophy and Literature, the American Association of Research in Education, the State University of New York at Binghamton's annual Philosophy and Interpretation Conference, the African American Studies and Research Center at Purdue University's annual African American Philosophy and Culture Conference, the American Political Science Association, and the Annual Conference of North American and Cuban Philosophers at the University of Havana. I thank those organizations for providing forums in which to present my work.

Finally, I would like to thank my mother Pat Garel, my grandmothers Sylvia Crosdale and Gertrude Stoddart, my mentor Maurice Natanson (who passed away in August 1996), my aunts Lola Blair and Ruth Ann Jarvis, my brothers Mark and Robert Evans, my cousin Tameka Solomon, my wife Lisa C. Gordon and our children Mathieu and Jennifer Gordon. All of my work ultimately springs from the love they have given me and the love I have for them.

FOREWORD

RENÉE T. WHITE

Some years ago I found myself sitting in many meetings on problems ranging from health care for young black women to network resources for
indigent AIDS populations. Strange activity for a graduate student. I was
not alone. In the midst of that struggle was a fellow graduate student who
it seemed was often too busy to write. His name was Lewis Gordon. We
spent many hours working together in the New Haven community back
then, co-organizing a cross-cultural educational program with an activist
by the name of Vicki Sheppard, developing links with Latin-American
solidarity groups, and forging alliances with some local churches. Gordon
also had a jazz quartet at the time: the Greg Hampton-Lewis Gordon Quartet. It was not unusual to find them performing benefits. There was always
much to do. Gordon quickly completed his doctorate, however, and announced that he was headed to the Midwest because he felt he would be
more useful there and he was excited about the possibilities it offered for a
young scholar.

We never lost contact. A stream of books followed. And now, he has
asked me to write a foreword for this book, a book of sketches he has been
working on for the past two years.

When I read these "sketches" (Gordon's word for essays that are at
times aesthetical and phenomenological), I wondered: Why a discussion of
racism and colonialism? Aren't we already aware of how race is used as a
tool of oppression within and among nations? Are you born black or
brown, or do you become black or brown? Isn't it interesting that one can
be accused of being too much of a particular race, or too little? That one
person can become the very embodiment of an entire race of people?

According to some social and cultural critics, we live in a postmodern
age. In this age, gender, race, and class matter in a way that has new significance. They are important and need to be studied and celebrated. We live
in an age of at least the avowed value of tolerance and acceptance. Individual perspective, experience, and difference matter. Racial identity is to be
celebrated. Racism is intolerable.

People are seen as falling very neatly on either side of this ideological
divide, this battle of the "-isms." Such a neat view of the world doesn't

begin to account for, or to be accountable to, the many men and women who find themselves "simply" negotiating the land mines. These land mines occasionally break through the social fabric—to be seen and named—only to fall back slowly underground, where they remain unseen by many, forgotten by some, but felt by the rest.

The sketches in this book attest to the political, ideological, philosophical, and often very personal ways such mine fields have been confronted. What these essays challenge us to do is to theorize about the essential lived-experience of antiblackness. While there is a place for celebrating difference, such celebrations do not necessarily look critically at the way antiblack racism operates, and how black and brown men, women, and children continue to confront the minefields.

Gordon asks us to face the minefields: What is it to be black or brown in a world of antiblack racism? In a world where one must first survive in order to have the luxury of existence? Humanity is fundamentally about the acknowledgment of one's right to exist. One can only have rights, and exercise true choice and freedom, when one is seen as human. Herein lies the irony. Black and Latin-American men and women are charged with responsibility for effecting change in their lives: in family, community, and nation. They are charged with the challenge of survival amid antiblackness. Such a charge denies the historicity—the very institutional nature—of the denial of black and Latino existence.

How can one be denied the right to exist? How can a nation, country, or people deny others this right?

As we know, this is a world of hierarchy. Race has become defined, and is manifested, as one mechanism of this hierarchy. We organize the world into social categories because these categories enable us to figure out what is expected of us, as well as what we expect of others. In this way, we are all made to function in social strata, to interact with each other on the basis of social meaning assigned to these social locations.

It has become standard to claim today that race is constructed, that race is a human creation, a social fiction, but one with deep societal meaning and resonance. Despite attempts to define and redefine race—consider the call to eliminate race as a social category, to be, in other words, color-blind—race continues to have value and purpose in our lives. Many claim that race only has meaning within a particular historical context, and thus racism is historically bound as well.

How, then, do we explain the persistence of racism and colonialism across the ages? Why is racism endemic to the social conditioning of black, indigenous, Asian, and Latin American peoples around the globe? How is it that racism manifests itself in each generation? How do and should those of us who live within a racist and neocolonialist reality survive?

In our social world are many racially defined and determined "oughts," "shoulds," and "woulds." We define our expectations in accordance with what we have learned to expect of each other. Although we all have a modicum of independence we can exercise on a situation-by-situation basis, we also know that, for good or bad, the rest of the world is watching to see whether we will tow the line or reject it.

As children we learn about the social world. We watch our elders for cues. They are our guides. As we venture out into the social world, we begin to understand the complicated nature of social engagement. Nothing is as simple as it once seemed to us. Our first engagement into the social world starts while we are very young, probably when we are preverbal. We see and are seen. We react to our physical, emotional, and social environments before we can even express what it is we react to.

The question, then, is this: How do we travel from those preverbal days to a world in which race and racism are clearly understood, articulated, and experienced? Essentially, as Gordon asks, at what point do people of color discover their invisibility?

Race does not exist, someone will argue. As a physiological, genetic, or genotypic category, it is a falsehood. Racism is a *social* construction, one developed within a particular sociohistorical context. Whether or not any of this is true, people still live in a world in which race is important. If we accept the constructionist argument as true, and we were to discover tomorrow the exact moment when race and racism were "invented," how important would this discovery be? If the biologically deterministic nature of the way race sometimes functions could be challenged on "traditional" scientific grounds in a way that challenges the assumptions of even the most trenchant racist, would that mean that race and racism would eventually cease to have meaning? Obviously, race operates within a very complicated web of social definitions, personal meanings, and political realities. So much of the world functions within this dynamic that the conceptualization of a race-free world may be neither possible nor useful. The conceptualization, though, of a racism-free existence is both appealing and constantly fought for. The problem is that the very institutional and structural nature of, for example, the United States and the United Kingdom is predicated on race and racism.

The very fact that as children we all understand not only how to distinguish what characteristics are associated with a particular racial group but also what race represents speaks to the effectiveness of our racial miseducation. Consider the well-known "Bluest Eye" experiment conducted by an elementary school teacher in the U.S. soon after Dr. Martin Luther King Jr. was assassinated. Her aim was to teach her students about the ease with which they can accept being made someone's social, political, and intellectual superior (or inferior).

She divided students in her class by eye color. Ones with brown eyes were supposed to be subservient to those with blue eyes for a few days, then she would reverse the power base for these students. Eye color determined entitlement. Within a few hours of the first day of the experiment, children were fighting each other, crying, and asking the teacher to stop the game.

Those who were empowered by virtue of their eye color literally transformed on camera. They were fearless in their aggression. Their "birthright" enabled them to behave as they wished without retribution or punishment. They knew the teacher would automatically support them, regardless of the circumstances. Other children, those *born with the wrong eye color*, had to develop ways to get through every moment of the day, knowing that in any one of those moments they could be under assault from either the teacher or the blue-eyed group. They had to find alternate means of survival. For them, authority counted as little more than agents of the status quo—agents of their group's prevalent oppression.

What would any child do in that situation? What do children of color do?

So then, where and how can black and brown people create and recreate themselves in their own nonracist images? How can they maintain humanity in the realm of anonymity and the ordinary? Consider this: If you are not defined as human, by virtue of your biological makeup, then being seen as part of humanity and the human condition just might be an exercise in futility. Imagine your birthright: invisibility, nonentity, nothingness, and absence. If faced with the systemic and systematic denial of the right to choose one's very existence, one is left in anguish.

Why discuss humanity when we are all obviously human and all agents of our own existence? This question assumes that humanity is a natural byproduct of human existence. However, in reality, humanity is a complicated matter indeed. As Gordon points out, the fact that people of color exist is regarded by the racist as justification for excluding them from humanity. If one is one too many, then what is there to prevent the negation of the existence of millions?

If nothing else, talking about race is filled with contradiction and paradox. Let us return to one of the many important questions addressed by this book: If race is problematic as a social category, then why not eliminate its use? Once this is done (if, in fact, it were possible) what happens next?

Since race exists in a multifaceted web of meaning, what this question posits is eliminating the definition of race without remembering that the reality of racism can outlive the definition and manifestation of race, that racism functions within and even beyond the sociohistorical moment. Opting to be colorblind is not the same as deciding to reject the institution of racism. Race by itself is not the problem. The use of race within a racist context is the issue at hand. Racism is used as a tool that bifurcates society into good and bad, healthy and unhealthy, included and excluded. If one can choose to operate in racist, antiblack ways, can one also choose to reject racism?

Options, opportunity, and choice are factors of sociality that exist within socially proscribed parameters. Being an actor, an agent (or whatever other terminology you prefer) implies something very basic. Agency is shaped within a particular social context. What one could do and what one is able to do are very different issues. Colonialism, oppression, and antiblack racism create the context in which choice is either available or not. Most of us would choose to be free, but many of us don't have options that make our choices relevant. The only way to be actively antiracist is to be actively opposed to the structures of society in which racism flourishes.

We are faced with the ultimate question: What is this process of rejection and subsequent social and political transformation? On a basic, but not simple, level, survival is fundamentally revolutionary. It flies in the face of all social expectations regarding race. Racism should lead to the failure of people: it should lead, in a sense, to their destruction. Sometimes this may be physical destruction, but often it is emotional, psychological, and economic. Inhumanity is violent. Poverty is destructive. Illiteracy is destructive. Denial is destructive. Forgetting the past is destructive.

How does one live in a world with such regular destruction? Love, forgiveness, trust, and faith have been used as tools of survival, but how do they connect to revolutionary change in our society? People have engaged in protest, been angry, and been (non)violent. Is this revolution? People have created and maintained families, worked, lived in communities, and by so doing recognized their right to be. Is this the first revolutionary step?

It is imperative that scholarship begins to confront racism in its mundane, ordinary embodiment. That scholarship must be receptive to the lives of many men and women who do the extraordinary every day and are critical of the deceptively ordinary.

Renée T. White
Hartford, Connecticut
March 1997

INTRODUCTION:

HER MAJESTY'S OTHER CHILDREN

I remember, as a child, looking at a penny on which stood the staunch profile of Queen Victoria of England. She was indeed an ugly, imposing figure. Her profiled face was so stern that it seemed to have carved itself into the coin. It is odd how both recent and past that experience was. Since I was about three years of age, it must have been about 1965. The island of Jamaica was then "independent" for a total of three years. My second brother, Mark, was due to be born. The house in which I and my mother lived was more of a commune, with my maternal great-grandmother and great-grandfather serving as its matriarch and patriarch. The rest of the house consisted of my great-grandparents' many daughters and their children.

My great-grandmother, "Granny Bea," as I remember her, was always very busy with the business of maintaining order in the community. She was so busy that I have no memory of her sleeping. My great-grandfather, Uriah Ewan, who spent many hours sitting on the veranda, was blind by that time. I used to sit on his lap and pray for him to regain his sight. He seemed to like me a great deal. I amused him. He had a walking stick, which helped him around. His trembling eyelids, darkest brown skin, and gentle smiles are among the many fond memories that have left a permanent impression on me.

The extent to which gentleness shines through the heart of some children depends on the spiritual resources offered across generations. I didn't receive much by way of material things from my great-grandparents (modest as their income was). But the spiritual sustenance I received was always rich.

Today, I find myself thinking back to those times as I try to recollect some experiences that led to the composition of this book. The work is dedicated to my grandmothers and my son and daughter. For it is through these sets of generations that my wife and I have found ourselves, over the past couple of years, thinking about the generations that preceded them and those who we hope will come into being and succeed them. My grandmothers were born in colonial times. They were born in an age in which their perspectives were contextualized by what Enrique Dussel calls "the underside of modernity," the context by which the modern, for them, was marked by the defining, military moment of Christopher Columbus' setting foot on Caribbean shores.[1] European modernity's self-reflection prefers to look at that moment as an age of exploration, as an age of courage, fortitude, and faith. Yet for those whom they met, it was an age marked by the prophetic image of Bible and sword from whose reflection against the sun portended a time of suffering, disease, and death. My grandmothers managed to see independence day on their island and the subsequent bitter dependence that became more evident with each passing day.[2] Their great-grandchildren were born in a neocolonial age in the nation that stands as the heart of a new world and "new world order" of military and multinational-corporate assaults on many other nations' sovereignty and independence. It is no accident that another age of exploration was set afoot by two competing empires in the 1960s. "One small step for. . . ." Our age seeks legitimacy in repetition. Old exploration and new exploration carry the ideological burdens of their times: a flag on the moon hardly stood as a cooperation of nations as much as the supremacy of one. "One giant step for mankind" required, as we find in science fiction fantasies, that the foot that makes that step be an Anglo-American one. Recall that the black foot that first stepped on the North Pole remains a forgotten and therefore invisible one. The print made by that foot seemed untranslatable into man*kind*.[3]

My paternal grandmother, Ms. Gertrude Stoddart, is a feisty Chinese Jamaican. Tall, beautiful, and proud, she raised six boys and one girl, suffered from betrayal and abandonment throughout her life, and managed to show her children, their children, and their children's children much love, albeit most of the time from a great geographical distance. Ms. Sylvia Crosdale, alias Sylvia Solomon, alias Sylvia Ewan (her maiden name), is the beautiful daughter of that powerful matriarch, Beatrice Ewan or "Granny Bea." The death of my grandfather, Edgar Solomon, led to a series of events that brought Sylvia to the United States, where she met a man whose last name she now bears. "Mama," as her children, grandchildren, and great-grandchildren now call her, is a spiritual lady. Like her mother, she has offered me and my children that gift that, as we say, money cannot buy.

So I find myself now thinking about my grandmothers and their mothers as I write this introduction to a book of philosophical sketches or essays from a neocolonial age. I wrote this book in an aytpical way. I simply responded to concerns I had along its themes over the past two years. The queries emerged along a neocolonial-postcolonial divide. An impetus to this project was the observation that although we live in neocolonial times, many of our most influential scholars who theorize about conditions of colonization and domination are reluctant to admit it. In the wake of decolonization, it is far more comforting to advance our age as "postcolonial," although power relations worldwide continue to support colonial realities. In the world that my grandmothers will be saying goodbye to and their great-grandchildren have greeted, there is bewilderment as such forces of domination and oppression do more than preserve themselves. They prosper.

I recall answering a caller during an interview on a radio program entitled *Focus 580* in Champaign-Urbana, IL. The year was 1995. The caller wanted to know why the U.S. government prefers to spend money on maintaining the living conditions of wealthy Europeans (and certain wealthy Middle Easterners) instead of indigent Americans, particularly Native, African, and Latin Americans. I asked the caller to consider the following: In the interest of making a little bit more profit, large multinational corporations sometimes decide to "downsize." What that means is that employees will be fired for the sake of an immediate increase in profits. Now, since our world is a transnational economic world—a world, that is, in which a decision made in Tokyo, London, Berlin, or New York City can affect people who live in Calcutta, Nairobi, or Champaign-Urbana—we may need to ask ourselves who a local mayor, senator, governor, or president should consult when such decisions are made. It used to be that sovereignty—authority, legitimacy, power—was in the hands of sacred symbols and then governmental ones.[4] But today, even priests, kings, presidents, legislators, and judiciaries are under market influence. All are asked, in the now popular adage, to "show us the money." Given such a circumstance, where can accountability lie? For if one were to contact multinational corporations and similar market forces, one will find that they are hardly persons of flesh and blood.

So where do we go?

In my first book, *Bad Faith and Antiblack Racism*, I made two claims that particularly riled some readers.[5] The first was that we need to deal with the flesh-and-blood embodiments of our institutions in their historic moments, and those are the people who present themselves as though they live through those institutions instead of embodying them. In our age, heavily influenced by systems and poststructural analyses, the prevailing approach to institutions is to treat them as autonomous sites of activity. Instead of social agents, the prevailing approach is to focus on social agencies. Power, under such a scheme, is an anonymous resident. Yet, although the nation-state may function as if power were anonymous, the fact remains that the influences of multicorporate interests are still administered through state apparatuses, and those state apparatuses have grown to the point of representing a bureaucracy whose distance from people of political sentiments on both the left and the right has led to widespread bewilderment and hostility regarding whom it supposedly serves. In search of the "who" behind these institutions, right-wing militia voice anger against governmental resources for the colored poor, whose role in this drama is often reduced to mere instruments of a great conspiracy. Then there are theorists on the left who have even gone so far as to argue that the governmental bureaucracy *is* a socialist bureaucracy, albeit so on behalf of the wealthy. North American and European "bail-outs" of large lending institutions and other corporate entities, followed by restructuring of their economies to facilitate global profit for those institutions, hardly stand, however, as contradictions to that thesis.[6] Thus, my answer to the caller had a second part: that in spite of government officials' being influenced by decisions that emerged outside their borders, they are nevertheless responsible for the resources they issue as a response to such circumstances. It is still up to the nation-state to play its role in the lives of its citizens and residents in far more responsible ways. The struggle here is one of developing political responses to political problems. In my home city, New York, for instance, there has been a direct correlation between the growing number of students of color in the City University of New York and the full-scale assault on that institution by the state, the municipal government, and even media resources such as the *New York Times*. The same correlation relates to public hospitals and other social services. These are politically effected problems whose ideological force depends on the population's lack of faith in political solutions to those problems. The caller's intimation of racism as an influence on policy decisions requires little effort to substantiate in these cases, and it is the racist dimension of their assault that encourages the politically nihilistic attitude that these problems cannot be resolved since the underlying sentiment on racial matters is that they, too, cannot be resolved.

Recognition of racism as an influence on policy leads to my controversial second claim: racism is a white–black phenomenon with enough semiotic flexibility to mask itself as living "beyond" such a dichotomy. It is fashionable today to speak of racism beyond its black-white manifestation in a way that racializes nearly every identity formation. Today, the term "ethnicity" has lost nearly all its meaning. My argument, however, was that both white and black are extremes that are flexibly occupied by logics of distance and nearness. One is black the extent to which one is most distant from white. And one is white the extent to which one is most distant from black. What this means, then, is that if we take any other "racial formation," we will find that its members' identity is a function of its distance or nearness to the two extremes, which means, in the end, that if the extremes are eliminated, new extremes will emerge. Every "in between" is a whiteness or blackness waiting to emerge. A consequence of these two phenomena of hidden institutional responsibility and shameful dichotomous hierarchy is a whole world premised upon perverse, anonymous, invisible, below-otherness. That world is a consequence of what was openly called "imperialism" in another age, but these days has learned to conceal itself and present itself as many other things. It has learned to conceal itself so well, in fact, that some theorists have felt compelled, almost as a knee-jerk reaction, to ascribe the prefix "post" to nearly every dimension of contemporary human life, signaling and wishfully relegating most of such realities (if we can any longer call them "realities") to the past. Yet there are certain conditions that persist, and they have even intensified. Among them is the lived reality of the people who actually occupy these spaces designated anonymous, invisible, Other, and even below-Other.[7] It is they to whom I refer in the present work as Her Majesty's other children.

For such children, who are actually subordinated in the present age in such a way that their ages do not matter, the prefix "neo" is persistently appropriate in the ongoing folly of labeling. For such children, there are *neohunger*, *neoexploitation*, *neomortality*, *neoviolence*, *neoinvisibility*, and *neoetcetera*, all of which are bitterly familiar manifestations of supposedly much older régimes.

For such children, there is a closing gap between each generation that paradoxically creates a greater chasm between generations. For as the negative conditions faced by the younger become no different than the older, the older generation begins to lose ground as a source of spiritual strength. How can they pass a baton of hope to their children when they have not yet had the opportunity to seize their own?

I have found, as I get older, that the best gift my grandmothers and my great-grandparents nurtured in me is a profound love for elderly people, for the (often) wise, in spite of Ralph Ellison's and our contemporary youth's suspicion against the aged. In *Invisible Man*, Ellison's alienated protagonist found himself in a struggle against elderly generations who commanded respect in spite of their cowardice and pettiness. Yet his protagonist was such that, like a recent alienated generation who once trusted no one over thirty, he knew that he would one day have some "pearl of wisdom" to offer another generation. It is so tough to live as a person of color in this world that one can always see some wisdom in a black person who has achieved old age.

Whether it be Queen Isabella, Queen Victoria, or the White House and Capitol Hill, Her Majesty has never had concern for children like my grandmothers' children. Think here as well of the contradiction between Lynden B. Johnson's Great Society and the Vietnam War. There have been times, mostly for convenience's sake—like the many wars or the many projects that demanded manual labor or the many bits of ingenuity to steal—when some claim is made to a broader human family. At those times, Her Majesty's other children are urged to come in through the back door, show what is left in their pockets, pick up a few scraps brushed from the dining room table, and be grateful and forgetting.

The aims of this book are to articulate philosophical contradictions and challenges raised by recent philosophical treatments of race, racism, and intellectualism and to pose some critical amendations, especially by way of black aesthetics, against some of those contradictions. This project can be characterized as a work in Africana philosophy. Africana philosophy pertains to the thought that has emerged from the culturally and linguistically rich African diaspora. In the words of Lucius T. Outlaw, Africana philosophy is

> a "gathering" notion under which to situate the articulations (writings, speeches, etc.), and traditions of Africans and peoples of African descent collectively, as well as the subdiscipline- or field-forming, tradition-defining or tradition-organizing reconstructing efforts, which are (to be) regarded as philosophy. Use of the qualifier "Africana" is consistent with the practice of grouping and identifying intellectual traditions and practices by the national, geographic, cultural, racial, and/or ethnic name for the persons who initiated and were or are the primary practitioners—and/or are the subjects and objects—of the practices and traditions in question (e.g., "American," "British," "French," "German," or "Continental" philosophy). However, "Africana philosophy" is meant to include, as well, the work of those persons who are neither African nor of African descent but who recognize the legitimacy and importance of the issues and endeavors that constitute the philosophizing of persons African or African-descended and who contribute to discussions of their efforts, persons whose work justifies their being called "Africanist."[8]

Africana philosophy addresses problems across a wide range of philosophical and social issues. In part I, the most obvious of social territories are race and racism. There, Her Majesty's other children's theorists find themselves in a heated battle over their racial identity, their antiracial identity, and the plethora of alternatives available with which to theorize about those identities themselves. The most influential figure in part I, and most of the volume, is Frantz Fanon, primarily because he is the most influential theorist on colonialism, neocolonialism, and postcolonialism in the second half of the twentieth century. The reader may wonder why I didn't place my discussion of Fanon in part II, "The Intellectuals." The reason is because his insights are such that they lay some important foundations for analyzing intersections of philosophy and racism. Moreover, his influence on my thought has been such that he has been a presence in nearly all of my published work. To place him under the intellectuals would be redundant here. I then move on to other theorists and their struggle to transcend idealism and inaction in the present age. The journey comes to an end in part III, where the democratic and aesthetic assumptions behind criticizing the exclusion of children are considered through heartbeats that beckon toward the soul of another mother and father, a mother and father who call to us these days through those dynamics that move our soul. For theorists like Sylvia Wynter, this beckoning voice emerges from what she calls "liminality," epistemic boundaries in which the connections between the array of calamaties—political and spiritual—that besiege us emerge over a struggle for the meaning of life. She writes:

> Once we identify the connection and correlations between the contemporary state of Africa and the United States' Black jobless inner cities and their correlated prison system, we can link them to the state of the Third World and its large-scale shanty-town/favela jobless *archipelagoes*. . . . Any strategy to deimmobilize Africa will, therefore, necessarily entail a move, beyond our present epistemological order. Specifically, beyond its foundational premise that the truth of the human lies in its biogenicity as a natural organism rather than in the culture-systemic and, therefore, meta-organic processes by which it auto-institutes itself as specific modes of subjectivity and sociality and, therefore, as specific "forms of life."[9]

The struggle is, indeed, for "forms of life." It is for no less than the self-reflection of the human species in the *Geist* War, the war of the spirit, the war over who constitutes who "we" are and who "we" shall be. Theorists have a special place here. These days, however, the question of the theorist usually occasions accusations of privilege; as a consequence the term "privilege" has gained some currency in critical political discourse. It is a term I have never liked. Its ascent parallels the descent of the term "right." There *are* privileged people in the world, truly. But that is because they have things to which they have no right, simply opportunity. As for the rest of the world, and especially Her Majesty's other children, there is no time for such rubbish. They know what they have a right to.

In "Cumbia & Jazz Fusion," Charles Mingus announced that Mama's little baby doesn't like shortenin' bread. He provides a list of the things that Mama's little baby likes that includes caviar, Mercedes-Benz, education, African gold mines, and all the "fine things in life."[10] They have a right to it all. Not the scraps. No. But the table. The house. The supermarkets. The jobs. The value of their labor. The books. The media resources.

The gods . . .

Humanity . . .

The doors have to be watched while the borders are denied. The servants must now be embraced while they sleep outdoors. Dream, servants, the world now beckons, dream that you are awake.

Notes

1. See Enrique Dussel, *The Underside of Modernity: Apel, Ricoeur, Rorty, Taylor; and the Philosophy of Liberation*, trans. Eduardo Mendieta (Atlantic Highlands, NJ: Humanities Press, 1996).

2. For discussion of this bitter dependence in Jamaica, see Claremont Kirton, *Jamaica: Debt and Poverty*, with additional material by James Ferguson (Oxford: Oxfam, 1992).

3. I return to this problem in chapter 2 and chapter 7, where the universality of the underside is hidden by the pretense of its particularity. We see the phenomenon well in Hegel's reflections on historical universality.

4. I leave aside here the complicated issue of the viability of sovereignty as a guiding principle of contemporary political organizing. Locked in modern liberal paradigms though it may be, the insult of hegemony is that *de jure* sovereignty in the face of a *de facto* lack of sovereignty is the rule in many "developing" nations. The concept of sovereignty—"legitimate" rule—is found often to be idealistic where there is no power to effect that legitimacy. In modern political thought, the concept has been struggled over by Thomas Hobbes, John Locke, and Jean-Jacques Rousseau, and criticisms of legitimacy without power undergirds the work of Karl Marx, Max Weber, Antonio Gramsci, Hannah Arendt, and Enrique Dussel, all of whose contributions to this concept will emerge in the course of this volume.

5. Lewis R. Gordon, *Bad Faith and Antiblack Racism* (Atlantic Highlands, NJ: Humanities Press, 1995).

6. See, for instance, Donald Hodges, "Post-Marxist Political Economy," presented at the Eastern Division meeting of the American Philosophical Association in Atlanta, Georgia (December 28, 1996). Hodges argues that we in fact live in socialist times—which he defines as bureaucratic control of the economy—and we need now to start the project toward communism. His post-Marxism then is perhaps more rigorously Marxist. He is against the more humanistic Marx, however. There he sees a diversion. Communism requires the more "scientific," later Marx. In the course of our discussion of Hodges paper, it became clear, also, that Hodges prefers ascetic ethics instead of humanistic ones. It was clear that Hodges position was in the camp of what existentialists call *the spirit of seriousness*, where values are treated as material conditions of the world. His antihumanism is clearly in this camp. But the irony is that *for Hodges*, that is hardly a criticism. It is a compliment.

7. The skeptic need simply consult the Oxfam series *Oxfam Country Profiles* and the array of recent studies on the increasing number of poor people in the midst of increased wealth for the few. For a discussion of the U.S. situation, see Herbert J. Gans's *The War Against the Poor: The Underclass and Antipoverty Policy* (New York: Basic Books, 1995).

8. Lucius T. Outlaw, *On Race and Philosophy* (New York and London: Routledge, 1996), p. 76. Revised reprint of Outlaw's article, "Africana Philosophy," *Philosophical Forum* 24, nos. 1–3 (1992–1993), with relevant citation appearing on p. 64. The form of racism I will focus on in this volume is *antiblack racism*. My reason is that the category of *the black* is broader in scope than the category Africana. And as we progress, it will become clear that by *black* I do not simply mean *Negro*. I mean, instead, the negative pole of Western (and often Asian) binary opposition, where the positive and highest pole has been designated *white* for over a millennium. But since Africana philosophy constantly raises the question of blackness, that distinction will not be of great consequence here. For discussion, see Tommy L. Lott's "Du Bois on the Invention of Race," *Philosophical Forum* 24, nos. 1–3 (1992–93): 166–87, and see *Bad Faith and Antiblack Racism*, introduction and part III.

9. Sylvia Wynter, "Is 'Development' a Purely Empirical Concept or also Teleological?" A Perspective from 'We the Underdeveloped,' " in *Prospects for Recovery and Sustainable Development in Africa*, ed. by Aguibou Y. Yansané (Westport, CT, and London: Greenwood Press, 1996), p. 301.

10. See *The Charles Mingus Anthology* (Santa Monica: Atlantic Records and Rhino Records, Inc., 1993).

Part I

Philosophy, Race, and Racism in a Neocolonial World

Chapter One

Context: Ruminations on Violence and Anonymity

"We would like an essay on black men on love and violence," declared the editor.

I was spending much of my time on philosophical questions of anonymity and violence. That project brought me to the work of Frantz Fanon, the philosopher, psychiatrist, and revolutionary from the island of Martinique.

Fanon was a humanist who argued that most basic human problems lay at the heart of our understanding of the human being and humanity. For him, violence is a form of dehumanization; but worse, our efforts to eliminate it, to forge a human place, often lead to a swirl of continued violence. This is because inhumanity, dehumanization, is a tragic affair. It is the human being thrown into the absurdity of action and reaction, out of which emerges, it seems, almost no chance of ever again having clean hands.

Growing up in a tragic world is full of cruel reality. It marks the core of oppression. I think Fanon is right when he says, in *Les damnés de la terre*, that oppression forces upon us constantly the question, "In reality, who am I?"[1] Or worse: "What am I?" For in an oppressive environment, one slips into a sea of absurd invisibility. One patters through the world like mice when the lights are turned on, leaving, that is, only droppings behind. Occasionally, there is identification—"Look! *Un Nègre!*"—although such occasions are loaded with a rancid odor of sadism. For there are many ways to look without seeing, and for those caught in the web of oppression, not being seen is so familiar that it, too, ceases to function as a seen circumstance. Invisibility loses its extraordinary dimensions.

I was spending much time on the ordinary. Ordinary existence is an immersion in the bosom of anonymity. Anonymity literally means to be nameless. The context of anonymity with which I am here concerned is an antiblack society. The result in such a society is a violent namelessness committed against blacks whose familiarity is so familiar that it transforms the protective dynamics of anonymity itself. Yet anonymity is not in itself the cause of this violence. Anonymity by itself doesn't *cause* anything.

In a humane world, anonymity is a blessing that offers human possibility and understanding. For as we go about our business in the world, we often stop here and there and take in a moment's glimpse of other human beings. As we look at them, we keep ourselves aware of the limitations of such encounters. I can see that the fellow across the way is a custodial worker, a father with his children, an African American, a baseball enthusiast, as he discusses baseball cards with his children. He is all these descriptions that situate him in various types of human being, but above all, he is someone I do not know. To know him requires effort on my part, which reminds me of his humanness as a limitation of my presumptions.

An antiblack racist would see our African American differently. He is, after all, a black man. For an antiblack racist, to see a black *as black* is to see enough. He requires nothing more. All else will follow like effect to cause in the mechanistic world. What's more, there is the endorsement of an array of institutions and prevailing ideologies to discourage many efforts at human contact. A crushing weight of predetermined identification grows to the point of limiting options in an antiblack world. This limitation un-leashes itself with bitter, sadistic irony. For after all, in the midst of all this, there is the prevailing, existential reality:

"Well, you always have a choice. . . ."

Choice. It teases, caresses, punishes, intoxicates the oppressed individual. For he knows that no matter how many limited options are thrown at him, he faces the bitter reality of always having to choose how he lives his op-tions. Does he live them as defeat or occasion through which to assert his freedom?

For my part, I've always tried my best to refuse to surrender. There are, however, times at which I wonder. . . .

"Bad faith" is a term that lurks in the philosophical undercurrents here. It is a lie to oneself that involves the effort to escape one's freedom, choice, and responsibility. Can I choose not to choose? As I face all those limited options thrown at me, those limitations that tell me each day what I cannot be, what my son cannot be, what my daughter cannot be, my brothers, my sister, my aunts, my mother, what members of the community of blackness of which I am but a fragment cannot do, as I face all these, don't I, in trying to make sense of it all, find myself constantly facing the questions:

"Who am I? . . . *What* am I?"

I had received a brutal welcome to the United States in 1971, at age nine.

"Don't you know you're a nigger?"

"A nigger." Sounded like the Jamaican word *neeyga*, which meant those other, dirty, lower-class types of Jamaicans—Jamaicans who were always conspicuously the darkest. "What's a nigger?" I asked.

Eyebrows rose as smirks permeated the classroom. I asked around, until one boy, black like me, explained. It is a bad way of saying black person. So I returned to my seat.

"So, what's up, nigger?" repeated the little white boy who sat next to me.

My fingers scratched through his skin when I grabbed his neck.

I beat him twice that day. The first was then, the second was after school.

Everyone was shocked to see a white boy running from a black one, especially into an Italian neighborhood in the Bronx.

My teacher rebuked me. "I didn't expect this from you," she said.

I didn't expect otherwise.

Still, neither "neeyga" nor "nigger" became standard speech in that classroom again. But outside, it was everywhere, assailing me from every direction from across the full spectrum of color. Not only did everyone become "niggers," but it seemed also that everyone believed that *others* were "niggers."

So later that year, I received another surprise.

"Get out of the park, you fucking Puerto Rican!"

I looked around and saw black and white boys, with sticks and pipes in their hands. Perhaps I could have told them I wasn't a Puerto Rican. I could have told them lots of things. I could have run. But at that point I thought I had had enough. Against whom was this encounter? The "Puerto Rican Nigger"?

I didn't realize it then, but I had decided at that moment to *be*, for that moment, a Puerto Rican because "they"—those anonymous, hating "they," since to this day I don't know who those boys were, which in a way is how all oppressive souls continue to be, who "they" are and how they remain—yes, those they whose anonymous, hating consciousness is saturated with American false idealities promising them, at the end of all the misery and suffering, a promised land of the "we," for them I shall be whoever *they* hated. Throughout the years, I've made sure never to apologize for their perception of me, since ultimately that was their sickness, not mine. So, I was blackest when they hated my blackness; Jewish when they hated my Jewish ancestry; Jamaican when they were troubled by my accent; a question mark when they were curious about my sexual orientation; whatever they were attempting to evade through making me what they wanted to see, hear, or smell, I refused to indulge through an exit into convenient identity.

But such a battle is tiring, is it not?

It became apparent that, as I looked around me at all the hostility, I needed to rest. Somewhere out there, there must be space for everyday existence, a place simply for living.

Therein is the dream, is it not?

I remember lying on a park bench on a hot summer's day, closing my eyes, and simply taking a moment to sleep under the warmth of the caressing sun. I woke from the pain of wet heat burning my legs as tar burned its way through my skin, and I looked over at the fleeing, laughing "they."

"They" come around when you least expect them. "Come on!" I sometimes hear. "Why are you people so sensitive?"

I remember being an adolescent of thirteen standing at the edge of my school door. I was with three friends. We stared at the white members of the community who gathered at the edge of the school. They were there to deal with our "black presence." They were about three blocks' full. Their ages ranged from ours to the elderly. Some had bats; others, chains; some, metal paddles; others, pipes; all had hatred in their eyes. A product of busing and having missed the announcement of an early departure, we found ourselves alone.

Yeah, many of us are very sensitive people.

"Ricky, please call. *C* has left us." Ricky, my childhood name. It was as if hearing that name, my name, was a way of calling me back. The message on the answering machine was gray, as all things appear when steeped partially in reality and the unreal.

My wife looked at me, her eyes swelling.

"No," I said. "He must have moved out."

C was my best friend of fifteen years. We met as early adolescents wrapped in a shared world of jazz and funk. We played music together under the most arduous of conditions, and we embraced each other's joys and sorrows. Eventually, we formed a close knit of five friends: a bassist, a clarinetist, a saxophonist, a trombonist, and a drummer. *C* played the bass. He was a somber soul with whom I shared everything. But over the years, his life slipped into a violent storm of inner turmoil. He saw a woman for a while who reminded him of his mother. That relationship devolved into physical abuse. We parted company with a great deal of pain, with my urging him to seek psychiatric help, with his being disgusted at my nerve. Eventually, he and that love parted after having a child, and he found himself wrought with shame and a desire to "fix" himself. He was never going to be abusive again. He met a woman to whom he gave and gave and gave until it killed him.

I approached the message on the answering machine with denial. "No, you know how he is. He must have just broken up with his recent flame. He must have . . . he must have . . . he must have. . . ."

The phone rang. "He's dead. He died yesterday from a bullet wound to the heart."

So began one of my worst years' encounters with violence and death. I received the news of my friend's death after coming from a park in which I and some men, Brothers Getting Busy, spent the day cleaning up for a community rally, the purpose of which was to retrieve the park from the neighborhood crack dealers and give it back to the children who used to play there. The year was 1991.

I had first refused to deliver the eulogy for my friend. I took his death harder than any death I had ever experienced. The circumstance was surreal; there he was, stiff as dried wood, his face so swollen and full of anger. Worst of all was the moment of placing his coffin into the ground: There, in the earth, was a line of other coffins. In the midst of all that death, my friend, with all his unique talents—a would-have-been architect, a would-have-been-famous bassist, a would-have-been who knows what else—was laid to rest as a dull, blank, anonymous nothing. Beneath the earth, sealed in their coffins, the dead all reduced to the same, all ripped out of the drama of life; it became clear to me why tombstones are so important—they are cries out of the nothingness, cries to be cherished in the heart, cries to be remembered.

As the tears flowed down my face in that August heat, a friend of the family walked up to me and said the most asinine words, revealing the degree to which the understanding of unique contact with other human beings is being swallowed into a mire of a society so lost that it is practically socially brain-dead:

"Don't worry. You will have other friends."

I found myself sitting three years after my friend's death with the question: What was *I* to say on violence? At the time of his death, I was a graduate student in New Haven, CT. I was studying philosophy. I had gone there to delve more deeply into the philosophical dynamics of human evasion. Today, I find human evasion to be such a mundane feature of our world that the possibility of its being an extraordinary feature of human reality seems also an extraordinary thought.

I now stand as a black man of thirty-five years. As I walk through the world, I find myself trying to suppress the gnawing sense of being an existential anomaly advancing further and further across enemy lines.

"Why are you still here?" the voice asks.

To have survived this far!

Many others have fallen along the way. A friend's older brother—a tall, dark, handsome fellow who loved to play basketball comes to mind. He always gave a kind hello in the afternoons as he passed our building with the regularity of the famous philosopher whose afternoon stroll was a means of villagers' setting their watches. One day he didn't appear. Stabbed in the chest. Lost into the bleak nothingness that has become obscenely familiar.

The bodies are mounting up. Our clarinetist, my friend *Sn*. Beautiful *Sn*, whose smiles were so bright and full of cheer that we used to call him "Jaws."

"Did you hear about *Sn*? He's gone. AIDS."

"We're dying," the trombonist, Richard, declared. He and the saxophonist jumped ship to The Netherlands. Now, the thought gnaws . . . two of the five haven't reached thirty . . . who will reach forty? . . .

Pn', the drummer who sold me my first set of Zildjian cymbals; saw him on *Soul Train*. AIDS. Gone.

Community activist. Came up to Yale to study for his ministry. Dropped out and became a dreadlocked community preacher. Was to show up for a Brothers Getting Busy rally. Heart attack while watching television the previous day. Gone.

A brother went nuts the next week. Shot his wife in the face and then himself. Craziness.

Then there was *Sz*, my comrade in arms in the streets of New Haven. The hours he spent on the streets, in the prisons—many hours, for the sake of what? One day he showed me. He lifted his shirt.

"See this," he said, pointing at his stomach that bore horrible, violent scars and the absence of a great deal of flesh. "This is from my gang days. I crossed enemy territory. They caught me and tied me to the bottom of a car. Then they drove down the street as fast as they could. Good thing I was wearing a thick coat. I felt it peel away until my skin began to go. They stopped the car and set it into reverse. But they got stuck. I hollered and hollered so loud that finally some people came out. Fortunately, the gang got out of the car and ran. The people who came to help me picked my insides up off the street and got me to the hospital. . . ."

The phone rang on a Sunday morning that was so gray it felt like twilight.

"Did you hear about *Sz*? . . ."

A drunk white lawyer ran into *Sz*'s van on the highway. The engine of the car broke through the front and crushed his wife. *Sz* and his wife had been together since they were twelve years old. They had five children, all boys, and another on the way. Their eldest was twenty.

Sz suffered an understandable deterioration from that point onward. I would visit him and the boys and talk with him, as his face trembled with pain and sorrow. We became family in a way, until I left New Haven. *Sz* was left always on the edge. I think his family was prepared for *his* death, but not his wife's. There isn't much by way of resources and moral support for widowers, particularly black ones. He was feared, he was pitied, he was supposed to be able to work and bring in all the resources, as though there were a world of great, paternal, patriarchical opportunities available to black family men. Had he died, there was a community on the alert with a great deal of practice on how to deal with a widow and her children, but a man who also suffered from the accident—"No one stopped as I flagged for help. I had to ask the white man who knocked us off the road to flag down help. That's when someone stopped," he had told me—such a man, plagued by violent intrusions into his skull, from operations after operations. . . .

Recent news. "Did you hear about *Sz*? The papers said he stabbed a man to death who shouted insults at him while waiting to use a phone at a public booth. . . ."

Yeah, I am studying Frantz Fanon quite a bit of late. Fanon was a firm believer in social illness. In his resignation letter from the colonial hospital in which he was the directing physician, he declared that the very notion of well-adjusted human beings under oppressive conditions amounts to the accomplishment of happy slaves. He considered that an obscenity. I agree.

We live in a sick society. I have always known this, as we theoreticians say, "theoretically." After having had the opportunity to travel a bit and gain a different grounding of the reality of our disease, I've found too many confirmations of my judgment. Perhaps the most vivid for me was returning from my first trip to Cuba. I was invited to the University of Havana to present my work on Fanon and to learn about the Cuban dimension of Caribbean philosophy. There, I saw many things that have left a lasting mark on me. Perhaps the most significant was the scarcity of one kind of poverty there, poverty of the human spirit, though as is all too well known, spirits can be broken.

There was constant talk about the children there, about the importance of leaving the legacy of a human project for them, a legacy that they hope will fortify them against the assault of the liberty without freedom that is promised them when the U.S. affirms its hegemony *within* the island again. Whatever one thinks of the Cuban people—the people of that island whose racial constitution the U.S. Congress debated at the turn of the century, that Cuba whose division into a white and a black side, as in Haiti and the Dominican Republic in San Domingo, was proposed by the U.S. Congress then, as well—whatever one thinks of what Cuba represents to its critics and proponents, there was one uncontested feature of the world as lived on that island, and that was the ever-present question of a human agenda in its public sphere. Whatever happens to Cuba politically, its judgment rests, ultimately, on the degree to which it can forge a human agenda throughout the state of war issued against that island by the U.S. and U.S.-Cubans who encourage the continuation of that war.

History has no mercy for failure.

I landed on U.S. shores again—the USA, which, when all is said and done, after twenty-six years, is also where I am from as much as I am from other shores. Here, I was greeted by a hurricane of madness. Here, on a television screen, was a white Bronco being followed by a team of black-and-white police cars. On both sides of the highway's divide were people of color cheering on the Bronco. Inside was a black man with a black shotgun, a man whose name is also a nickname for orange juice. Various rationalizations and irrationalizations surfaced coverage of the "chase," like frequencies caught through a roving tuner on a radio. Antimiscegenation snippets here and there; an opportunistic district attorney "speaking out" against domestic violence at a news conference, although I thought it was standard procedure to say "no comment" until apprehension of the suspect; carefully guided efforts to avoid the *race* word as the image of a dead white woman and her dead white male friend permeated television screens, news-papers, and magazines; editorials on women, mostly white and battered (which raises questions about the black face of the batterer versus the bat-tered), everywhere; and on and on; switch the channel, turn the page, turn the dial, and there we find that one cannot simply turn off reality, however absurd and surreal it may be, and then . . . and then the awkward sense of the constant rationalizations here and there for complicity in oppression; this stuff is marketable; a *Time* letter from the managing editor saying that no offense was intended by the "blackened" mugshot of the black man of the week; then the thought that struck me, of how that black man never seemed so black until he was so obviously down; then the whole absurdity of trying to say something then, say something while I searched within myself for a response to the question,

"For what reason?"—"In reality, who/what am I?"—"Who/What are *we?*"

There is nothing to say against a businessman in a world in which business rules. There is supposedly a world of difference between the businessman who makes his profit off the backs of laborers in other countries—laborers with not much to eat and not much to hope for—and the businessman who makes his profit off the local vices. The Phillip Morris Corporation makes money legally off cigarette addictions; the dealer on the corner makes his money illegally off illicit addictions. But when all is said and done, what can we say against the street dealer when even our values are out for a buck? Isn't there moral bankruptcy here? For the street dealer knows that he is not even close to the reality of Bob's and John's and Henry's and Tony's profits on illicit vices, but he bears the face for the crime. He knows as he raises the question of who he is that he constantly encounters what he is. He is crime.

I am a crime. I have known this since my first encounter with the po-lice—their attacking me in junior high while I was defending myself against a group of adult whites; their stopping me on the New Jersey Turnpike for driving too slowly after a drunk driver nearly knocked me off the road; their accosting me and my friends while we moved our instruments into our rehearsal place; their pulling me over (again on the New Jersey Turn-pike) while I was driving to North Carolina to see my brother, who was losing his mind after the absurdity of "our" second intervention into the Persian Gulf; their sadistic grins as they attempted to confiscate my car in freezing Connecticut weather while I held my four-year-old son in my arms, and on and on. Hot pursuit is the rule of thumb. What can I think when police officers pursue me because they see me, when what I have supposedly done is determined by police officers after I have been stopped—what can I think but that they lay in wait, confident that there is a problem with my very existence that will emerge and provide them with what they already know, and that problem, without anything else to offer beyond my existence itself, is that I exist?

The black's everyday, if he or she ever really has an everyday, will be an extraordinary achievement. Think of it. To face social problems, not as flickered responses that are declivities in understanding that emerge from problematized blackness, but purely and simply because they are realities through which human beings must negotiate their way.

I hear that I, by virtue of my kind, am a violent type of being. Bigger

Thomas lurks within my veins, and my cowardice forces me to live out my fantasies against "them," whites, in mad barbarism against my brothers. I don't have disputes. If against whites, it's racial; if against blacks, it's black-on-black violence. I stare constantly in the face of a causal-racial explanation of what I do, where I'm from, and where I am going. In those eyes that fail to see beyond the perverted anonymity of my appearance, I become the problems I face. So the communities in which I live become Joseph Conrad's Congo—stared at from without, decided by the garbled imagination that hears only gibberish from my mouth, and condemned to the rhythm of natural forces against which our punctual eighteenth-century philosopher once suffered and trembled from the sublime—oh, yes, the violent din that claws at who I am, that din that makes me constantly the anomalous "survivor," yes, violent with fury, violent with that ever-present call to *destiny*.

They are waiting. For they know I have to be on the alert. I have to be on call—no respite, no letting my guard down. Somewhere out there, until the day I die, there is the weight of predistined failure. To be black is to *be*, as Du Bois observed, a "problem." I have seen many black men struggle, struggle hard, and then just when they are about to achieve their goal, they go to pieces. They slip into a horrid absurdity.

"What's up with that?" a friend once asked.

Yeah, what's up with that? But he knew. He knew what it was to be the exemplification of sin. To be, that is, guilty in advance. It waits. Guilty of what? Time will tell. Out there, hooking an index finger, calling us into full view of the storm, calling us to explode: "Yeah, violent, criminal, sexually deviant black man, come to me, I await you—yes, me, your *destiny*. . . ."

We've seen the explosions. We've seen the eruptions, the onomatopoeic eruptions of destiny . . . of blackness in its fusion with black death through black guns in the night . . . of shiny knives taking on a promise of permanent darkness . . . oh, yes, of the thickness of a racist cloud hovering in the skies and swooping through windows, into lungs, into hearts, with a promise of violent destiny.

Yes, "Who am I?" "Do I mean all these things—do I?"

So I, like many before me, reached out. To reach out is an act of faith. There are black people in the U.S. and other affluent parts of the world whose lives are predictable enough to cushion them, to some extent, from the experiences I have been describing. Perhaps, even, their access to a seemingly safe world has enabled them to imagine themselves protected by their own *accoutrements* of class or ethnicity to avoid, or at least evade, the lurking antiblackness that simmers in the distance. To them, however, I do not know what to say. For I suspect they will be willing to listen when the weight of destiny invades their sanctuary. After all, even they will discover, albeit occasionally, the importance of being alert. For there is a form of groping going on, and in the midst of it nothing falls but crumbs.

I return to anonymity, for it taps me on the shoulder now and then when I realize how extraordinary it would be to be extraordinary in an ordinary way. In the midst of all this, there isn't much time, like life during wartime, to sulk. We must destroy destiny, and in that victory will stand, albeit fragile, the possibility of a kind of wonderful affirmation of our strength and willingness to love.

Note

1. Frantz Fanon, *Les damnés de la terre*, préface de Jean-Paul Sartre et présentation de Gérard Chaliand (Paris: Gallimard, 1991; originally published by Maspero in Paris in 1961), p. 300.

Chapter Two

Fanon, Philosophy, and Racism

Only for the white is the Other perceived on the level of the body image, absolutely as the not-self—that is, the unidentifiable, the unassimilable. For the black, as we have shown, historical and economic realities come into the picture.
> —*Frantz Fanon*, Peau noire, masques blancs

At times, this Manichæism goes to its logical conclusion and dehumanizes the colonized, or, to speak plainly, it turns them into animals. In fact, the terms the settler uses when he mentions the colonized are zoological terms.
> —*Frantz Fanon*, Les damnés de la terre

They issue orders without providing information.
> —*Toni Morrison*, The Bluest Eye

"Ordered you?" he said. "He ordered you. Dammit, white folk are always giving orders, it's a habit with them. Why didn't you make an excuse? . . . My God, boy! You're black and living in the South—did you forget how to lie? . . . Why, the dumbest black bastard in the cotton patch knows that the only way to please a white man is to tell him a lie! What kind of education are you getting around here?
> —*Ralph Ellison*, Invisible Man

We begin with philosophy and racism in a neocolonial world. Our task calls for a marked break from past misconceptions of the nature of philosophy and the nature of race and racism. Philosophy, it is often believed, is not of the world, whereas problems of race and racism are firmly rooted in the most tenuous of worlds, the social world.

What could possibly be philosophical about problems of race and racism?

To that query, philosophers in the field of critical race theory can respond, What isn't racist about philosophy?

Or perhaps worse, given racism's well-rooted place in the modern and contemporary worlds, how can we be certain that racism doesn't ultimately

render much of modern and contemporary philosophy serious to the foolish and irrelevant to the wise?[1]

I am in an awkward position when I raise these questions. After all, I am
a philosopher. And I am a critical race and liberation theorist. I consequently face the risk of a performative contradiction, if I were to take
too skeptical a stand. Yet, as a philosopher committed to a conception of
philosophy that is ultimately a form of radical critique, I need consider
these questions with all the gravity they occasion. How are theorists such
as I—black and philosophical in theoretical orientation—situated by such
questions?

I recall discussing, in a session of a course I taught on Africana existen-
tialism, passages on blacks from the work of G.W.F. Hegel and Friedrich
Nietzsche. Not a pretty affair. Consider the following passages from Hegel's
Philosophy of History:[2]

> The peculiarly African character is difficult to comprehend, for the
> very reason that in reference to it, we must quite give up the principle
> which naturally accompanies all *our* ideas—the category of Universal-
> ity. In Negro life the characteristic point is the fact that consciousness
> has not yet attained to the realization of any substantial objective exis-
> tence—as, for example, God, or Law—in which the interest of man's
> volition is involved and in which he realizes his own being. . . . The
> Negro, as already observed, exhibits the natural man in his completely
> wild and untamed state. We must lay aside all thought of reverence
> and morality—all that we call feeling—if we would rightly compre-
> hend him; there is nothing harmonious with humanity to be found
> in this type of character (p. 93).

> But from the fact that [among Negroes] man is regarded as the High-
> est, it follows that he has no respect for himself; for only with the
> consciousness of a Higher Being does he reach a point of view which
> inspires him with real reverence. For if arbitrary choice is the abso-
> lute, the only substantial objectivity that is realized, the mind cannot
> in such be conscious of any Universality. The Negroes indulge, there-
> fore, that perfect *contempt* for humanity, which in its bearing on Justice
> and Morality is the fundamental characteristic of the race (p. 95).

From these considerations in the text's introduction, Hegel concludes:

> At this point we leave Africa, not to mention it again. For it is no
> historical part of the World; it has no movement or development to

exhibit. Historical movement in it—that is in its northern part—belongs to the Asiatic or European World. Carthage displayed there an important transitionary phase of civilization; but, as a Phoenician colony, it belongs to Asia. Egypt will be considered in reference to the passage of the human mind from its Eastern to its Western phase, but it does not belong to the African Spirit. What we properly understand by Africa, is the Unhistorical, Undeveloped Spirit, still involved in the conditions of mere nature, and which had to be presented here only as on the threshold of the World's History (p. 99).

Hegel has ironically done us a great service. He has clarified some themes of racist theorizing by embodying those themes so well in his thought. One of those themes is rooted in the relationship of History to universality. History, with a capital H, is universal and marches a course toward absolute self-realization. White people are universal, it is said, and black people are not. A people's greater universality and another's greater particularity are contingent upon their closeness to whiteness in the former and distance from blackness in the latter. "Colored" people of the Asiatic varieties have periodic appearances on the Historical stage, having at times stood below universality but not to the point of being without relevance to the charted course of universality. Beyond universality and particularity, however, are the nonhuman zones of, at most, human similitude. In those zones, there is no History. In classical Aristotelian logic, the syllogistic divide between universality and particularity is as follows:

(a) Universal Affirmative (All Xs are Ys)

(b) Universal Negative (No Xs are Ys)

(c) Particular Affirmative (Some Xs are Ys)

(d) Particular Negative (Some Xs are not Ys)

The logic is familiar. A particular negative (d) is the contradiction of a universal affirmative (a). To refute the statement that "All Xs are Ys," one need only show that at least one X is not a Y. And for the universal negative claim (b) that "No Xs are Ys," one need only show a particular affirmative (c), that at least one X is a Y. Universal affirmatives and universal negatives are each other's contraries. And the particulars relate to their correlated universals as subalterns. Thus, the particular of (a) is (c). And the particular of (b) is (d). Note also that if the universal categories, the contraries, are both false, it doesn't follow that the particulars are false. Some trees are not green is true in a world in which it is false to claim that all trees are green and that no trees are green.

Returning to Hegel, where History is a universal affirmative embodiment of world spirit (which is Western European), his judgment on Asiatic civilization becomes one of a universal to its subaltern. Hegel's claim is, however, stronger than a regional or cultural claim. That is why he made sure to distinguish the cultural genesis of the northern regions of Africa. He is in fact talking about blacks, and Africa south of the Sahara is being considered a nadir zone because of its concentration of blacks. Europe or the Occident is here read, then, as white, with its "other" being the Orient and its neither-Other-nor-self zone being "below," "southward," "dark," and eventually "black." The black is left to stand, then, as either Europe's contradiction or its contrary. A problem with central and southern Africa's being Europe's contradiction is that they would only stand as an instance of World spirit that is not European. Hegel's claim, however, is that the truth of World spirit can only be embodied in the European. So the (black) African contradiction must be false. If there is not at least one case of a black embodiment of universality, then in Hegel's system, the (black) African stands also as Europe's contrary. The divide between the worlds is therefore not one of Being and less-Being but instead one of Being and *no-Being*. Its divide is absolute. It is a divide between Being and Nothingness.

Since Eurocentric History (here capitalized to signify its centrism) supposedly emerges on the level of the universal, blackness or *the black* (*le Nègre*), as Frantz Fanon would say, is locked in a pit of *ahistoricity*. One would think that being ahistorical would mean that blacks could claim at least another form of universality, a universality that is not conditioned by the relativism of historicism; however, as we shall see, when it comes to racism, it is the nature of the beast to be not only perverse and cruel, but also ironic. The black's ahistoricity is ironically conditioned by History. Thus, even Hegel's declaration of there being no History in "black Africa" (an ascription with a drama of its own) was, unbeknown to many black Africans, one of their historical moments. [3] Since Hegel's no-History-there was, as we have seen, an antithetical *Keindasein* (no-being-there), it facilitated a consciousness of black Africa as a humanless place, a place without God and, hence, a place below and without humanity. On that basis, all the rest, namely the stereotypes about blacks, was granted.

Nietzsche, thick-browed and thick-mustached and utterly in love with the notion of Aristocratic values, provides a conclusion to the dialectic. Why should whites condescend to engagement in a struggle for recognition with blacks? Would not a collision of claims to universality with one's potential equals make more sense, as in the case of, say, whites of lower social and class status? For Nietzsche, blacks are, in the final analysis, irrelevant.[4]

Here we have two Manichæan points of relevance and irrelevance that place blacks in a peculiar relation to philosophy. Named after the Persian Mani, "the Apostle of God," Manichæism is the doctrine that espouses a world of "objective," material good and evil.[5] In a Manichæan world, there are physically evil objects, physically evil "things." From such a perspective, there are people who are materially good and others who are materially evil, not because of their actions and deeds but because of *who or what they are.* Existential philosophers refer to this attitude as the spirit of seriousness. It is the value system in which values are regarded as material conditions of the world. In such a world, notions of physical purity are paramount and must be maintained at all costs. Thus, bringing blacks "in" is on the level of miscegenation; it subverts philosophical purity and relevance, whereas keeping blacks "out" maintains those dimensions of philosophy. Here, there is a rigid ontological divide between being and nonbeing, with the manifestation of both in the evaluation of reason, nonreason, and unreason. Fanon puts this attitude another way: When blacks walk in the door, Reason walks out.

If our project is the exploration of philosophy and critical race theory as compatible projects, the obvious concern that emerges is the classical theoretical problem of defining our terms. Much of what can be done hinges upon what we mean both by philosophy and by critical race theory. Although philosophy and critical race theory have been developed by many theorists—from the European "Giants" and the classic Africana liberation theorists Wilhelm Amo, David Walker, Maria Stewart, Martin Delany, Edward Blyden, Alexander Crummel, and Anna Julia Cooper of the eighteenth and nineteenth centuries, and such twentieth-century luminaries as W.E.B. Du Bois, Alain Locke, Léopold Senghor, Aimé Césaire Almicar Cabral, C.L.R. James, and Sylvia Wynter—the rest of my discussion will focus on the exploration of this question of reason and unreason as it manifests itself in a particular dimension of the work of perhaps the twentieth century's greatest critical race and liberation theorist: Frantz Fanon.

Fanon was an explosion in the philosophical study of race and racism. His thoughts and deeds manifested a full-scale war against the forces of oppression. We can summarize his position on racism by his deceptively simple formulation of racism as fundamentally misanthropic. He writes in *Peau noire, masques blancs* (*Black Skin, White Masks*):

> All forms of exploitation resemble each other. They all seek their necessity in some decree of a Biblical order. All forms of exploitation

are identical because they are all applied against the same "object": man. When one tries to examine the structure of this or that form of exploitation on an abstract level, one masks the major problem, the fundamental problem, which is to restore man to his proper place.[6]

We see from this passage that Fanon's normative position is a form of existential humanism. His call for the "restoration" of humanity makes his existential humanism a form of *revolutionary* existential humanism. Restoration is here full of irony, for Fanon would have nothing to do with what humanity may have been but what humanity ought to be and possibly could become. It is a restoration of what has never been. It is to struggle toward a new kind of future. For him, the Rousseauean remark of a humanity in chains is a lived reality, and the demand for a freedom achieved by greater *humanization* is a lived obligation of every human individual.[7]

Fanon was born on the island of Martinique in 1925, the same year in which, farther north, Malcolm Little, who was to become El-Haji Malik El-Shabazz (better known as Malcolm X), was born. Like Malcolm X, Fanon was a restless spirit. Like Malcolm, his struggle with himself and with others against the dehumanization of his fellow human beings took him across three continents, into the hearts of many devotees, and against the grain of many enemies. Both were actively engaged in liberation struggles. Both focused much of their energy on Arabic culture—Islam in Malcolm's case, the Algerian struggle in Fanon's. Unlike Malcolm, however, Fanon was not assassinated, although there were many attempts and the circumstances of his death suggest pernicious forces at work. He died in Bethesda, MD, from pneumonia stemming from leukemia after being held for questioning ten days without treatment by C.I.A. agents. Fanon had an interesting life that has been embellished in several biographical texts, including a recent film by Isaac Julien.[8] Since my concern is with his contribution to the philosophical study of race, racism, and colonialism, I will not say more about his biography here.

To illustrate Fanon's significance to the philosophical study of race and racism, consider what the "discourse" on colonial and racial oppression was before he came on the scene. That situation was much like a Trinidadian story of an Anglican clergyman inspecting an Anglican school for boys. Entering the school's corridors, he encountered a little boy who regarded himself as minding his own business. The clergyman decided to seek some fruits of the queen's labors. "Young man," he asked the little boy, "could you tell me who knocked down the walls of Jericho?"

Our young man thought for a moment and gave what he considered an appropriate response to authority. "Not me."

The clergyman became outraged. "Who is your teacher?" he demanded.

"Mr. Smith, sir."

He dragged the boy to Mr. Smith's room, burst in, and asked, "Are you Mr. Smith?"

"I am, sir."

"Well, Mr. Smith, I just asked this boy who knocked down the walls of Jericho, and do you know what he told me?"

Mr. Smith became perplexed. He looked at the boy and then at the clergyman. "No, sir. What did he tell you?"

"He told me he didn't do it."

Mr. Smith got up slowly. He took off his glasses and looked at the boy and then at the clergyman. "I've known this boy throughout the time he has attended this school, sir. He is a boy of good parentage. If he says he didn't knock down the wall, then he didn't do it."

The clergyman then dragged the boy, followed by Mr. Smith, to the headmaster (principal) and complained, "I asked this boy who knocked down the Wall of Jericho and he told me he didn't do it. Then I asked his teacher and you know what he told me? He said the boy didn't do it!"

The headmaster, dark-skinned and proud, a stern and fair fellow, stood up. His eyes met the eyes of the frightened little boy and then the concerned teacher's. "Father," he declared, "Mr. Smith has worked here for over ten years. I've known him for a longer time than that. He is a man of great integrity. If he has vouched for the boy, I see no reason not to stand by him."

The clergyman then decided to appeal to "higher authorities." After a few heated moments on the telephone, he got the office of the Minister of Education.

"Hello. I am at the Anglican School. I've asked repeatedly, but nobody here can tell me who knocked down the Wall of Jericho."

"Just one moment," answered the Minister of Education. "I'll put you on to Buildings and Water Works. . . ."

Philosophical encounters with racism have for some time now functioned like an Anglican minister in a colonial school. Its modern epistemological dimensions have been such that its messengers have tended to ask questions without an appreciation for context, and the questioned are often those who feel as though they are perpetually on trial. By the time Fanon came along, there was a shift in inquiry. We see this when he writes:

From all sides tens and hundreds of pages assail me and impose themselves on me. Still, a single line would be enough. Supply a single answer and the black problem will lose its seriousness. What do human beings want? What do blacks want? (*Peau noire*, pp. 5–6).

This passage reveals a provocative challenge to the intersection of philosophy and racism. For in raising the question of desire, of a point of view of the questioned, Fanon here also raises the matter of black subjectivity. But black subjectivity is an ironic proposal here, for there is, after all, a structural humanity that challenges the formation of what blacks want. The structural humanity is that universal spoken of earlier, that universal that lays claim not only to what human beings really want, but also what counts as really human.

"What do blacks want?"

A black philosopher taps away at the keyboard while a white plumber is busy in the bathroom working on the toilet in the philosopher's drab old apartment. (Strange class dynamics here, given American folklore on race and class that demand a reversal of roles.) The plumber decided to pass time with some small talk. He noticed a pile of papers on the floor by the philosopher's computer and asked him what he was working on. The philosopher, regarding himself as organically rooted with working–class sensibilities, told him that it was a book on antiblack racism. After exchanging a few words, the plumber's face tightened as he let out, with an irritated huff: "What do blacks *want*?"

Did he *really* want to know? Listen to Jean-Paul Sartre:

When you removed the gag that was keeping these black mouths shut, what were you hoping for? That they would sing you praises? Did you think that when they raised themselves up again, you would read adoration in the eyes of these that our fathers had forced to bend down to the very ground?[9]

Indeed, what do black people want?

Fanon asked the question, but in his typical penchant for irony, Fanon ultimately put the question on its head; for in Fanon, whose colonized person recognizes the need for "replacement," for the last's becoming the first, there is ultimately no point pursuing *that* issue of desire, since the question itself is rhetorical and therefore requires the revolutionary recognition and response: "Not what you, whoever you are on top, the first, are willing to give up."

We are now experiencing a period of heightened attention to Fanon's work. The standard description of this development is that it is a "resurgence" in Fanon studies. In my research on Fanon scholarship, however,

I've noticed a steady stream of articles and books since the early 1960s. As for articles and substantial sections of monographs and anthologies in political theory and Africana studies, the list has made a sizable bibliography of secondary material.[10]

The secondary literature reveals that Fanon studies have undergone five stages of development. The first stage, occasioned by such strange bedfellows as Albert Camus, Jean-Paul Sartre, Simone de Beauvoir, Huey Newton, Hannah Arendt, and Jack Woddis, was primarily reactionary: Both Fanon and his thought were either monsters or our saviors.[11] The second stage, inaugurated by Renate Zahar's *Kolonialismus und Entfremdung: Zur politischen Theorie Frantz Fanons*, published in Frankfurt am Main in 1969, focuses on Fanon's significance for political theory. That stage was in full bloom by the mid-1970s, with excellent work by such theorists as C.L.R. James, Pietro Clemente, Ato Sekyi-Otu, and Emmanuel Hansen, and has remained influential to the present.[12] The third stage, set in motion by David Caute, Peter Geismar, and Irene Gendzier, is Fanon as good biography. His life as a revolutionary who conversed with the foremost African, French, Cuban, and African-American intellectuals of his day provides much informative and "sexy" material for anyone interested in twentieth-century intellectual and political history. In addition, he was an attractive, irascible, complex, courageous personality, the stuff that makes great biography. The fourth stage has accompanied the emergence of postcolonial studies in the *academy*. Although dominated by work of people such as Edward Said, Neal Lazarus, Benita Parry, Homi Bhabha, and Abdhul Jan-Mohamed, the major metatheoretical text on this period is an essay by Henry Louis Gates, Jr., entitled "Critical Fanonism."[13] This stage is marked by the peculiar absence of monographical studies on Fanon and, among some of its adherents, a peculiar absence of memory and at times clear hostility to the historical-racial reality signified by Fanon—in a word, his *blackness*. There, Fanon as text emerges in the midst of a derision, except for Said's, Parry's, JanMohamed's, and Lazarus's works, which are perhaps the most in stream with much of Fanon's thought, of liberation theory and praxis.

The more unfortunate side of this turn is perhaps best illustrated by an account I received of a three-day workshop on Fanon conducted at the University of Chicago by Homi Bhabha and his adherents. The presenters were either East Indian, Middle Eastern, or Euro-American. The audience consisted of instructors from colleges, many of whom were black. Bhabha opened his talk with a quip that he is known for being abstruse, so he won't disappoint his audience by being otherwise. When asked by a member of the audience to relate Fanon's relevance to the black American experience, Bhabha's response was that it wasn't his area of interest. That East Indians, Middle-Easterners, and Euro-Americans were on the panel wasn't the problem. The outrage was the absence of the black dynamic, whether in representation or thought.

There are many black philosophers, sociologists, and literary theorists who do work on Fanon in the United States. Many of them would have perhaps told Bhabha, as I know I would have, that what they have to say on identity issues, which are Bhabha's "interest," may be highly relevant. I suspect, however, that the exclusion of blacks may have been connected to the current climate of treating black participation as intrusion. Blacks might, that is, make the identity waters murky with talk of racism and struggles for liberation. Or, what has become popular, discussions of racism must learn to go beyond the black–white dynamic. We also find that many writers who dominate the postcolonial stage, when they do raise issues of liberation and blackness, often raise them *against* Fanon and other black liberation theorists by reconstructing them as essentially misogynous and homophobic.[14]

It is an irony of postcolonial studies that perhaps no group is more alienated from its developments than black people, the people from whose history, experiences, and bodies a thinker like Fanon emerged.

Then there is the current stage. This stage, which also had its roots in the mid-1980s, consists of engagements with Fanon's ideas in a multitude of fields. The first major work of this period is Hussein Abdilahi Bulhan's *Frantz Fanon and the Psychology of Oppression* (1985).[15] There, Bulhan not only discusses Fanon's life and work but also pursues their implications for the problem of developing a social psychology of liberation. Adele Jinadu's *Fanon: In Search of the African Revolution* (1986) and Tsenay Serequeberhan's *The Hermeneutics of African Philosophy* (1994) are also worth mentioning in this regard, for they explore the relevance of Fanon's *ideas* for the project of an African revolution.[16] In the 1995–1997 period, however, there was an explosion of representative work. My book, *Fanon and the Crisis of European Man,* appeared in fall 1995, and in a way signaled the beginning of a new stream of literature from authors such as T. Denean Sharpley-Whiting and Renée T. White. I have edited *Fanon: A Critical Reader* (1996), a work that presents the first collective philosophical effort, from a variety of disciplinary perspectives (philosophy, literature, and the social sciences), in Fanon studies. That anthology was followed by Alan Read's *The Fact of Blackness* (1996), a volume that focuses on cultural studies and film representations of Fanon.[17] In addition, there were Ato Sekyi-Otu's beautifully written *Fanon's Dialectic of Experience* (1996), T. Denean Sharpley-Whiting's critical engagement, *Frantz Fanon: Conflicts and Feminisms* (1997), Sylvia Wynter's discussions of Fanon's sociogenic turn and its relevance in the struggle to forge new conceptions of life, and Paget Henry's stream of important articles on the relevance of Fanon's thought for the development of Afro-Caribbean philosophy.[18] And then there are the many texts to come, which include Nigel Gibson's *Rethinking Fanon* and *Beyond Manichaeanism*.[19] Again, the primary feature of this period is that there is more engagement of and with Fanon's ideas than commentary on Fanon himself.[20] The work in this period focuses on the usefulness of Fanon's ideas.[21]

Now, the reader may wonder why a short statement on the literature that constitutes Fanon studies precedes our discussion of Fanon's contribution to the study of philosophy and racism. It is because in these stages we also can observe the routes usually taken by any thought-provoking theory and, consequently, critical race theory. Critical race theory took a path of first responding to reactionary responses to its goal of a *critical* positioning of race matters. It then undertook overtly political explorations of race— explorations usually rooted in sociology and public policy. A shift to biographical or "experiential" accounts of race and racism then emerged. Then there was the turn to metatheoretical questions of the Kantian form: How might so-and-so, that is, a critical theory of race and racism, be possible? Immanuel Kant, we may recall, changed the course of Western philosophy by raising the question of how synthetic knowledge without prior experience is possible. Similarly, in critical race theory, its own metatheoretical assumptions became the focus of its critique. We can consider this dimension to be the positive outcome of the turn to postcolonial theory. And finally, there is the point of simply theorizing itself, where a response to the previous question is performative, where its assessments are left to emerge from its practice. In Fanon's biography and thought, then, there is a portrait of the study of philosophy and racism in all of its dimensions. More, in Fanon, at least for our topic, there is the dramatic edge of his not only being a psychiatrist and revolutionary, but also his being a social theorist and philosopher.[22] Fanon embodies the tension between the universal and the particular in a profound way. Consider the following disjunction of the question of philosophy and racism: "Fanon or Kant, Hegel, Marx, Nietzsche, Heidegger, Dewey, Wittgenstein, Sartre, Foucault, or Derrida." Except for Marx and Sartre, explorations on philosophy and racism lead to Fanon through a classic disjunctive syllogism.[23] Many thinkers have explored racism and many thinkers have explored philosophy. But philosophy *and* racism, treated as a conjunctive analysis, calls for Fanon as it does for no other.[24]

What do we find in Fanon's work?

In Fanon we find an arsenal of criticisms of three fundamental assumptions of Western philosophical attitudes toward the study of racism. The first assumption is that racism is irrational. The second is that modern Western human sciences can present a rigorous portrait of racism. And the third is that racism is a conflict between the self and the Other. All these assumptions explode from three of Fanon's theoretical advances: the sociogenic dimension of racism (and all forms of oppression that appeal to a conception of human nature), the existential reality of oppression, and the phobogenic dimension of antiblack racism. These theoretical advances emerge through a phenomenological consideration that governs antiblack reality: the *epidermal schema*. On the epidermal schema, Fanon writes:

> An unusual clumsiness came upon me. The real world contested my place. In the white world the man of color encounters difficulties in the assimilation of his bodily schema. Consciousness of the body is a uniquely negating activity. It is a third-person consciousness. . . . Then the bodily schema, attacked from several points, collapses and gives way to a racial epidermal schema. In the train, it is no longer a matter of knowledge of my body in the third person, but in a triple person. In the train, instead of one, I am left with two, three places (*Peau noire*, pp. 89–90).

Fanon has here described what can be called, in phenomenological language, a form of perverted anonymity. To be anonymous means literally to be nameless. Namelessness is a mundane feature of the way in which we each move through the social world. Our fellow human beings, as Alfred Schutz, Merleau-Ponty, and Maurice Natanson have observed, pass by us, and at times they say hello to us as nameless types—people of definite description with an inner life-world of mystery: the cashier handing us our change, the student hurrying to class, the unfortunate stranger whose hat was blown off on a cold, windy day, the attractive man or woman who gave us a smile. Our ancestors and our descendants, whom Schutz called our predecessors and successors, are part of this anonymity: think of the joy of finding dusty letters in the attic, messages that give us a glimpse beyond the named namelessness of old black-and-white pictures; the archaeologist's shock in finding ancient graffiti and pornographic sculptures and paintings in ancient temples. And our successors? Well, there we find a profound level of anonymity; neither named nor understood beyond the fact that they will, or, in more skeptical times, may one day exist.

Fanon is not, however, concerned primarily with these forms of anonymity. He is concerned with forms of anonymity that constitute forms of closure, where the epidermal schema plays an ironic game of cat and mouse. These are *perverse* forms of anonymity. In such cases, social relations are saturated with bad faith; they manifest an opposing rationality. Things become what they are based on what they are not, and they become what they are not based on what they are. The black is invisible because of how the black is "seen." The black is not heard because of how the black is "heard." The black is not felt because of how the black "feels." For the black, there is the perversity of "seen invisibility," a form of "absent presence." How is this possible?

I have argued elsewhere that seen invisibility or absent presence is possible through a form of believing what one does not wholly believe. This phenomenon is bad faith. Bad faith manifests itself in convincing ourselves of the nonhumanity of others and ourselves. In ordinary anonymity, the human being is a form of presented invisibility. Part of what it means to be human is to be beyond, though not without, one's "outside." It is, as Merleau-Ponty observed, to have an "other side" of one's body. Thus, in typical human encounters, there is always a presumption of transphenomenal experience: there is always more about the human other that each of us could learn. With antiblack encounters, however, the mystery or riddle of blackness is a function of its supposed worthlessness. Hegel's rejection of black Africa could, after all, be translated as *Es gibt kein Geist dort* ("There is no Spirit there"). Fanon summarizes the matter this way: "For Hegel there is reciprocity; here [with the enslavement of black Africans] the master mocks the consciousness of the slave. He doesn't want recognition from the slave but work" (*Peau noire*, p. 179, note 9). The correlate is what the farmer wants from the ox. Frederick Douglass articulated this form of consciousness well when he wrote:

> In a very short time after I went to live in Baltimore, my old master's youngest son Richard died; and in about three years and six months after his death, my old master, Captain Anthony, died, leaving only his son, Andrew, and daughter, Lucretia, to share his estate. . . . Cut off unexpectedly, he left no will as to the disposal of his property. It was therefore necessary to have a valuation of the property, that it might be equally divided between Mrs. Lucretia and Master Andrew. I was immediately sent for, to be valued with the other property. . . .

We were all ranked together at the valuation. Men and women, old and young, married and single, were ranked with horses, sheep, and swine. There were horses and men, cattle and women, pigs and children, all holding the same rank in the scale of being, and were all subjected to the same narrow examination. Silvery-headed age and sprightly youth, maids and matrons, had to undergo the same indelicate inspection. At this moment, I saw more clearly than ever the brutalizing effects of slavery upon both slave and slaveholder.[25]

The epidermal schema represents a perverse reality of a denied "inside" to the life of the black. The antiblack racist regards the black world as a world of "surfaces." Listen to Fanon:

I am overdetermined from outside. I am not the slave of the "idea" that others have of me but of my appearance. I move slowly through the world, accustomed to aspiring no longer to appear. I proceed by crawling. Already the white looks, the only true looks, are dissecting me. I am *fixed*. Having prepared their microtome, they slice away objectively pieces of my reality. I am disclosed. I feel, I see in those white looks that it is not a new man who enters, but a new type of man, a new genus. Why, a Negro! (*Peau noire*, p. 93).

The black, Fanon observes, is locked in a world governed by a natural attitude of surfaces. The black is an epistemologico-ontological ideal. One can study the black, it seems, as one studies the surfaces of "things." This attitude governs the framework of normality in such a world; it infects and perverts what constitutes the "normal." It is on this basis that Fanon declares that a "normal" black child growing up with "normal" black parents in an antiblack world will still be an "abnormal" human being (*Peau noire*, p. 117). How could such a circumstance emerge? What can be done toward its *lysis* or elimination?

The first task is to recognize what Fanon calls the "sociogenic" dimension of the situation. In one sense, sociogenesis refers to the human contribution to human institutions. On another level, sociogenesis refers to the role of human institutions in the constitution of phenomena that human beings have come to regard as "natural" in the physicalist sense of depending on physical nature. Sociogenic dimensions are meaning-constituting features of social life. To understand antiblack racism in this regard, we need to go through a thought exercise on the creation of the "object" of antiblack racism: the black.

In the history of racist literature, there is the structural posing of a rather odd question: How and when did black people come into being? (Note here the normative presumption of white people's having always existed.) Now, although the history of this question is also a portrait of pathology, where the decoded originating query of the black is "Where did humanity go wrong?" there is a legitimate variation of this question through the lives and history of black people. If we shift from perverse anonymous behavior to the phenomenological sociological technique of imaginative deployments of anonymity, where we imagine what a typical human being would do in a typical instance of the social situation in question, we find an unusual tale. Nonperverted or ordinary anonymity calls for us to imagine being in the place of another. For ancient and even medieval people of the continent that we now call Africa, there may have been multitudes of ethnic groups, but there was no reason to see a continental racial identity of any sort. If we were to employ this interpretive phenomenological technique radically, it may be the case that we cannot even imagine what those people ultimately saw in terms of color.[26] For, locked in the epidermal schema, _our_ imagination of "seeing," "smelling," and "feeling" heads straight to the skin—at least where Africans and their descendants are concerned. But the exercise is instructive, since it behooves us to raise the question of what social forces were set in motion to articulate an identity that blocks our perception so severely. From the sociogenic approach, there has been a transformation of social reality itself, a transformation on both the ontogenic (individual) level and the phylogenic (group, species) level. It is a convergence of individual involvement in social processes and the imposition of social processes on individualization. It is, in other words, an existential sociodiagnostic.

Having stated the sociogenic dimension of antiblack racism, the other considerations and their significance become evident through a summary of Fanon's argument in his first major work, _Peau noire, masques blancs_. The work itself has received much attention over the past ten years, but unfortunately for many of the wrong reasons. Commentaries range from discussions of Fanon's supposed Lacanianism to his Hegelianism and his Sartreanism. Such elements are there, true. But I suspect that the power of the book goes beyond these features. Its power, ultimately, is that it is a beautifully and provocatively written _theoretical_ statement on the human condition in the face of unyielding obstacles. One is not used to seeing theory written this way, save, perhaps, in some of Du Bois's classic engagements, especially _The Souls of Black Folk_. _Peau noire_ is a bold text, with irony, pathos, fear, trembling, and hope. I say this even though the text itself issues its call through an unabashed pessimism toward any response short of revolutionary struggle against what Fanon regards as the murdering of humanity. In that regard, one cannot help but agree with Derrick Bell, who observed:

> Fanon's book was enormously pessimistic in a *victory* sense. He did not believe that modern structures, deeply poisoned with racism, could be overthrown. Yet he urged resistance. He wrote a book—perhaps to remind himself that material or cultural fate is only part of the story.[27]

Fanon's project in *Peau noire* is to read how occidental thought has read the lives of black and other colonized folk. The reading of reading here is a theoretical move in which the metatheoretical question of theoretical legitimacy emerges. How does the introduction of the black or the colored affect the ways in which we read and write our conceptions of the human being?

Here is Fanon's argument: Blacks have attempted to escape the historic reality of blackness through language, which offers semiotic resources for self-deluding performances of emancipation. If blacks can speak the European language well enough and even use it against the European with the ferocity of Shakespeare's Caliban, perhaps they will "become" European and, consequently, "become" white. Value-neutral semiotic resources do not exist, however, in an antiblack world. Signifiers that overtly deny color are thus governed by a colonized life-world. On the level of class, for instance, a person who speaks the national language well is, from the proletariat's perspective, someone who "speaks like a book." Racial impositions lead to a different formulation: A black who speaks the national language well is, from the perspective of many blacks, someone who "speaks like a white person." Think of the discussion over Bryant Gumble's supposed "whiteness." Should a professional journalist speak otherwise? What should Gumble speak otherwise? Yet the discussion on Gumble emerges from the identity formation he is claimed to have transcended. It is because Bryant Gumble *is* black that his failure to speak "black speech" becomes pronounced.

Fanon provides many examples of the black's effort to escape the reputation of the black's relation to language. The black is, from the antiblack racist's perspective, an "eater of language." The effort to escape blackness through mastery of the national language leads to a comic-tragedy of escapism. For the more the black has mastered the colonizing language, the more obscene the black becomes. The language games that emerge are too serious to be ordinary manifestations of the language. The semiotic turn leads, in other words, only to phony whiteness and pitiful blackness. In poststructural parlance, the black chases the signifer in the hope of becoming the signifier. The black discovers, however, that he or she is always already negatively signified by the system of signs that constitute antiblack racism.

The failure of such an avenue of escape in the public sphere leads to a retreat into the private sphere of love. Toni Morrison summarizes Fanon's position well in *The Bluest Eye* when she observes: "The best hiding place was love. Thus the conversion from pristine sadism to fabricated hatred, to fraudulent love. It was a small step to Shirley Temple. I learned much later to worship her, just as I learned to delight in cleanliness, knowing, even as I learned, that the change was adjustment without improvement."[28] Perhaps one can escape racial stratification in the eyes and bosom of a white lover and the gift of acknowledgment it offers from a white world. Fanon's point is not that blacks should not be romantically involved with whites. He argues instead that the effort to escape blackness through such liaisons is a form of unhealthy behavior. For the white lover's desire to serve as a transformation of blackness, it requires either (1) loving blackness or (2) hating blackness but failing to see it in the beloved. The failure of the effort strikes both possibilities: If the lover loves blackness, that would devalue the lover's affections in the pathological black's eyes, for the pathological black's efforts were aimed at rejecting blackness in the first place. In the second instance, a white lover who hates blacks while denying the blackness of a black lover is lost in a game of self-deception. What is lost in both instances are what Willy Apollon has described in Lacanian psychoanalysis as "a certain quality of love—more precisely, words of love, certain words addressed to them as subject."[29] The antiblack context subordinates words of love into words of transformed, epidermal existence—words of assured whiteness:

> In fact you are like us—you are "us." Your thoughts are ours. You behave as we behave, as we would behave. You think of yourself—others think of you—as a Negro? Utterly mistaken! You merely look like one. As for everything else, you think as a European. And so it is natural that you love as a European. Since European men love only European women, you can hardly marry anyone but a woman of the country where you have always lived, a woman of our good old France, your real and only country.[30]

In psychoanalysis, one must distinguish between what a woman wants and what a man wants. But the intersection with racism raises new forms of "unhealthy" behavior for women and men.[31] The effort to escape blackness

through a lover's words of whiteness perverts love. The psychological resources needed to preserve the bad faith of such relationships require more
than the private dimensions such relationships can sustain. Fanon provides
examples of the pathological black's eventual efforts to seek *public* approval
of the relationships—a black woman who insists on going to an elite ball
with her white lover, a black man who seeks approbation through his lover's brother—which returns the black to the forces of institutional imposition. The desire marks the internal limitations of the relationships. They
are not relationships premised on love.

The black may then try to evade the *historical* dimension of antiblack
racism. Appeals to constitutional theories of oppression, such as Dominique
O. Mannoni's, emerge. The argument is that blacks are oppressed because
of the type of people they *are*. Here, we are reminded of W.E.B. Du Bois's
observation in *The Souls of Black Folk*: Antiblack racists treat black people
as problems instead of recognizing the problems faced by black people.
That ideological rationalization recurs in many forms. The vogue of the
culture-of-poverty argument is one instance. Writers such as Dinesh
D'Souza attempt to defend American racism by rendering black people as
producers of pathological culture. Fanon's response was that *historical* forces
come into play here, without which the *racist* dimension of the situation
cannot be articulated. His example of Malagasy children's dreams is a telling
case. Without the imposition of social-political racial realities, their dream
contents appear to be symbols of phallic and paternal orders. Fanon points
out, however, that the black images wielding guns in those children's
dreams are not symbolic but "real": the French used Senegalese soldiers to
do their dirty work. A collapse of symbolic resources into material realities
emerged. The "black" dimensions are claustrophobic.

By the time we arrive at the fifth chapter of *Peau noire*, "The Lived-
Experience of the Black," we find, then, that semiotic, erotic-narcissistic,
and constitutional resources are ultimately irrelevant to the matter.[32] The
black lives on a collision course with Western rationality. A total retreat
from Western rationality *as* rationality leads to a glorified blackness (négri-
tude) that inevitably realizes its self-deception: An essentialized blackness
that intensifies white hegemony. The isolation of black specificity intensifies, and it is an isolation that continues to chase Reason and eventually
consciousness out the door. As Fanon observes, in discussing Jewish phobia
and Negrophobia, "The Negro is fixed at the genital [level]. . . . There are
two domains: The [Jewish] intellectual and the [black] sexual [danger].
Think of Rodin's *The Thinker* with an erection; there's a shocking image!
One cannot decently 'have a hard on' everywhere" (*Peau noire*, p. 134).

The situation is moribund from the following *évidence*: "*Wherever he goes, the Negro remains a Negro*" (p. 140; italics in original). In these times of metaphorical blackness, where even rich, conservative white men can be found complaining about being treated "like the blacks," Negroes signify a convergence of these metaphors to the point of stepping out of metaphors.[33] Negroes are, in other words, significations of the blackest blacks.

Fanon describes the isolated anonymity of this schema:

> I feel in myself a soul as immense as the world, truly a soul as deep as the deepest rivers, my chest has the power to expand without limit. I am a master and I am advised to adopt the humility of a cripple. Yesterday, awakening to the world, I saw the sky turn upon itself utterly and wholly. I wanted to rise, but the disemboweled silence fell back upon me, its wings paralyzed. Without responsibility, straddling Nothingness and Infinity, I began to weep (*Peau noire*, p. 114).

Fanon's conclusion leads to a profound critique of the use of the symbolic in the analysis of antiblack racism. For the black lives not as a symbolic reality but as what Fanon calls a "phobogenic" reality. What this means is that the black stimulates anxiety. In his play, *The Respectful Prostitute*, Sartre used the character Fred as a spokesman for what we may call the antiblack phobogenic consciousness. Declares Fred, "A nigger has always done something." Fanon adds the black's perspective in the play:

> A feeling of inferiority? No, a feeling of nonexistence. Sin is Negro as virtue is white. All those whites in a group, guns in their hands, cannot be wrong. I am guilty. I do not know of what, but I sense that I am no good (*Peau noire*, p. 112).

The police officer follows the black, because the black has crossed his path. The white woman fears rape, because the black is close enough to touch her, if he tried. The black is unqualified because a white wanted that job. The black is unintelligent because, as Kant once observed, he or she *is* black and, therefore, anything coming forth from such a mouth must be utterly stupid. "Research" emerges that explores black propensities for violence, laziness, idiocy, and pathological sex—lots of pathological sex. The black thus becomes the material manifestation of pathology, and mythopoetical "facts" of blackness emerge that run counter to the lived-reality, the lived-experience, of the black. What phobogenesis allows is the breakdown, then, of theory into a perverse play of terminology. Phobogenesis refers to the Manichæism, the spirit of seriousness, we discussed earlier; it locks the black outside symbolic reality and ensnares the black in materially constituted realms of evil. The black *is* rape, nymphomania, crime, stupidity, moral weakness, and sin.

Where does all this lead?

Perhaps Fanon's most enduring contribution to philosophical considerations of race has been his sociogenic critique of traditional ontology and his critique of European Reason. On that matter, Fanon admonishes us against the use of traditional ontological claims:

> There is, in the *Weltanschauung* of a colonized people, an impurity, a defect that forbids any ontological explanation. Perhaps it will be objected that it is so with every individual, but that is to mask a fundamental problem. Ontology, when it is admitted once and for all that it leaves existence by the wayside, does not permit us to understand the being of the black (*Peau noire*, p. 88).

The reader will note Fanon's proviso, "when it is admitted once and for all of leaving existence by the wayside." Here, we find the classic critique of system-centric ontology. Ontology is the philosophical study of being or, as W.V.O. Quine puts it, what there is.[34] Then there is existential ontology, an ontology that recognizes the being-there of the human being as a question to the questioner. This form of ontology takes seriously the meaning of what there is and what there is not.[35] In Hegel's world, from where we began our discussion, there was no-one-there when it came to the question of the black. There was no Other. Antiblack racism, then, becomes unintelligible without the reality of this denial. Hegel saw no Other and therefore saw no reason for a dialectic of recognition with the black. The antiblack epidermal schema, properly understood, takes the form of such a denial. Recall Hegel's encouragement to "leave Africa, for there is no History there." Fanon's reply? "Let us decide not to imitate Europe but combine our muscles and our brains in a new direction. Let us try to create the whole human being, whom Europe has been incapable of bringing to triumphant birth."[36]

Fanon's response, through black existence, requires an ontology of admission (critical good faith), context (situation), and social existence (sociogenesis of lived-experiences). Philosophy that fails to account for existence is, therefore, trapped in a bad-faith claim to universality. In Fanon's critique, then, there is a perspective beyond particularity and universality, a perspective that sees multiple worlds.

We shall return to Fanon here and there through the course of these philosophical sketches of racism in a neocolonial world. Let us close for now with his two famous encomia that are important for understanding philosophy as both a love and a struggle for wisdom and, therefore, a radical practice that must be lived. He asks, at the end of *Peau noire, masques blancs*:

Was my freedom not given to me then in order to build [to edify, to inspire] the world of the *You*?

And in that regard, he prayed:

O, my body, make of me always a man who *questions*.

Like Fanon, philosophy must decenter itself in the hope of radical theory and become, in its embodiment, a critically self-questioning practice.

Notes

1. Think of the contrast between Western philosophical conceptions of its modern icons and its philosophical underside's conception: In most Western philosophy curricula, modernism is constituted by the thought of Descartes, Hobbes, Spinoza, Leibniz, Locke, Smith, Hume, and Rousseau. For Dussel, as we saw in our introduction, European modernism is marked by the deeds of Columbus, Cortés, and Pizarro. He writes, "Modernity was born in 1492 with the 'centrality' of Europe[;] eurocentrism originated when Europe was able to dominate the Arab world, which had been the center of the [European] known world up to the 15th century. The 'I,' which begins with the 'I conquer' of Hernán Cortés or Pizarro, which in fact precedes the Cartesian *ego cogito* by about a century, produces Indian genocide, African slavery, and Asian colonial wars. The majority of today's humanity (the South) is the other face of modernity," *The Underside of Modernity*, p. 20.

2. G.W.F. Hegel, *The Philosophy of History*, trans. with a preface by J. Sebree, a preface by C. Hegel, and a new intro. by C.J. Friedrich (New York: Dover Publications, 1956).

3. Culture in Africa literally was defined as non-African. Thus, *black Africa* called for a search for culture that was uniquely African. But since culture itself was defined as European or Asiatic, black Africa was considered, and to some extent is still considered, a cultureless place. The black contributions to Northern African society (which isn't called *white Africa*) is thus glossed over in the designation. North Africa, although spoken of in terms of European and Asiatic cultures, is designated a racial identity of whiteness.

4. For discussion, see William Preston's "Nietzsche on Blacks" in *Existence in Black: An Anthology of Black Existential Philosophy*, ed. with an intro. by Lewis R. Gordon (New York and London: Routledge, 1997), and his *Nietzsche as Anti-Socialist: Prophet of Bourgeois Ennoblement* (Atlantic Highlands, NJ: Humanities Press, 1998).

5. For a discussion on Manichaeism, see R. McL. Wilson, "Mani and Manic-haeism," in *The Encyclopedia of Philosophy*, vol. 5, ed. by Paul Edwards (New York: Macmillan and The Free Press, 1967), pp. 149–50.

6. *Peau Noire, Masques Blancs* (Paris: Editions de Seuil, 1952), p. 71. All translations of Fanon's work throughout this volume are mine except where otherwise noted.

7. For Rousseau's view, see *Du contrat social*, chronologie et intro. par Pierre Burgelin (Paris: Garnier-Flammarion, 1966). Many English translations are available on the title *The Social Contract*. See also the thought of Karl Jaspers, where a similar view of humanization is advanced in, for example, *Reason and Existenz*, trans. William Earle (New York: Noonday Press, 1959).

8. The most popular biographical accounts are David Caute, *Frantz Fanon* (New York: Viking, 1970); Peter Geismar, *Frantz Fanon* (New York: Dial Press, 1971); and Irene Gendzier's *Frantz Fanon: A Critical Study* (New York: Pantheon Books, 1973). The film version is Isaac Julien, *Frantz Fanon: "Black Skin, White Mask"* (1995), a film that, when screened at the Black Harvest Film Festival (Art Institute of Chicago, 1996), was described by an audience member as "covering up more than uncovering Fanon." For "uncovering" Fanon, I recommend Hussein Bulhan, *Frantz Fanon and the Psychology of Oppression* (New York: Plenum, 1985); *Fanon: A Critical Reader*, ed. by Lewis R. Gordon, T. Denean Sharpley-Whiting, and Renée T. White (Oxford: Blackwell, 1996); and *Franz Fanon: Conflicts and Feminisms* (Lanham, Md.: Rowman & Littlefield, 1997).

Fanon and Feminisms: Theory, Thought, Praxis (Lanham, MD: Rowman & Littlefield, forthcoming).

9. "Black Orpheus," trans. by John MacCombie, in *"What Is Literature?" and Other Essays*, ed. by Steven Unger (Cambridge, MA: Harvard University Press, 1988), p. 291. This essay is Sartre's famous preface, "Orphé noir," to Léopold Sédar Senghor's edited collection of black poets, *Anthologie de la nouevelle poésie Nègre et malgache*, which was originally published in Paris by Présence Africaine in 1948.

10. For a recent survey, see the bibliography in *Fanon: A Critical Reader*, ed. by Lewis R. Gordon et al.

11. For discussion of some of these views, as well as the postcolonial view discussed below, see Lewis R. Gordon, *Fanon and the Crisis of European Man: An Essay on Philosophy and the Human Sciences* (New York and London: Routledge, 1995), chap. 5.

12. See C.L.R. James' pamphlet, *From Du Bois to Fanon* (East Lansing, Michigan 48823: PLSI East Lansing, no date); Pietro Clemente, *Frantz Fanon, tra Esistenzialism e Rivoluzione* (Bari: Casa Editrice Guis, 1971), Ato Sekyi-Otu's "Form and

Metaphor in Fanon's Critique of Racial and Colonial Domination," in *Domination*, ed. by Alkis Kontos (Toronto and Buffalo: University of Toronto Press, 1975), and Emmanuel Hansen, *Frantz Fanon: Social and Political Thought* (Columbus: Ohio State University Press, 1977).

13. Henry Louis Gates, Jr., "Critical Fanonism," *Critical Inquiry* 17 (1991): 457–78.

14. For examples of these interpretations, see Gwen Bergner, "The Role of Gender in Fanon's *Black Skin, White Masks*," *Publications of the Modern Language Association of America* 110, no. 1 (January 1995); Mary Ann Done's "Dark Continents: Epistemologies of Racial and Sexual Difference in Psychoanalysis and the Cinema," in her *Femmes Fatales* (New York: Routledge, 1991); Clarisse Zimra's "Right the Calabash: Writing History in the Female Francophone Narrative," in her *Out of the Kumbla: Caribbean Women and Literature* (Trenton, NJ: Africa World Press, 1990); and Marie-Aimée Helie-Lucas, "Women, Nationalism and Religion in the Algerian Liberation Struggle," *Opening the Gates: A Century of Arab Feminist Writing*, ed. by Margot Badran and Miriam Cooke (Bloomington: Indiana University Press, 1990). There are many more. See T. Denean Sharpley-Whiting, *Franz Fanon*, for a full bibliography and response. Sharpley-Whiting points out not only that many of these writers misrepresent Fanon's thought, but also that they often extol white male writers who have been influenced by Fanon as "feminist," in spite of those writers' often clearly misogynist declarations. Jean Genet, for instance, used many of Fanon's ideas and was much admired and respected by Euro-feminists and gay theorists, although he declared that what was positive about him was his having only passed through a woman by the necessity of birth. See discussion in Sharpley-Whiting's text and also Edmund White's award-winning biography, *Genet: A Biography* (New York: Vintage, 1994). Think also of the Euro-feminist use of the thought of Kant, Nietzsche, Heidegger, Foucault, or Derrida, without apologies. In the end, the question is unavoidable: Why is Fanon's thought on women misogynist and Angela Davis's and Genet's feminist, when they argue the same case, with the same conclusions? The visceral response to Fanon on the part of Euro-feminists is ultimately black-male phobic: Fanon was a black man and, as such, was being rebuked for speaking beyond his "place." The racist conclusion is that the discourse on women is reserved for white women, white men, and women of color. Finally, we should observe the politics here. The attack on Fanon is also linked to an attack on liberation theorists. If revolutionary politics of the left is rewritten as intrinsically misogynist and homophobic, what kind of politics remain as acceptable political alternatives? For discussion of the political significance of these criticisms, see Joy Ann James, *Transcending the Talented Tenth: Black Leaders and American Intellectualism*, foreword by Lewis R. Gordon (New York and London: Routledge, 1997), and for more on the context of this discussion, see *Spoils of War: Women of Color, Cultures, and Revolutions*, ed. by T. Denean Sharpley-Whiting and Renée T. White (Lanham, MD: Rowman & Littlefield, 1997).

15. Hussein Abdilahi Bulhan, *Frantz Fanon and the Psychology of Oppression* (New York: Plenum Press, 1985).

16. Adele L. Jinadu, *Fanon: In Search of the African Revolution* (London: KPI/ Routledge & Kegan Paul, 1986) and Tsenay Serequeberhan, *The Hermeneutics of African Philosophy: Horizon and Discourse* (New York and London: Routledge, 1994).

17. *The Fact of Blackness: Frantz Fanon and Visual Representation*, ed. by Alan Read (Seattle: Bay Press, 1996). See also *Mirage: Enigmas of Race, Difference and Desire*, ed. Ragnar Farr *(London: Institute of Contemporary Arts, 1995), which features the provocative art work that accompanied the conference from which the Read volume emerged.*

18. *Ato Sekyi-Otu's Fanon's Dialectic of Experience* (Cambridge, MA: Harvard University Press, 1996). Sharpley-Whiting's book has already been cited above. Sylvia Wynter's articles are many, but "Is 'Development' a Purely Empirical Concept or also Teleological?" (1996) is representative. Paget Henry's articles are also many, but see especially: "CLR James, African and Afro-Caribbean Philosophy," *The CLR James Journal* 4, no. 1 (Winter 1993); "African and Afro-Caribbean Existential Philosophy," in *Existence in Black*; and "Fanon, African, and Afro-Caribbean Philosophy," in *Fanon: A Critical Reader*. See also Paget Henry and Paul Buhle, "Caliban as Deconstructionist: C.L.R. James and Post-Colonial Discourse," in *C.L.R. James's Caribbean*, ed. by Paget Henry and Paul Buhle (Durham, NC: Duke University Press, 1992), which, although focusing on James, contextualizes Fanon's contribution as well.

19. *Rethinking Fanon*, ed. by Nigel Gibeson (Atlantic Highlands, NJ: Humanities Press, forthcoming) and *Beyond Manichaeism* (forthcoming).

20. Sharpley-Whiting reports, by way of bell hooks, that there was hostility toward hooks's presentation of Fanon's work in a spring cultural studies conference on Fanon's work in England. The Euro-feminists at that conference attacked hooks for engaging Fanon's ideas instead of "working him over." See Sharpley-Whiting's discussion of Fanon's influence on bell hooks's thought in her final chapter of *Fanon and Feminisms*.

21. For a review of some of the books published during this period, see Anthony C. Alessandrini's "Whose Fanon?," *The C.L.R. James Journal* 5, no. 1 (1997).

22. "Philosopher" here means something more than a person with a doctorate in philosophy. I regard many individuals with that title to be scholars of or on philosophy instead of philosophers. Philosophers are individuals who make original contributions to the development of philosophical thought, to the world of ideas. Such thinkers are people whom the former study. It is no accident that philosophers in this sense are few in number and many of them did not have doctorates

in philosophy, for example, René Descartes, David Hume, Søren Kierkegaard, William James, Edmund Husserl, Karl Jaspers, Jean-Paul Sartre, Simone de Beauvoir, and Alfred Schutz.

23. The secondary literature on Marx and Sartre are dotted with excursions into theoretical discussions of race. For a bibliography, see Lewis R. Gordon, *Bad Faith and Antiblack Racism.*

24. Cornel West is another philosopher who may come to mind. Yet, in spite of his being well-rooted in discussions of race, West's major contribution in the end may be his effort to forge a genealogy of modern scientific racism in his *Prophesy, Deliverance!: An Afro-American Revolutionary Christianity* (Philadelphia: Westminster, 1982). For discussion of West, see our discussion of black academic intellectuals in part II of this volume. See also James's discussion of postmodern black intellectuals in her *Transcending the Talented Tenth.* A problem with West's account is that it tells us less about what racism is than about its evolution in a particular form of discourse. The problem is that black inferiority was a part of European discourse before the emergence of modern science, and even if it were concomitant with modern science, there is still the need to explain its existence among populations who were not even aware of natural scientific developments and assertions. Did slave traders read Buffon, Gobineau, and Kant? Maybe some did, but that hardly explains whether the texts were cause or ideological rationalization (effect).

25. Frederick Douglass, *Narrative of the Life of Frederick Douglass, an American Slave, Written by Himself* (New York: New American Library, 1968), pp. 59–60. [Originally published in 1845.] See also his discussion of his recognition of the similarity between his condition and the ox in his later narrative, *My Bondage and My Freedom,* ed. with an intro. by William L. Andrews (Urbana and Chicago: University of Illinois Press, 1987), chap. XV.

26. See *Bad Faith and Antiblack Racism,* pp. 95–6.

27. Derrick Bell, *Faces at the Bottom of the Well: The Permanence of Racism* (New York: Basic Books, 1992), p. x.

28. Toni Morrison, *The Bluest Eye* (New York: Washington Square Press, 1970), p. 22.

29. Willy Apollon, "Four Seasons in Femininity or *Four Men in a Woman's Life,*" *Topoi* 12, no. 2 (September 1993): 103.

30. René Maran, *Un homme pareil aux autres* (Paris: Editions Arc-en-Ciel, 1947), pp. 152–3. The translation is Charles Lamm Markmann's.

31. I return to these dynamics in chap. 4 below.

32. This chapter has been translated in the Grove edition by Charles Lamm

Markmann as "The Fact of Blackness," which has generated a slew of misinterpretations of Fanon's thought in the English language. The French, "L'expérience vécue du Noir," is rooted in a phenomenology of lived-experience (*expérience vécue*) with a drama of its own. For discussion, see Ronald A. T. Judy, "Fanon's Body of Black Experience," in *Fanon: A Critical Reader.*

33. Craig Kilborn of the Comedy Central television station's *Daily Show* made the following remark about the Republican Primary Convention, at which reportedly one out of five delegates was a millionaire and over 90 percent of the delegates were white male: "This is a party for everyone. We don't care if you are a rich white male from Palm Springs, Florida or a rich white male from Palm Beach, California." In a different context, the cry against so-called "reverse discrimination" manifests this ideology. Whites have been racialized as a discriminated-against group by virtue of an egalitarian positioning with blacks. See Robert Westley's essay, "White Normativity and the Rhetoric of Equal Protection" in *Existence in Black*, for a development of this argument.

34. See Quine's *From a Logical Point of View* (Cambridge, MA: Harvard University Press, 1953).

35. A classic example is Sartre's *L'être et le néant: essai d'ontologie phénoménologique* (Paris: Gallimard, 1945), trans. by Hazel Barnes as *Being and Nothingness: A Phenomenological Essay on Ontology* (New York: Philosophical Library and Washington Square Press, 1956). For an existential phenomenological discussion of Quine's view of ontology, see *Bad Faith and Antiblack Racism*, pp. 81–2.

36. *Les damnés de la terre*, p. 373. *Les damnés* is translated into English by Constance Farrington as *The Wretched of the Earth* (New York: Grove Press, 1963).

Chapter Three

RACE, BIRACIALITY, AND MIXED RACE—IN THEORY

"You, who are a doctor," said I to my [American] interlocutor, "you do not believe, however, that the blood of blacks has some specific qualities?"

He shrugged his shoulders: "There are three blood types," he responded to me, "which one finds nearly equally in blacks and whites."

"Well?"

"It is not safe for black blood to circulate in our veins."

—Jean-Paul Sartre, "Return from the United States"

An African American couple found themselves taking their child, a few months of age, to a physician for an ear infection. Since their regular physician was out, an attending physician took their care. Opening the baby girl's files, he was caught by some vital information. The charts revealed a diagnosis of "H level" alpha thalassemia, a genetic disease that is known to afflict 2 percent of northeast Asian populations. He looked at the couple.

The father of the child, noticing the reticence and awkwardness of the physician, instantly spotted a behavior that he had experienced on many occasions.

"It's from me," he said. "She's got the disease from me."

"Now, how could she get the disease from you?" the physician asked with some irritation.

"My grandmother is Chinese," the father explained.

The physician's face suddenly shifted to an air of both surprise and relief. Then he made another remark. "Whew!" he said. "I was about to say, 'But—you're *black*.'"

The couple was not amused.

Realizing his error, the physician continued. "I mean, I shouldn't have been surprised. After all, I know Hispanics who are also Asians, so why not African Americans?"

Yes. Why not?

The expression "mixed race" has achieved some popularity in contemporary discussions of racial significations in the United States, Canada, and the United Kingdom.[1] It is significant that these three countries are marked by the dominance of an Anglo-cultural standpoint. In other countries, particularly with Spanish, Portuguese, and French influences, the question of racial mixture has enjoyed some specificity and simultaneous plurality. For the Anglos, however, the general matrix has been in terms of "whites" and "all others," the consequence of which has been the rigid binary of whites and nonwhites. It can easily be shown, however, that the specific designations in Latin and Latin American countries are, for the most part, a dodge and that, ultimately, the primary distinctions focus on being either white or at least not being black.

We find in the contemporary Anglophone context, however, a movement that is not entirely based on the question of racial mixture per se. The current articulation of racial mixture focuses primarily upon the concerns of *biracial* people. Biracial mixture pertains to a specific group within the general matrix of racial mixing, for a biracial identity can only work once, as it were. If the biracial person has children with, say, a person of a supposedly pure race, the "mixture," if you will, will be between a biracial "race" and a pure one. But it is unclear what race the child will then designate (a mixture of biraciality and *X*, perhaps, which means being a new biracial formation?).

To understand both mixed race and its biracial specification and some of the critical race theoretical problems raised by both, we need first to understand both race and racism in contemporary race discourse.

Much of contemporary race discourse is muddled, confusing, and premised on an ongoing project of evading the core issues of race and racism. Texts that racialize everyone with equal-opportunity racism tend to achieve some popularity because of the carrot they offer the contemporary sentiment on race matters. There is desire to speak about race, that is, but not about racism. Consequently, as race is spoken of in ways that offer multiple sites of oppression (consider the current vogue of the term *racisms*), we find persistent racializing of every site of oppression. Thus, even where race isn't the proper marker nor concern, the terms *race* and *racism* are evoked as legitimating expressions for acts of condemnation. One reason for this tendency is the historic role race and racism have played in the construction of oppression in Anglo societies. For example, given the historical significance of slavery and the civil rights struggle in the United States, the operating metaphor for oppression has been and continues to be race and racism.

Thus, race discourse is projected onto any location of group oppression, the consequence of which is that race and racism are spoken of in contexts ranging from Irish-Anglo conflicts to black-Korean conflicts.

Yet, if we were to deconstruct the order of racial signifiers in these contexts, we will notice the persistence of the metaphor "the blacks of. . . ." If one has to be "the black" in or of a particular context in order to designate a racial and a racist formation, then the rug that slips away beneath one's feet becomes apparent with the Fanonian historical "lived-experience" (*l'expérience vécue*) of the black: Although there are people who function as "the blacks" of particular contexts, there is a group of people who function as the blacks everywhere.[2] They are called, in now-archaic language—*Negroes*. Negroes are the blacks of everywhere, the black blacks, the blackest blacks.

Blackness functions as the prime racial signifier. It is, the element that enters a room and frightens Reason out. The popular effort to articulate racial specificity through rubrics such as "racial formation," as emerged in the 1980s in work like that of Michael Omi and Howard Winant, fails, then, to address the lived reality of what race and racism are about.[3] Their theory, which they call racial formation, is premised on the view that race must now be analyzed beyond its historical associations with ethnicity, class, or nation.[4] The biological paradigm of racial formation is limited and limiting, they argue, because it supposedly presumes a static meaning to a historically shifting concept. "*Race is,*" they claim, "*a concept which signifies and symbolizes social conflicts and interests by referring to different types of human bodies. . . .* We define *racial formation* as the sociohistorical process by which racial categories are created, inhabited, transformed, and destroyed" (p. 55, emphasis in original). They define racism thus: "A racial project can be defined as *racist* if and only if it *creates or reproduces structures of domination based on essentialist categories of race*" (p. 71). Fanon's sociogenic turn supports this interpretation. But the historical specificity of blackness as a point *from which* the greatest distance must be forged entails its status as metaphor. The formal structure of racism could be articualted thus:

The underlined blanks are asymmetric points. The arrow points to a direction at which to aim. That direction goes away from the direction to avoid. Color contingently occupies these relations. Distance is relationally understood here, as are race and racism. This distance transcends logic ironically through a logic of its own. For intance, the call for black existence as unjustified existence need not appeal to essentialist racial categories.[5]

Couldn't a structure of domination based on an *absence of essential categories* emerge—especially where an essential category is "humanness"?

Note further that the concept of racial formation is based on a distinction between social constructivity (which is an ontological claim about reference) and racial meaning (which pertains to the concept of race and is a claim about sense). Omi and Winant are antipathetic, on social constructivist grounds, to biological interpretations of race, even though a social construction can have biological connotations or senses. It is like a physicist who claims that what is meant by "table" is its collection of atoms. It may be correct that physical particles comprise a table, but that in no way determines the table's meanings. Thus, although meaning may be a function of societal conditions—how, for example, language is manifested—it doesn't follow that what is "meant" is social. Think of the distinction between a belief and a belief about or on the basis of that belief. Both race and racism, for instance, emerge when the physical or the biological is invoked. Groups are therefore racialized at the point at which the values attributed to them are treated as material attributes of who or "what" they are. There are formations that will not collapse into the "racial" category without a special set of signifiers, which the racial formation theory was designed to reject.[6]

In his famous *Oration on the Dignity of Man*, Pico Della Mirandola constructed a schema that is instructive for the understanding of race and racism.[7] According to Pico, the human being stood between the gods above and animals below. Although racism is generally spoken about in terms of hatred of other races, one should note the difference between hatred of other races and racism. One can hate another race on the basis of the conviction that that other race is one's racial superior. With such hatred there is no construction of the other race as less than human. In fact, with such a construction, there is danger of one's own race being less so. To be more precise on our use of the term *racism*, then, we shall use racism to refer to (1) the conviction that there is a race that is superior to other races and (2) the institutional practice of treating that race as superior to others. Pico's schema becomes instructive, in that the implications of a superior race and an inferior race fall onto the schema, in terms of which each group is pushed in relation to the gods and animals. The teleological implication of a superior race is its closer place to the gods, and the implication of an inferior race is its closer place to animals.[8]

The consequence of such a schema is that the conditions of being human are transformed into conditions of being gods or at least godlike. An instructive example of such conditions is Hitler's logic in *Mein Kampf*.[9]

There, Hitler argues that the proof of a superior group's superiority is its ability to exercise its will over inferior groups. Thus, a superior group "is" superior by virtue of its place under the status quo. An implication of this superiority is its freedom from constraints. The superior group is literally boundless. It thus serves as the criterion for its own justification, whereas the inferior groups can only be "justified" in terms of the superior group. In effect, then, the category of superiority demands the impossible of the inferiors. They are to prove the validity of their existence, which, in effect, means to demonstrate, beyond using themselves as justification, that their existence is justified. Recall that Fanon identified this phenomenon in *Les damnés de la terre* when he writes:

> Because it is a systematic negation of the other, a resolute decision to refuse the other all the attributes of humanity, colonialism compels the dominated people constantly to ask the question: In reality, who am I? (p. 300).

Although Fanon is talking about colonialism, his points have a corollary in racism. For racism compels the designated inferior race to ask constantly not only in reality who am I, but also, "In reality, *what* am I?"

Without the transition of an interrogated "what," a what that signals a call for one's place in the scheme of human identification, neither racism nor race is born. On the same page, Fanon adds a distinction between domination and colonialism. To be dominated is not identical with being colonized, for it is still possible for one's humanity to be acknowledged (as, for example, in the case of being under the authority of a legitimate government). It is when one's humanity is wiped out of the scheme of human affairs, to the point of functioning as a natural phenomenon among other natural phenomena—in other words, among the land, plants, and animals—that the racist schema evinces itself. Both race and racism, then, are functions below the sphere of normativity. The consequence is that the dominant "race" is, as it were, *raceless*.

Race-neutrality is loaded with coded racial designations. If the standpoint of "man" is the dominant group, then that group stands as the leitmotif of all human significations. If white stands at the top of the value scheme of a society, we will find that many supposedly racially neutral terms also carry a white subtext. Arguably, in most of the world, except northeast Asia and India, the terms *man, woman, person, child*, and a host of other supposedly racially neutral terms, usually mean white man, white woman, white person, and white child.[10] Thus, to be equal to white means to be raceless. Race, then, is a feature of all other groups, and racism be-comes a uniquely white possibility and perspective on these groups.

We can now explore the question of how both mixed race and biraciality can be understood in this context. In the United States, the significant factor of differentiation is premised on whites in an epicenter of swirling colors. In effect, then, to be "mixed" is a function of colored realities, not white ones, on the level of "race." Although whites may speak of being "mixed" with various European ethnicities and religions, racial mixture and white identity are antipathetic to each other. Whiteness, in other words, usually signifies purity. The "child," if you will, of white-nonwhite liaisons exists as an onto-biological point of difference from at least one parent. One finds, in such circumstances, a rigid order of hierarchies ac-cording to social subordination. Thus, in all matrices it is the white parent who loses onto-racial connection to her or his offspring. But in other ma-trices—for example, Northeast Asians ("mongoloids") with blacks—it is the Asian parent who loses the connection.[11] In terms of membership, then, the black parent finds a permanent racial connection with the child. (Of course, there are children who reject the racial designation and, in effect, reject, although not intentionally, their parents. But our concern here is the social reality of the hierarchies.)

One finds, then, that offsprings who are biracial mixtures with blacks are pretty much excluded from most racial categories except for black. Although it can be shown that among Native Americans the story differs—for Native American and African American offsprings are often both (Na-tive American and black)—there is still the social reality of the different quality of life available for a child who is a result of Native American unions with whites or Asians versus blacks. I recall speaking at a state university in Tennessee. A member of the audience introduced himself as a redneck with a Confederate flag on his truck. He also identified himself as part Cherokee by virtue of his grandmother, and he added that that has posed no problem at efforts to recruit him at Ku Klux Klan and right-wing militia rallies. I asked him to consider what his affiliations may have been if his grand-mother were black or Asian. I also asked him to think about the signifi-cance of his Confederate flag as a sign of willingness to join right-wing and racist organizations. And finally, I asked him why he was so proud of being taken by such people as someone who is ideologically in their camp. Before he could respond, a woman in the audience, who announced herself as part Cherokee as well, voiced her objection. "Indians aren't white," she said.

"There are whites with some Indian in them. But to be Indian, that's another story. Go to the reservations. You'll see."

Later that year, I found myself having lunch with a prominent couple from Toronto, Canada, one of whom regarded herself as being a biracial mixture of European and Chinese parentage. Her husband was white. As we discussed matters of race and theory, I eventually asked her and her husband to consider this: Most racially mixed marriages in North America occur between white men and Asian women. I recall a Chinese male associate in San Francisco lamenting that, in order to marry an Asian woman in California, he would have to find a way to become white. If the possibility of having children is still a central concern in most marriages, and if people also consider the possibility of desirable children in their choice of matrimonial partners, why don't white men seem to worry about having children with Asian women? Why is the least mixture between blacks and every other group, and the highest mixture between whites and every other group except blacks?[12] And finally, why is there such a qualitatively different life in racial terms for Asians who are mixed with blacks versus Asians mixed with whites? Do we find Asians (and Latin Americans) rushing to wed blacks to uplift their gene pool, as seems to be the case with their marrying whites? Blackness, in the end, functions as a constant, underlying mark of racialization as does no other racial designation. Its persistence suggests that the fluidity of racial identities points upward in continuing spirals of potential whiteness.

But blackness also points to a history of mixed racialization that, although always acknowledged among blacks, is rarely understood or seen among other groups. I have argued elsewhere, for instance, that to add the claim of "mixture" to blacks in both American continents would be redundant, because blacks are their primary "mixed" populations to begin with. Mixture among blacks, in particular, functions as an organizing aesthetic, as well as a tragic history. On the aesthetic level, it signifies the divide between beauty and ugliness. On the social level, the divide is between being just and unjust, virtuous and vicious; "fair skin" is no accidental, alternative term for "light skin." And on the historical level, the divide signifies concerns that often are denied. Consider the striking similarity of the subtext of the following two observations—the first by El-Haji Malik El-Shabazz and the second by Frantz Fanon:

> Out in the world later, in Boston and New York, I was among the millions of Negroes who were insane enough to feel that it was some kind of status symbol to be light-complexioned—that one was actually fortunate to be born thus. But, still later, I learned to hate every drop of that white rapist's blood that is in me.[13]

And Mayotte Capécia has [a good] reason [for being elated at having a white grandmother]: It is an honor to be the daughter of a white woman. That shows that she was not "made in the bushes." (This expression is reserved for all the illegitimate children of the upper class in Martinique. They are known to be extremely numerous: Aubery, for example, is reputed to have fathered fifty.) (*Peau noire*, p. 37, n. 5)

In these two passages, we find both an aesthetic and moral tale that is indicative of the dynamics that emerge on questions of racial mixture. On the one hand, there is the prevailing significance of what Fanon calls "de-negrification" (*dénégrification*), the phenomenon in which blackness is treated as a Manichæan quantity to be either eliminated from one's body or at least reduced. But on the other hand, there are the facts of historical social reality. In the El-Shabazz/Malcolm X passage, there is the historical reality of rape that signals the wisdom of the contemporary black expression, "All of us have a little bit of white in us." In Fanon's discussion, however, there is the more nuanced reality of the dynamics of power and gender difference. For Fanon's point is not only that social status enables one to "have one's way" with groups of lower social status, but that even among the upper classes, gender genealogies are of differing significance.[14] A white female parent or grandparent shifts the meaning of the source of whiteness. It is not that one's genesis cannot have a history of violence (for the source of violence could also be from the black father and forefathers), but that if violence were present against a white forebear, consequences would have been different. The victimological narrative on both rape and lynching are so focused on white females for the former and black males for the latter in the Americas that an invisible history of predatory white males reaping the advantages of legally rejected black female bodies became the organizing principles behind any social consciousness of interracial realities. We find, then, a history of a touch of whiteness being a mark of blackness in the Americas.[15] As one U.S. woman of African descent puts it:

While some have recently overthrown this term [Black American] in favor of African American, I have not. I find it too simplistic. I am not an African with American citizenship. Please do not misunderstand. I embrace my African roots. However, the term African American excludes the Native American, White Protestant, and Jewish components of my distant ancestry. And, I identify most strongly with a culture rooted in the American South. Since I have not yet thought up a term that I like better, I still call myself Black.[16]

This woman makes no denial of being "mixed." Yet she defines herself as black, and she uses the term *black* in the way most U.S. blacks actually use the term. (In countries like Brazil, however, blackness refers to a mythical, "pure" blackness because of the existence of the various populations of recognized mixtures that differentiate themselves from blacks. To this point we shall return.) In the North American context, then, awareness of being mixed has taken on a kind of banality in black communities. What is often overlooked, however, is the extent to which mixture-in-itself also has functioned as a site of value. The general view is that people of color's preferential treatment for lightness of skin and eyes and straightness of hair are signs of their preference for or desire to become white. Consider Fanon's rather pithy observation:

> For several years, some laboratories have been trying to discover a serum for "denegrification"; these laboratories, with all the seriousness in the world, have rinsed their test tubes, checked their scales, and begun research that might make it possible for the miserable Negroes to whiten themselves and thus to throw off the burden of that corporeal malediction (*Peau noire*, pp. 89–90).

These remarks on the technology of denegrification signal the matrices of value in a world that is conditioned by two fundamental convictions: (1) it is best to be white, and (2) it is worst to be black. The logic leads to obvious conclusions of rational action. Failing to become white, one can at least increase the distance between oneself and blackness. Thus, there are skin creams for lighter skin, hair devices and chemicals for straight, "pretty," more "manageable" hair, blue- and hazel-eyed contact lenses, and surgical techniques for the transformation of lips, hips, thighs, and any dimension of the body that is interpreted as a signifier of blackness.[17] Yet in spite of the seemingly obvious aim of becoming white, I suggest that another step in the analysis is needed to understand how such phenomena are, in phenomenological terms, *lived*. The way such phenomena are lived alludes less to becoming white than to gaining certain aesthetic and political-economic resources that pertain to being white. Many blacks, in short, simply want to be beautiful and successful. But because no black can be white, it follows that there must be some *other*, achievable point of being beautiful and successful that is aimed at in such activity, and I have argued that that achievable point is ironically one that is already embodied by the people trying to achieve it. One has, in other words, a phenomenon of black people aiming not to pass for being white, but instead to pass for being *mixed*, which is ironic because most people of color in North and

South America as well as Europe and Australia, are, in fact, already mixed. That being mixed needs to be made apparent—that is, it is important to *look* like one's mixture, to be, in a word, "authentically" mixed—provides a demand for the technology of mixed-race constructions.[18] Within the white social sphere, the technological innovation is ironically similar: The objective, whether in Bo Derek's wearing corn-rows or the current wave of hairstyle and tanning techniques to don the *look* of mixed race, is not to be taken for being mixed in the sense of parentage or heredity, but in the sense of *playing* mixture—literally, wearing it.

Appearing mixed offers something for both poles of the racial matrix. A touch of mixedness, which announces blackness, functions like black leather or lingerie in a bedroom—wearing it elicits associations and desires that are necessary but purged and relegated elsewhere in a bad-faith social order.[19] If blacks are socially acceptable sites of sexual and biological release, then one needs to wear one's blackness to be set "free."[20] The mixture emerges, then, as whiteness in colored clothing. In popular culture, examples abound: Whites in "darky" or blackface makeup, superheroes and heroines who don dark garbs, sexy vampire ghouls in dark clothing, or even the recent popular film, *The Mask* (1994), in which the personality released by the protagonist's wearing the possessed mask during the night abounds with peculiarly African American and Afro-Caribbean cultural formations, music such as jazz, rhumba, salsa, and the language of hipsters' like Cab Calloway and the youthful Detroit Red (Malcolm X). The libidinous release achieved through rock 'n' roll has its genesis, after all, in white participation in black musical productions.[21]

In black communities, power and superiority have long been invested in children whose mixture was, let us say, phenomenologically apparent. To wear one's mixedness offered instant satisfaction. Even if one were not affluent or successful, simply appearing mixed signaled that one ought to have been so. One's existence takes on that added, almost-human element that shifts one's condition from the banal to the unjust and eventually to the tragic—as in the case of the "tragic mulatto."

Recall our discussion of Pico's schema. Individuals who are a mixture of white and black find themselves in more than a construction of mixture in and of itself. They find themselves facing a mixture of clearly unequal terms. For even if their whiteness is toppled from the stage of whiteness, it will stand, nevertheless, on the level of a human existence. But the prevailing ideology offers no hope in the other direction, where blackness is located on a lower point of the evolutionary scale. The conclusion is devastating: One is more of a human being to the extent to which one is less black.

The consequence of such an ideology is a set of existential and political considerations that provide tensions in the current movements of mixed-race identifications, to which we shall now turn.

Race talk is dirty business, primarily because race discourse exists in a racist context, a context that is occasioned by such a desire to deny what it is that its mode of operation is to play on ambiguities of the human condition in order to avoid getting to the heart of the matter. Consequently, diversions constitute a vast body of the literature. One is on the road to sobriety, however, when one begins to interrogate the keepers of the gate, for at least then one can discern the purpose of the practice.

Race discourse today can be divided into groups who find the very concept of race repugnant and groups who find race itself to be less an issue and racism to be the primary concern.[22] Between these two groups of theorists, however, I would add a group I shall call *everyday people*. For the most part, everyday people do not think about races. They instead think about groups of people who are identified as races by people who theorize about what human beings are and what they do. Thus, for the typical antiblack racist, it is not races that bother him. It is *the blacks*. *The blacks* are an idealization that is seen in the body of certain people throughout the day. *The blacks* signal the extreme category of the nonwhites. As a character announced in a wonderful German cinematic allegory on racism and immigration: "As if it weren't bad enough that we had the Italians and the Turks. Now we have the Africans!"[23] Similarly, children learn about groups to hate, although they have no clue about what races are. I make these remarks because it is important to understand the extent to which race is a designation that usually emerges in contexts of explanation, whereas racism is simply the lived, ongoing practice that stimulates such explanation. The antirace people therefore miss the point. Even if they show that race is a social construction, even if they show that races are no more than cultural or social formations, even if they show that races are pseudoscientific fictions, they still need to address the ways in which phenomena understood as racial phenomena are lived. Not all black people know what races are, but they know what hatred of black people is. They read it in the symbols of value and the objective sites of power and lack thereof in which they are immersed in their waking moments, and even in their dreams. Even if every scientific claim about the existence of races is true, the antiracism people can retort, and rightly I would say, that such claims will have no impact on the task of fighting racism.[24] The fight against racism is an existential/moral phenomenon. Proof is found in the nineteenth century, when people who actually believed in the scientific validity of the concept of race simultaneously fought against slavery, genocide, and exploitation, and the myriad of ways in which *racism* is made manifest. Against Anthony Appiah's position then, where it is claimed that racism needs to be rejected because of the scientific invalidity (which for him constitutes the ontological illegitimacy) of the concept of race, the obvious conclusion here is that the scientific invalidity of races is not the relevant point.[25]

The antirace gatekeepers have had an unfortunate relationship with the evolution of one dimension of mixed-race movements and contemporary biracial politics. As we've seen, the whole point is not to be the darkest/most inferior.

So, given the existential dimensions of what we have discussed thus far, what, may we say, are the goals and possibilities available for a critical theory of mixed race?

Some claims that can be asserted in favor of a critical race theory premised on mixed-race identity are:

1. Accuracy and consistency of racial ideology demand a mixed-race standpoint, for if whites and blacks are "pure," then mixtures signify "other" forms of race. (This argument supports the reasoning behind constructing separate racial categories for mixed-race people.)
2. The question of accuracy raises questions of affiliation: Filial recognition plays an important role in our self-identities. The need to recognize fully one's ancestry calls for recognition of mixture. Saying that one's ancestry is all-black because of the "one drop rule," for instance, fails to identify relatives whose lineage is multiracial beyond their African ancestry.
3. On the biracial end, there is the fact of converging embodiments to consider: A biracial offspring "is" biologically and often culturally both of her or his parents.
4. If race *means* black or white, then mixture becomes an enigma. It signifies "racelessness." (This argument goes both ways. In favor of a separate category for mixed-race people, it is advanced as a way of eliminating their exclusion from racial matrices by making such a provision. Against a category of mixed-race people, it is advanced to claim that even a racial designation will be an inaccurate articulation of their reality. And there are those who argue that it provides a

critique of racial categories to begin with and perhaps point to a [raceless] future.)[26]

5. On the practical end, biraciality and mixed-race designations can serve an antiracist strategy: recognition of racial mixture dilutes identities premised on conceptions of "purity" and can therefore be an important stage on the road to a raceless or more racially free future.

6. And finally, but not exhaustively, there is the existential claim: Mixed and biracial people have unique experiences that can be shared and cultivated through a recognized group identification. (This existential turn is also, of course, support for the political implications designated by the first claim.)

Now, recall my point about the two dominant principles of racist ideology: (1) be white, but above all, (2) don't be black. We can call the first *the principle of white supremacy*; and we can call the second *the principle of black inferiority*. Given these two principles, the following responses can be made to our six aforementioned claims.

First, we have already shown that to be racialized means not to be "white." And in fact, when white is spoken of as a race, many whites experience discomfort for good reason; it violates their place in the social order. Thus, when all is said and done, the question of mixed-race people being an "other" race is only significant in regard to principle (2), which signifies the importance of not being black. Now, although this principle doesn't apply to biracial and mixed people along Euro-Asian or Euro-Native American lines—and given the racial hierarchies, it is rare, very rare indeed, that we find principle (2) being articulated in relation to any group other than blacks—it becomes clear that the "other" race argument is really about not being black.[27] Since the practice is geared toward adhering to principle (2), the political consequence will be an institutionalization of a certain place in the racial hierarchy. There will, in short, be an institutionally recognized group of nonblacks. One can readily see why certain groups of blacks are very suspicious of such a move, for its consequence is, after all, a quantitative reduction, by a legal stroke, of the population of designated black people. A whole group of black people will, that is, legally disappear.

Perhaps the best critical response to this move stems from our articulation of racism as a desire for black people to disappear. The first claim about accuracy requiring a mixed-race standpoint has the consequence of facilitating such a process, at least in terms of legal measures that can be taken. Such a consequence clearly violates W.E.B. Du Bois' famous admonition against problematizing people instead of responding to the social problems that people experience.[28] There is nothing in the first claim that can reject the conclusion that the world will be better off if it had a lot less black folks, especially since the number of white people in the world will in no way diminish from such a move.

The second claim about affiliation seems to me to be correct but also in need of other considerations, for the question of filial recognition pertains primarily to *white* affiliation. The history of ancestral denial and rejecting descendants hasn't been a problem of colored folks. It is a white problem. There are whites who deny black ancestry and whites who reject black descendants; the issue pertains to the principle of white supremacy. But the principle of black inferiority also emerges through the lack of appreciation of black filial recognition. In black communities, for instance, talk of ancestry nearly always pertains to nonblack ancestry. It was only during brief moments of African ancestral pride, periods under attack today as "nationalist" and "Afrocentric," that a search for specificity of African lineage emerged. There are, however, surprising sites of such recognition. On a research visit to Cuba, for instance, my U.S. colleagues and I were astonished by a tour guide's response to a question raised by a member of our delegation: "Are there any Cuban Indians still around?" The guide, without missing a beat, responded, "Native Caribbeans were killed off within a century of Columbus's landing. All Cubans are of African and European ancestry." Because Cubans, at least the Cubans who remain on the island, are for the most part a "colored" people, the point of colored recognition is here affirmed. But even in Cuba, there are clearly black-designated people. There, as in most of the Caribbean, Central America, and South America, such people hardly stand as racially superior. The project of the ancestral claim, then, is to affirm *mixture* itself, which is to establish the force of the principle of black inferiority.

The third claim is clearly true. Biracial offsprings are from both parents biologically and often culturally. But again, once one introduces a racial designation other than white, the principle of black inferiority becomes the dominant factor. The biracial person can embody white superiority if the current group of people who are designated white people disappear. But in that case, whoever is next on the racial hierarchical scale will become white people. This turn, then, affirms the principle of black inferiority only because of the *current* limitations of embodying the principle of superior whiteness. In countries such as Brazil and Mexico, this is exactly what occurs. I recall a colleague of mine being shocked, for instance, while staying with a family in Guatemala. The family, whom he saw as not only colored but "mixed," categorically hated black people. What were they? Their answer was simple: white.

Moreover, the biracial offspring who attempts to affirm both identities faces the social reality of both identities existing on unequal terms. In short, to affirm whiteness on the level of blackness has the consequence of equalizing whiteness, which, in effect, is to "blacken" it. There is thus the catch-22 of being unable to affirm their white side *as white* without encountering two perversions of reality: Either the white side is treated as superior or it is treated as a form of nonwhite whiteness; as, in a word, colored. These considerations bring us to the fourth claim, which addresses the supposed racelessness of mixed groups.

The fourth claim is subject to all the criticisms of race-neutrality. Since whites function as normative standpoints of humanity, they normally live as raceless. Angela Y. Davis, in a public lecture, phrased the situation thus: If colored means not to be white, then white means to be colorless.[29] Thus, to declare, as Michael Jackson did in his song "Black or White," "I don't want to spend my life being a color," means, in effect, to spend one's life surreptitiously being white. The problem with using this route as a means to a raceless future, then, is that it affirms a future premised on both principles by ultimately advocating the elimination of black people.

In an essay entitled, "White Normativity and the Racial Rhetoric of Equal Protection," Robert Westley unmasks some insidious dimensions of racelessness in the present age. [30] When the search for a legal remedy to racism took the form of *equal* protection, many whites suddenly gained the consciousness of being *racialized*. In the previous world, there were only human beings and coloreds—at the bottom of which were *the blacks*. Today, the law says that blacks are equal to every other group, which for these groups means that the law considers them equal to blacks. A strange equality: blacks move up while everyone else moves "down." For many whites, the metaphor of being treated "like the blacks" became a source of deeply rooted anxiety. In effect, social policy demanded that they to take, as Adam and Eve apparently did, a "fall." Needless to say, many whites couldn't take it, and a full-scale attack on affirmative action and an array of antirace and so-called reverse-discrimination constructions emerged. The goal of this attack is supposedly a raceless future, but because racism can persist without race, such a future holds the key to a special nightmare of exploitation and invisibility without reference. It problematizes race, ultimately, to preserve racism.

The fifth claim, which sees an antiracist strategy in which racelessness is the carrot at the end of the rod, is problematic for the same reasons as the fourth one: It portends a world without blacks.

The sixth claim, that biracial and mixed-race people have a unique existential situation, strikes me as correct. Mixed-race and biracial people do have unique experiences that are functions of their existential situation. For the biracial child, the anonymous white man may be, in his specific instantiation, Daddy. And all the literature and cultural knowledge of victimized feminity—white, pure, rapable—may be Mommy. Similarly, the complex social forces that say that one is more one's black parent than one's white parent (or one's Asian or Native American parent) raises a complex question of who one is by virtue of one's choice and that choice's relation to one's social situation. Since black Americans and Native Americans are already mixed peoples (what is a "pure" New World black and Native American today?), the question relates, mostly, to people of color elsewhere: African Americans, for example, experience a profound anxiety when they travel to "black" countries; they seem, in those places, to be the least or lesser blacks; they carry with them, that is, the United States as a history of white domination and, for the most part, the masculine history of white "insemination."

On the existential level, biracial people at least have the unique experience of living the racial realities of more than one group in the course of their innermost private lives. That reality alone substantiates something unique, since among all other groups, "others" function anonymously. "God knows what they do in their homes!" is not a rhetorical appeal in biracial people's lived realities.

The question of the political significance of the sixth claim is undermined, however, by our critique of the other claims, especially the first. After all, having a unique situation does not mean that the principle of white superiority and the principle of black inferiority should be affirmed. For the biracial child stands below whiteness and, by virtue of biraciality, in affirmation of black inferiority. The impact of building policy on the uniqueness of biracial people, then, is that it fails to account for political realities that are already in place against people who are clear and present violators of the principle against blackness—in a word, *blacks*.

In spite of contemporary resistance to "binary" analyses, a critical discussion of mixed-race categories calls for an understanding of how binary logic functions in discourses on race and racism. Without binaries, no racism will exist. We have seen the politics of mixed-racialization come to the fore, for instance, on matters of legal recognition of multiple categories. There, principle (2), which affirms the importance of not being black, is the most significant principle. That is because there are social benefits in not being designated black. It is a waste of time to discuss the social losses of being designated white, since the distribution of resources on a global scale falls disproportionately in favor of whites. Affirming principle (2), therefore, affirms the whole racist hierarchy that we may be attempting to avoid. It solidifies the significance of the expression, "Well, at least you're not black."

The struggle against racism from a mixed-race critical position cannot work, then, through simply a rejection of principle (1). To reject the importance of being white in no way addresses the social revulsion with being black. A mixed-race racial position is compatible with the rejection of principle (1), but it is not compatible with the rejection of principle (2). That is because there is no way to reject the thesis that there is something wrong with being black beyond the willingness to "be" black—not in terms of convenient fads of playing blackness, but by paying the social costs of anti-blackness on a global scale. Against the raceless credo, then, racism cannot be rejected without a dialectic in which humanity experiences a blackened world. But therein lies the suicidal irony of a *critical* mixed-race theory.

Notes

1. See, for example, Naomi Zack's *Race and Mixed Race* (Philadelphia: Temple University Press, 1993) and her edited volume *American Mixed Race* (Lanham, MD: Rowman and Littlefield, 1995), as well as the February 13, 1995, issue of *Newsweek* for some discussion of this phenomenon. One also can argue that the popularity of the term *hybridity* in postmodern and postcolonial cultural studies is indicative of this phenomenon, where, in an effort to evade the peculiarly biological dimensions of race, *cultural* mixture becomes the focus in a tale of political ambiguity. That cultures are not homogeneous is not new to cultural anthropologists. Its contemporary popularity is premised on a false academic history of hegemonic purity. For discussion, see Paul Gilroy's *The Black Atlantic: Modernity and Double Consciousness* (Cambridge, MA: Harvard University Press, 1993). Although Gilroy's position is a sound critique of cultural reductionism and cultural purity (homogeneity may have been a value of cultures, but not a reality of their evolution), some of his readers' interests stem not from the social logic of his argument but from a fascination with a form of privileged hybridity or mixture. One need only consult the contemporary mystique of mixture, particularly of the female biracial variety in British popular films over the past two decades. For discussion, see Joy Ann James, *Resisting State Violence in U.S. Culture* (Minneapolis: University of Minnesota Press, 1996) and Lisa Anderson, *Mammies No More!* (Lanham, MD: Rowman & Littlefield, 1997). Finally, on the matter of political ambiguity, I think

context and relevance are the best appeals. Sometimes, circumstances are without ambiguity. Only those with tenuous access to power can afford ambiguity in their political relations.

2. See Fanon, *Peau noire, masques blancs*, chap. 5. For discussion, see *Bad Faith and Antiblack Racism*, part III.

3. Michael Omi and Howard Winant, *Racial Formations in the United States: From the 1960s to the 1990s*, 2nd ed. (New York and London: Routledge, 1994).

4. We argue that sex and gender are two categories that also apply.

5. I discuss this dimension of antiblack racism in parts III and IV of *Bad Faith and Antiblack Racism*. See also "Introduction: Black Existential Philosophy" in *Existence in Black*.

6. For discussion, see treatments of the spirit of seriousness in chap. 6 and the discussion of "meaning" and racism in Parts II and III of *Bad Faith and Antiblack Racism*, as well as the critique, in *Fanon and the Crisis of European Man*, chap. 3, of the current misuse of the term *social construction*. See also Fanon's discussion of blacks as an *"objet phobogène"* (phobogenic object) and the point at which *"commence le cycle du biologique"* (the cycle of the *biological* begins) in *Peau noire*, pp. 123, 131. For critical discussion of Omi and Winant's notion of a racial formation, see also David Theo Goldberg's *Racist Culture: Philosophy and the Politics of Meaning* (Oxford: Blackwell, 1993), especially p. 88.

7. See Count Giovanni Pico Della Mirandola, *Oration on the Dignity of Man*, trans. by Elizabeth L. Forbes, in *The Renaissance Philosophy of Man*, ed. by Ernst Cassirer, Paul Oskar Kristeller, and John Herman Randall, Jr. (Chicago: University of Chicago Press, 1939).

8. For some readers, Lovejoy's discussion of the Great Chain of Being may come to mind. For discussion of that ontological schema, see Daniel Wideman, "The 'African Origin' of AIDS: De-constructing Western Biomedical Discourse," in *Black Texts and Textuality: Constructing and De-Constructing Blackness*, ed. with an intro. by Lewis R. Gordon and Renée T. White (Lanham, MD: Rowman & Littlefield, forthcoming). See also Robert Westley, "White Normativity and the Rhetoric of Equal Protection" in *Existence in Black*.

9. For discussion of this "logic," see C.W. Cassinelli, *Total Revolution: A Comparative Study of Germany under Hitler, the Soviet Union under Stalin, and China under Mao* (Santa Barbara and Oxford: Clio Books, 1976), part II.

10. One can argue that they mean these categories in those other societies as well, but the argument requires a demonstration of the relation between historical reality and phenomenology of "race seeing." For such a phenomenology, see *Bad Faith and Antiblack Racism*, chaps. 13–14.

11. For some discussion of Afro-Asian dynamics, see Ernest Allen, Jr., "When Japan Was 'Champion of the Darker Races': Satokata Takahashi and the Flowering of Black Messianic Nationalism," *The Black Scholar* 24, no. 1 (Winter 1994): 23–46, and Joy Ann James, *Resisting State Violence in U.S. Culture* (Minneapolis: University of Minnesota Press, 1996), chap. 15. For specifically Northeast Asian encounters with racial mixture in the United States, see Stephen Satris, " 'What Are They?' " in *American Mixed Race: The Culture of Microdiversity*, ed. by Naomi Zack (Lanham, MD: Rowman and Littlefield, 1995), pp. 53–60. Satris argues that children of European (caucasion) and Northeast Asian (mongoloid) descent tend to be regarded as Asian only when mongoloid morphology is visually apparent. Children who don't appear as such are regarded and treated by the white and Asian communities as white.

12. According to the U.S. Census, as of 1993, only 2% of interracial marriages were between blacks and "other" races, 20% between blacks and whites, but the number of interracial marriages between whites and non-black "others" was 77%. See also Connie Leslie, Regina Elam, Allison Samuels, and Danzy Senna, "The Loving Generation: Biracial Children Seek Their Own Place," *Newsweek* (February 13, 1995), p. 72, where these figures also are cited.

13. From *The Autobiography of Malcolm X as Told to Alex Haley* (New York: Ballentine Books, 1965), p. 2.

14. The impact of class on interracial relationships hasn't received significant study. And in fact, most of the constructions of interracial liaisons are premised on either a white male boss with a colored female subordinate, or affluent men of color with affluent white women. But note: relationships are most likely to occur where people are compelled to live. Because the black poor and the white poor have few options over where they can live, and because the urban poor tend to be located in black areas of cities, it follows that interracial relationships should have a greater probability of emerging in poor or working-class communities: In fact, there are no black American communities that have not had a white population, however small.

15. For discussion, see Fanon's essay "Antillais et africains" in his *Pour la révolution africaine: écrits politiques* (Paris: François Maspero, 1979), pp. 22–31. The essay appears as "West Indians and Africans" in the English edition, *Toward the African Revolution: Political Essays*, trans. by Haakon Chevalier (New York: Grove Press, 1967), pp. 17–27. See also our chap. 4 below.

16. Victoria Holloway, "President's Message," *The Drum: The SNMA-Yale Chapter Newsletter* (October 1991): 1.

17. The question of transforming the body takes special forms with Northeast Asians. There is, for instance, the phenomenon of surgically "fixing" the eyes. But note, the normative point is white eyes. The probability of Asians transforming

their bodies to look more "black" is very small. For discussion of Northeast Asian Americans' identity formations, see Brian Locke, "The Impact of the Black-White Binary on Asian American Identity," *Radical Philosophy Review* 1 no. 2 (1998). Locke argues that an apocalyptic subtext of the U.S. black–white binary structures Asian Americans as foreign.

18. In this regard, the appeal to mixed race as a model for resisting appeals to racial and cultural "authenticity" appears misguided, for the problem of authenticity—as "being *authentically* mixed" demonstrates—is quite resilient.

19. For more discussion of playing blackness, see bell hooks, *Black Looks: Race and Representation* (Boston: South End Press, 1992), chap. 1.

20. See, for example, bell hooks's criticism of Camille Paglia: " 'Black' Pagan or White Colonizer?" chap. 7 of hooks's *Outlaw Culture* (New York and London: Routledge, 1994).

21. One also finds the phenomenon of mixture in philosophy itself, where there is antipathy on the part of the dominant, Anglo-Analytical philosophy toward any of the pluralistic, "mixed" conceptions of philosophy ranging from pragmatism and European continental philosophy, on the one hand, to Africana philosophies and Eastern philosophies on the other. Departments that offer both are "mixed." Interestingly enough, certain "mixtures" exist in the form of Anglo-Analytical approaches to Africana philosophy, the most noted proponent of which is Kwame Anthony Appiah and the analytical race theorists who follow his path.

22. Theorists who focus on the concept of race are Michael Omi and Howard Winant, K. Anthony Appiah, Jorge Klor de Alva, and Naomi Zack. Theorists who focus on racism are Lucius Outlaw, Paget Henry, David Theo Goldberg, Cornel West, and myself, among others. This distinction doesn't mean, however, that the two groups do not touch on dimensions of each other's position. The former group argues that the elimination of the discourse of race is a necessary step toward the elimination of racism. The latter takes two stands on that issue. First, some argue for the existential complexity of race. Second, some argue that racism can exist without race. In either event, both groups end up addressing race and racism, but the first group, unlike the second, wants to eliminate both categories.

23. *Schwartzfarhen* (1992). In contemporary Eastern Europe (and Europe generally), the digression seems to take a definite form: first, xenophobic (anti-immigration) and, eventually, racist (antiblack). The argument is that immigration policies pollute the state by leading to an influx of blacks. For discussion, see Paul Hockenos, *Free to Hate: The Rise of the Right in Post-Communist Eastern Europe* (New York and London: Routledge, 1993). We also may note that in California the pattern is strikingly similar: Proposition 187 is anti-immigrants legislation that has been followed by a so-called Civil Rights Initiative, which is an anti-Affirmative Action legislation that is primarily antiblack.

24. A classic instance of a thinker and activist against racism who nevertheless believes in races is Franz Boas. Boas believed not only in the existence of races, but also that blacks were to some extent less intellectually capable than whites, yet he fought vehemently against the status of second-class citizenship of blacks. For discussion, see Vernon Williams, Jr., *Rethinking Race: Franz Boas and His Contemporaries* (Lexington: University of Kentucky Press, 1996). See also Amy Guttman's "Responding to Racial Injustice" in Anthony Appiah and Amy Guttman, *Color Conscious: The Political Morality of Race*, with an intro. by David B. Wilkins (Princeton: Princeton University Press, 1996), p. 64.

25. For discussion, see K. Anthony Appiah's "Racisms" in *Anatomy of Racism*, ed. by David Theo Goldberg (Minneapolis: University of Minnesota Press, 1990), pp. 3–17; Appiah's *In My Father's House: Africa in the Philosophy of Culture* (New York and Oxford: Oxford University Press), pp. 13–15; and "Race, Culture, and Identity: Misunderstood Connections" in *Color Conscious*. We return to Appiah and scientific criteria of meaning in chap. 6, below.

26. All of these possibilities are discussed in Naomi Zack's *Mixed Race* and *American Mixed Race*.

27. On the nonracial level, a correlative is in religious-cultural affiliation, where the goal of the assimilating Jew is not to be Jewish. The closest similarity to the racial question emerges when the assimilating Jew of "mixed" Gentile-Jewish parentage experiences this question through having a Jewish mother. We return to this question in chap. 6, below.

28. W.E.B. Du Bois, *The Souls of Black Folks*, with introductions by Nathan Hare and Alvin F. Poussaint, revised and updated bibliography (New York and Scarborough, Ontario: New American Library, 1982 [originally published, 1903]), chap. 1.

29. Angela Y. Davis, Keynote Address, *10th Annual Empowering Women of Color Conference: Reaping Fruit, Throwing Seed* (22 April 1995), University of California at Berkeley.

30. Robert Westley, "White Normativity and the Rhetoric of Equal Protecting" in *Existence in Black*.

CHAPTER FOUR

SEX, RACE, AND MATRICES OF DESIRE IN AN ANTIBLACK WORLD

In appearance too a boy is like a woman, and the woman is as it were an infertile male; for the female exists in virtue of a particular incapacity, in being unable to concoct seed out of the nutriment in its last stage (which is either blood or the analogous part in the bloodless animals) owing to the coldness of her nature.

—*Aristotle,* De Generatione Animalium I

We are accustomed to say that every human being displays both male and female instinctual impulses, needs and attributes; but though anatomy, it is true, can point out the characteristics of maleness and femaleness, psychology cannot. For psychology the contrast between the sexes fades away into one between activity and passivity, in which we far too readily identify activity with maleness and passivity with femaleness, a view which is by no means universally confirmed in the animal kingdom.

—*Sigmund Freud,* Civilization and Its Discontents

. . . the Negrophobe is a repressed homosexual. . . . Is the lynching of the Negro not a sexual revenge? We know how much of sexuality there is in all cruelties, tortures, beatings. One has only to reread some pages of the Marquis de Sade and one will easily be convinced. Is the sexual superiority of the Negro real? Everyone knows that it is not. But that does not matter. The prelogical thought of the phobic has decided that such is the case.

—*Frantz Fanon,* Peau noire, masques blancs

To help give me perspective, I remember that for years, in the namecalling at school, boys shouted at Jonathan not—"your mother's a lesbian"—but rather—"your mother's a nigger."

—*Audre Lorde,* Sister Outsider

Our epigraphs are two classic statements on sex and sexuality and two classic, provocative statements on their intersection with race. In Aristotle's world, where the hierarchies of a mythology are writ large and are at the core of a rational ordering of the universe, we find that the question of sex is colored by an indirect reference to the cold and, consequently, the dark. In that world of biological convergence with reproduction, the female is worse than a derivative of the male; she also is a derivative of the human species. For whereas male stands as the formal constitution of human reality, female lays bereft as an undeveloped male and, consequently, an undeveloped human being, a less-than-human being. To be is to be both form and a mover, which Aristotle linked to fertility. The male was a fertile mover who brought form into matter (female) and hence the concrete reality of the human being. In that world, then, one does not see female as a gender at all, another constituent of the human species. One sees simply males/ human beings and less-developed-males/less-developed-human beings— that is, *one* gender.[1]

By the time of Freud, we witness a schism between reproductive capacities and gender, where male and female refer to realities that are fertile, in spite of the etymological link between *gender* and Greek words such as *gênesis* (birth) and *genos* (kind). For Freud, the psychological constructions of sexual identity need not be linked to the markers male and female. In Freud's world, then, a female can be what psychologists regard as masculine and a male can be what psychologists regard as feminine.[2]

Separating the gender-sex link does not entail, however, a schism between the acts signified by the previous relationship. Thus, the masculine performance of a female can restructure her relation to a feminine male. This coding becomes particularly multivalent when we add, as do Fanon and Lorde, racial significations to the context. If we make as our model the context that I have coined in *Bad Faith and Antiblack Racism* as an *antiblack world*, we can see immediately how Fanon's and Lorde's remarks come into focus. For if a group is structured, in a phobogenic, overdetermined way, to signify hot/active/masculine/white and another group is constructed as cold/passive/feminine/black, then relationships between males and females in such a world may be skewed, with subtexts of transformed sexual meanings (in spite of the normative significance of sex): White males and black males may relate to each other in homoerotic ways that may be more genital than social; on the social level, the level of signification, the relation may be heterosexual and misogynist.

I have explored the significance of intersections between sexual relationships and race before. My past discussions focused on their relevance to phenomenological ontology.[3] I would here like to provide a discussion of racial and sexual matrices and their significance for the understanding of phenomenological treatments of social role. It is my aim to show how the false reality created by such bad-faith forms of desire ironically provides a clue for richer understanding of desire and, consequently, racial and sexual roles.

Let us begin by articulating a few key concepts. In Freud's and Fanon's remarks, there are indirect references to the constructability of human identity formations. An implication of this conception of identity is the view that human identity is made or lived; it is not a "determined" feature of the world. Where it is treated as constituted by an already existing social order, we may call it a social identity or a social role. Where it is lived, we can simply call it an existential identity or existential reality.

Existential realities are transphenomenal realities. What this means is that how they are lived always surpasses how they are understood. Their existence precedes their essence or conceptualization. When the order is reversed, and the essence is treated or lived as preceding existence, we shall refer to that circumstance or attitude as *bad faith*. Bad faith closes human reality into an essential reality that precedes existence or lived reality.

A key feature of all social realities is that they are constituted realities. What that means is that they are *Geist*-realms or spirit-realms. They add nothing physical to the world, although they are positive, meaningful additions to reality. Two human beings standing side-by-side in love are no different from two human beings standing side-by-side in lust or hate from a physical point of view. From the point of view of intentionality, the point of view of realities conditioned by meaning-contexts, there are worlds of difference. In bad faith, we play upon the difference and try to evade ourselves; we treat social realities as either consequences of nature (and hence not constituted by human beings) or fiction (and hence nonexistent by virtue of being nonphysical). At the heart of bad faith, then, is a denial of agency in the human condition and a denial of the relationship between such agency and the constitution of meaning.

We find, then, in the advancement of bad faith as an index of human possibilities, a principle of positive contingency and agency: That although the human world may be contingently constituted (neither by necessity nor fate nor destiny), it is never accidental. It is a world of responsibility and the irony of limited choices. By limited choices, I mean decisions based on options available. Options are what are available *in* the world; choices are what we make on the basis of those options, including how we may interpret the options themselves.

To articulate options, choices, and meanings, our inquiry must make an appeal to context. For options are not conditions etched in stone. They are simply wherever we happen to find ourselves or whatever is most relevant for our inquiry here. (Irrelevance has, as Schopenhauer would say, no principle of individuation.)

To decode matrices of race and sex requires contexts premised on racial and sexual identities. The context that we shall here focus on is the context of the antiblack world. We shall focus on the antiblack world primarily because of its unique relation to the Western world. The Western world, as we saw in Aristotle's depiction but can also see in many other sources, structures itself according to a binary logic of opposition. What this means is that the system functions contextually by always placing any two terms as far from each other as possible by that which supposedly differentiates them. Since the Western valuative system has historically placed positivity and its self-identity on the value of the white, that means, then, that it structures its primary opposition on the level of the black. To speak of racial opposition, then, is to speak of white and black.

Now, although this may make it seem that one can immediately speak of race and gender simply by placing the opposition in respective lines, that would be an error. For although our antiblack world is also a misogynist world, a misogynist world is not necessarily an antiblack one. For instance, in Aristotle's world, there was simply one gender: male. What we call female was in that world simply not-male. Race, in that world, simply meant genus. Only males were considered really part of the human *race*. Women, as women are envisaged in contemporary Western society, had no meaning in Aristotle's world.[4] On the other hand, in an antiblack world, race is only designated by those who signify racial identification. A clue to that identification is in the notion of being "colored." Not being colored signifies being white, and, as a consequence, being raceless, whereas being colored signifies being a race. Thus, although the human race is normatively white, racialized human beings, in other words, a subspecies of humanity, are nonwhite. The negation is the supposedly opposite term—in a word, the black. In effect, then, in the antiblack world there is but one race, and that race is black. Thus, to be racialized is to be pushed "down" toward blackness, and to be deracialized is to be pushed "up" toward whiteness. So, we have:

Aristotle's world: to be gendered and to avoid being nongendered— that is, female (not-male-enough).

The antiblack world: to be raceless and to avoid being racialized—that is, black (being never-white-enough).

It is ironic that today when we say "gender studies" we invariably mean discourses on women. A lot has changed since Aristotle's time. The centered significance of gender has been pushed to a racial paradigm, where gender has begun to function like race. Consequently, the genderless designation has become a goal similar to the racial designation. How can this be possible without a shift in the binaries by way of a third factor?

Let us call this third factor *power*. What thus emerges is the following:

The antigender world: to be genderless and to avoid being gendered— that is, determined, powerless, defined, feminine.

The antiblack world: to be raceless and to avoid being racialized—that is, determined, powerless, defined, black.

The third factor of power: to be neutral, genderless, raceless—that is, self-determined, powerful, self-defined, neither feminine nor black, which amounts to being masculine and white.

There are obvious breakdowns of logic in this triad. Take the third. If to have the power of self-determination means to be white, what can be made of determinations not to be white? Although the determinations may be lived as raceless and genderless, the social meanings are clearly skewed, because the "meaning" of being white in an antiblack-infected social sphere equates whiteness with such neutrality. Clearly, then, all three worlds are bad-faith worlds. To analyze the world conditioned by all three, which is the focus of this sketch, requires multiple levels of analyses that correlate with the evasive nature of bad faith: One must, in other words, analyze a world lived as a world encountered; a world of contingency without accident.

How does desire correlate with sexual identities in such a world?

Desire is normatively constituted as avoiding *being* the black and feminized. What this means is that in such a world a rational person wants to be white and masculine. But since white and masculine are treated as positive variables, there is a short step in reasoning to white *or* masculine to white *as* masculine to white *equals* masculine and masculine equals white.

We find, in this logic, a complex framework of identity and desire premised on the context itself as *antiblack*. If white equals masculine and masculine equals white, then blackness and femininity become coextensive realities in an antiblack world. Such a world becomes diadic, with "mixture" being indexed by two polar realities as follows:

(Supposed) *Highest Nonmixture*: white/masculine. The claim to this position, in an antiblack world, is the white man. (We do not say

white male since we have already problematized the relationship between masculinity and maleness, although we concede, as did Freud,
that the tendency of masculinity to manifest itself in males must be
acknowledged.)

(Supposed) *Lowest Nonmixture*: black/feminine. The claim to this position, in an antiblack world, is the black woman. (We do not say
black female for the same reasons that we do not say white male.)

Mixture is now left for structures that cross the color-gender convergence.
Thus:

Mixture α: white and mixed with feminine. Claim to this position in
an antiblack world is not always clear. For now, we shall simply designate this α-mixture as white woman by virtue of the order of the
pairs white and feminine. (We do not say white female because the
significance of color/gender designation is already conditioned by the
context itself—an *antiblack world*. A white female is not necessarily a
mixture, since masculinity can attach to males and females; whereas a
white woman is necessarily a mixture.)

Mixture β: masculine and black. The claim to this position in an antiblack world is similarly problematized. (We do not say the black male
for similar reasons as in the α-mixture.)

Now, what should be apparent is that the highest nonmixture functions
as what Fanon calls a governing fiction over the mixed categories. Since
the mixed categories do not stand as "pure" and therefore extremes, then
we should have a proper hierarchical articulation in an antiblack world as
follows:

Highest nonmixture → *mixture* α → *mixture* β → *lowest nonmixture*.

The reason for this schema is that the antiblack world is conditioned by
what we have already seen are two principles of value:

(1) It is best to be white but (2) it is worst to be black.

When one fails to achieve whiteness (principle 1), it becomes vital to avoid
embodying blackness (principle 2). As in our previous chapter, we reform-
ulate our two principles thus:

(1*) "be white!" but (2*) "don't be black!"

Mixture in this world is conditioned by poles of negative blackness (principles 2 and 2*), as we have seen, more than positive whiteness (principles 1

and 1★). The impact on sex-race constructions thus follows from the extent to which the sex-gender relationship serves as a leitmotif for the identities. For the extent to which we separate sex from gender will make all the difference between certain coextensive realities being homoerotic and homophobic on the one hand, or heteroerotic and misogynist on the other.

Our concerns are problematized even more by the constructivity dimension of color itself. For it should be obvious that *black* and *white* are not here meant to refer to colors in any ordinary sense but to the valuative expectations placed on people who are meant to exemplify those colors. One doesn't "see" white and black people ordinarily but instead sees pink, gold, brown, and a host of other shades of people, shades that may not correlate with the color designation—as we see so well in cases of brown caucasians and pink, in a word, *Negroes*.[5]

The constructivity of color designation has led some critical race theorists to reject race itself by appealing to its social constructivity and natural scientific invalidity.[6] A problem with the appeal to scientific invalidity, however, is that it is of no consequence in any other world but the world of scientific positivism, for in effect it centers natural science as a model of assessment. But scientific positivism, as Edmund Husserl,[7] Alain Locke,[8] and Maurice Merleau-Ponty[9] have shown, is incapable of critical and, admittedly, *valuative* assessments of its own assumptions without contradiction. On the interpretive level, the basis of scientific meaning and value itself is at stake. To get to these questions requires metascientific considerations. We can see how the problem of a neopositivist and social constructivist approach to race plays itself out when we choose supposedly preferred descriptions such as "human being" and "person." To define the human being in biophysical terms is one thing, but to define what it means to "be" human is another. For assessments of the basis of adjudicating philosophical anthropological claims, more radical articulations of human "science" may be needed. Such radical articulations also demand interrogations of appeals to even the social constructivity of science itself. Our discussion suggests that the framework of the social is itself conditioned by intentional features that situate it on the level of constructivity as well. Thus, social constructivity amounts to asserting, redundantly, constructed constructivity.[10] To get at the heart of the matter requires, then, realization of both the active and passive components of social phenomena, that human communities maintain phenomena that are lived as pregiven phenomena. This pregiven dimension of phenomena carries reality principles and meaningful features that make them accessible to phenomenological reflection at disparate times. It is in this regard that phenomena such as language and humanity, albeit constructed, are not fictional realities; they are dimensions of social reality.

Now, in worlds where social reality has been skewed, where it has become aim-inhibited, where it has become antisocial, antihuman, anticommunicative, there are rigid, underlying themes of subverted recognition. What this means is that, although there may be human beings in such a world, the sociohistorical features of that world may be such that ordinary expectations of human contact are inhibited. In an ordinary human environment, for instance, human phenomena are accessible to all human beings and, as such, have an anonymous dimension to their meaning; they become, in a word, *typical*. In a skewed context, however, the typical has been transformed in such a way that the atypical becomes normative. Relationships are therefore skewed in such a world, and what counts as typical of certain groups hides, in effect, atypical realities. For example, in an antiblack world, to be a typical black is to be an abnormal human being. Thus, normativity is indexed by its distance from blackness. The black could at most hope to be a black who is typically white, which in effect is to be atypically white. To be black in that world is, therefore, to be trapped in an obversion of normative reality: To be an extraordinary black is to be an ordinary person; to be an ordinary black is to be an extraordinary person. "Normal blackness," as Fanon has shown in *Peau noire, masques blancs,* is to be locked in the absurdity of everyday or banal pathology. The implications of this absurdity become stark when we return to our matrices of value and consider them with the added element of desire.

Desire can be constructed along matrices of (a) *most-desired,* (b) *desired,* (c) *less desired,* and (d) *least desired.* Context will dictate what ideal types fall along each category. Since our context is an antiblack world, it should be obvious that, on the level of color, to be white is a conclusion of ideal desire (a) and to be black has its conclusion in no desire (d), because there is no desire that is less than no desire at all. When gender is colorized and treated as coded forms of color, we find ourselves facing a world with a number of social enigmas.

On the one hand, there are two groups: the white and the black. Whoever lays claim to being "in between" does so only as a matter of distance from the black or closeness to the white, which is, for the white, still too close to the black for comfort. Since mixture is ultimately a function of colored gender configurations, the notion of "white woman" carries within it a positive element of whiteness and a negative element of blackness. Now, although most day-to-day activities carry an air of anonymity, where typically women and men pass by, in an antiblack world blacks and whites do not typically pass by. For to pass by typically means to be situated as a limited place of epistemic clarity: One simply doesn't know much about the typical Other beyond her or his typicality. In an antiblack world, however, to see black is to see a typicality that is epistemologically conclusive. What this means is that to see black is to see all that needs to be seen. It is to see a superfluous existent, a plenitude. To see the whiteness of a white woman, then, calls for an act of epistemic closure on her blackness, to the point of closing off the color-coded dimension of her femininity— that is, to not see her femininity. With such a seeing, she will have become "purified." "She" will become desire. "She" will be a point at which more needs to be known. "She" will be an informant into her subjective reality, realities that, if known, will be of objective value because they will be realities onto which and from which action will be encouraged. If, however, the closure is not possible and the feminine dimension, her blackness, is acknowledged, then she becomes a form of tainted whiteness. Her power in an antiblack world becomes a denial of her femininity.[11] The conclusion? Her phallic order, power, becomes linked, fundamentally, to her skin, to her epidermal schema. In an antiblack world, the phallus is white skin.[12]

One may wonder what type of situation emerges when the white (woman) is declared rapable, for as we know, there is a rich history around the avowed protection of whites from rapacious blacks in antiblack worlds. The obvious conclusion is that the history has nearly nothing to do with white *women* at all. In *Peau noire, masques blancs*, Fanon has observed that white male's aggression toward black males is saturated with homoerotic content. In his discussion, "Le Nègre et la Psycopathologie," he points out that the black is a phobogenic object, a stimulus to anxiety, in negrophobic people.[13] For the negrophobe, the black is not a symbol of certain negative realities. The black *is* those negative realities. Thus, if femininity is regarded as a negative characteristic of that world, the black will "be" femininity. The white concern with rape in such a world is conditioned by the extrication of the feminine dimension of woman in white woman. Rape in such a world is thus premised on violating whiteness.

Since whiteness has been structured as masculine, the violation becomes a violation of masculinity. The rape of white women—translated into this schema simply as "whites"—ultimately becomes to white men the rape of white men. The violent response that has been the history of lynching in the name of redressing the offense of rape in the U.S. antiblack world is, therefore, indicative of the form of bad faith manifested in homophobia: Public violence locates the masculine identity's *rejection* of homosexual desire. But as is well-known, there is a twist to this affair, for the lynched black body often was mutilated in a ritual of surgical restructuring; genitals were often removed and holes gauged into the bodies to eradicate vestiges of claimed masculinity. The sexual dimension of lynching, in other words, had to be restructured into a heterosexual framework, where the black body becomes woman. Woman, as the body of clay on which any form can be forced, becomes the motif of lynching. As a result, we find the history of mutilation, a history of literally cutting away all protruding and active bodily appendages, in the lynching of blacks of all sexes and ages.

Rape, a form of violation, depends on human agency for its existence. In our portrait of criteria for rapability in an antiblack world, the place of subjectivity, and thus consent and dissent, was the highest point on the hierarchical scale: whiteness/masculinity. For the phenomenon to appear as a violation of an agent and hence have standing before law requires that it embody the phallic order in that world, that it be white. Where agency is denied, so, too, is violation. We can thus restructure our matrices as a portrait of rapability to "unrapability." In such a world, it would seem, black women (a redundant reality) are literally not rapable, for they supposedly lack the ability to dissent. A portrait of desire is implied by this conclusion.

Recall our two initial principles, that (1) it is best to be white and (2) it is worst to be black. We can add two correlates to these:

(1**) desire white and (2**) reject black.

Since the values of an antiblack world are existentially serious values—that is, values that are treated as material features of the beings who comprise that world[14]—we find ourselves encountering two more correlates:

(1***) whiteness is the desired desire and (2***) blackness is the rejected existent.

As the desired desire, the white man's relation to the black woman becomes obvious in such a world: He is incapable of raping her because she is incapable of not desiring him. He is constructed as her desired desire, and constructed as not having desired her in the first place. In effect, she would be constructed as having violated *him* if physical contact occurred.[15] Since the white female can only be recognized as rapable through suspending her womanness to the point of simply becoming "the white," then we find a similar derivation; "she" *must not have desired* the black and the black *must have desired* "her."

We find also that these considerations affect even avowed homosexual and lesbian structures in such a world. For white men in sexual relations with white men become the homosexual paradigm, whereas black women with black women become the lesbian paradigm. White female liaisons are restructured so that whiteness becomes the operative dimension of gendered identity; the relationship becomes, in a word, masculine and, therefore, homosexual—unless, of course, womanness is the operative dimension of the specific instance of that relationship. Likewise, black male liaisons are restructured so that blackness becomes the operative dimension of gendered identity; the relationship becomes feminine and, hence, a lesbian relation. We find even more twists in interracial relations, for the white female with a black female, given these matrices, becomes a "heterosexual" liaison; so, too, becomes the white male with black male liaison.[16]

Destruction of the link between the penis and the phallus and advancing an alternative configuration like white skin may, however, raise the following objection: Aren't black men nevertheless men by virtue of their chromosomal make up and their extended urethra, their penis? What about the extensive literature on the reduction of black males to their penis? On penis size?

Our analysis suggests that the significance of penis "color" must be brought into consideration in an antiblack world. Two penises of equal length are not of equal significance when they are of different "color." For, in an antiblack world, a black penis, whatever its size, represents a threat. Given our discussion of the black signifying the feminine, the underlying nature of the threat should be obvious: the black penis is feared for the same reason that a woman with a penis is feared. She represents a form of revenge. Literally, the very notion of a black *penis*, a demand *for* masculinity, spells danger. The rationale for lynching returns with an added dimension of prevention. In lynching and other forms of "castration" and bodily reconfiguration, the objective is to prevent the black from doing not what the black supposedly has done, but what the black *must want to do*. The black "penis" is phobogenically not a penis at all. It is a vagina bent on revenge.

Now the reader should bear some obvious facts in mind, given our discussion thus far. The first, and most obvious, is that our stated existential commitments entail that the portrait presented here is limited to realities that are conditioned by its context. As Fanon has cautioned all of us who tread along the critical race terrain, not everyone will find her or himself in such texts.[17] The antiblack world is what phenomenological sociologists call an *ideal type*.[18] An ideal type is a subjunctive reality. It is a world with a strict logic and strict rationality, a world that is governed by a specific ontology where the human being collapses under the weight of existence. Although in such a world there is only one perspective, the *critical* theorist who attempts a hermeneutics of such a world has the triple task of interpreting the two poles as perspectives and interpreting her or his own relation as a critical relation to such a world. By considering the perspective of the bottom-pole of such a world, the theorist raises the question that Fanon raised in 1952: What is "the lived-experience of the black"? The theorist will then find two directional poles of theocratic values:

> *The white*: It is desirable to be a human being, but it is undesirable to be black. Whites are human beings, but they are not gods, because to be gods would mean to be a desired desire; to be, in other words, better than human. Blacks, on the other hand, although humanlike, are less than whites and, therefore, less human—or at least not the type of beings to desire to be.

> *The black*: Whites are the desired desire. They are, therefore, better than human. They are gods.[19]

Although the theorist ascribes a point of view to both poles and to her or himself, in order not to slip into being the white, the theorist must be properly critical. What this means is that the theorist must not construct the theorist's position as a desired desire, or even a desirable position. Whether this is possible requires another discussion, but suffice it to say that a value-neutral theorist, even if desirable, is susceptible to our concerns about ideal typification and existence. As Merleau-Ponty cautions us in *Phénoménologie de la perception*, we should not lose existence for the sake of validity.[20]

So, what does our analysis offer for an understanding of social role? The first and obvious conclusion is that context is a complex existential affair. Although we have been speaking of an ideal type, an antiblack world, the existential significance of bad faith enables us to understand how the ideality of the types are concealed by how they are *lived*.[21]

Next, although it may be common knowledge that some identities are more basic than others, as is the general view toward sex and gender, the phenomenological critique of the mundane permits the extraordinary dimensions of the ordinary to make themselves manifest. When it comes to social role, the logic of gender in an antiblack world can be demonstrated to converge with the logic of race in ways that question the very meaning of sex.

Thus, third, the significance of social role emerges through the significance of context itself. The antiblack world is one context among many, but even in its case, the extratextual consideration of gender comes into play. Isolated meanings, although useful for modeling and assessments premised on formulating paradigm cases, will never achieve *social* significance without exhausting themselves.

Finally, as we saw in our discussion of desire, identities can be structured by multiple matrices of value. These matrices take multivalent forms of sexual, political, and theological economies of expression premised on centers of power. In the intersection of sex and race, we found not only white people and people of color, men and women, but we found also prosthetic gods and a dark continent of effeminate existent—a world, that is, of spirit and nature conditioned by identities that transform themselves along grids of institutional power.

Where do we go from here?

Our project at this point is primarily interpretative. The obvious methodological consideration is that theorizing sex, gender, and race in an antiblack world calls for understanding of ideal typifications of lived realities. It demands an existential sociology.

On the question of the antiblack/misogynist world itself, our existential concern, committed to preceding essence, beseeches us to admit to what we see as we attempt, in the spirit of an eleventh thesis of a century ago, to change our world.

Notes

1. Cf. Judith Butler, *Bodies that Matter: On the Discursive Limits of "Sex"* (New York and London: Routledge, 1993), "Introduction," where sex is deconstructed as normative: "The category of 'sex' is, from the start, normative; it is what Foucault has called a 'regulatory ideal.' In this sense, then, 'sex' not only functions as a norm, but is part of a regulatory practice that produces the bodies it governs, that is, whose regulatory force is made clear as a kind of productive power, the power to produce—demarcate, circulate, differentiate—the bodies it controls" (p. 1).

2. Teresa Brennan has argued that it is this disjunction of sex and gender that led to the Freudian riddle of femininity: "Why is [femininity] found in men?" *The Interpretation of the Flesh: Freud and Femininity* (London and New York: Routledge, 1992), p. 8. We also find an existential psychoanalytical dimension of this question in Simone de Beauvoir's restructuring womanhood away from birth and into the realm of project and historicity; see her classic *Le deuxième sexe* (Paris: Gallimard, 1949). But the prime space in which this disjunction is afforded semiotic analysis is Jacques Lacan's *Écrits: A Selection*, trans. by Alan Sheridan (New York and London: W.W. Norton, 1977), where, for instance, the subject/object relation is substituted by the signifier/signified relation (see especially p. 284).

3. For discussion and critique of that work, see, for example, Paget Henry, "African and Afro-Caribbean Existential Philosophies" in *Existence in Black;* William L. McBride, "Review of *Bad Faith and Antiblack Racism,*" *British Society for Phenomenological Research* (1996); Linda Alcoff, "Review of *Bad Faith and Antiblack Racism,*" *Canadian Philosophical Reviews/Revue Canadienne de Comptes rendus en philosophie* (1997); Patricia Huntington, "White Gods, Raw Desire, Misogyny: A Feminist Conversation with Gordon's *Bad Faith and Antiblack Racism*" (forthcoming proceedings of the 1996 meeting of the Society for Phenomenological and Existential Philosophy), *Philosophy Today* (1998).

4. The impact of the Aristotelian view is explored in Judith Butler's *Bodies That Matter,* which in turn draws on, among many sources, Luce Irigaray's ironically psychoanalytical neo-Aristotelianism in *This Sex Which Is Not One,* trans. by Catherine Porter and Carolyn Burke (Ithaca: Cornell University Press, 1985) and *Speculum of the Other Woman,* trans. by Gillian Gill (Ithaca: Cornell University Press, 1985). Particularly revealing is Butler's discussion of *hyle* (matter) in endnote 22 of chap. 1 of *Bodies That Matter.*

5. See *Bad Faith and Antiblack Racism,* chaps. 13–14, and Tommy Lott's "Du Bois on the Invention of Race," *Philosophical Forum* XXIV, nos. 1–3 (Fall-Spring 1992–93): 166–187. See also our chap. 3 above.

6. The most well-known proponents of this basis for rejecting the concept of race are Anthony Appiah and Naomi Zack. My criticisms of this position can be found in *Bad Faith and Antiblack Racism.* See also my discussions in our chap. 3 above and chap. 6 below. Zack's position also has an existential dimension. See her, "Race, Life, Death, Identity, Tragedy" in *Existence in Black.*

7. See Husserl's "Philosophie als strenge Wissenschaft," *Logos,* 1 (1910–11): 289–341. This essay also is found in *Phenomenology and the Crisis of Philosophy,* trans. and ed. by Quentin Lauer (New York: Harper & Row, 1965).

8. See Locke's essays "Values and Imperatives" and "Value" in *The Philosophy of Alain Locke: Harlem Renaissance and Beyond,* ed. with an intro. and interpretive essay by Leonard Harris (Philadelphia: Temple University Press, 1989), chaps. 1 and 7.

9. Merleau-Ponty's *Phénoménologie de la Perception* (Paris: Gallimard 1945), *passim; Phenomenology of Perception,* trans. by Colin Smith (New York and London: Routledge/Humanities Press, 1962).

10. See *Fanon and the Crisis of European Man,* chap. 3.

11. For a discussion and critique of this attitude toward femininity in an antiblack world, see Audre Lorde's essay, "Uses of the Erotic: The Erotic as Power" in *Sister Outsider: Essays and Speeches,* intro. by Nancy K. Bereano (Freedom, CA: The Crossing Press, 1983), p. 75 .

12. Although I discuss this conclusion in *Bad Faith and Antiblack Racism*, Patricia Huntington develops its implications for a critique of poststructural psychoanalyses of gender; again, see her essay, "White Gods, Raw Desire, Misogyny." In an informal discussion of the present essay, Cynthia Willett also reminded me that Lacan's analysis doesn't exclude multiple manifestations of the phallus because, as we have already noted, the signifier/signified relation is its hallmark, which means that the signifier could be any semiotically active designation. Most Lacanians do, however, work in a world in which sexual difference takes center stage. For discussion, see Patricia Huntington's "Fragmentation, Race, and Gender: Building Solidarity in the Postmodern Era" in *Existence in Black*. The multisignificative dimensions of the phallus are developed also by Tina Chanter in her provocatively titled article, "Can the Phallus Stand, or Shoud It Be Stood Up?" in *Returns of the "French Freud": Freud, Lacan, and Beyond*, ed. by T. Dufresne (New York and London: Routledge, 1997). And the complexities of sex, sexuality, and color converging along power lines are explored in many passages of Audre Lorde's *Sister Outsider*. My point here is not to reduce the phallus to white skin. It is to point out what emerges, hermeneutically, when the phallus is, in at least its instantiation in an antiblack world, white skin.

13. For discussion of Fanon's conception of phobogenesis, see chap. 2 above and my essays, "The Black and the Body Politic: Fanon's Existential Phenomenological Critique of Psychoanalysis" in *Frantz Fanon: A Critical Reader* and "Existential Dynamics of Black Invisibility" in *Existence in Black*.

14. See *Bad Faith and Antiblack Racism*, chap. 6, for a discussion of the spirit of seriousness, and part III for a discussion of that attitude in an antiblack world; also Linda A. Bell's *Rethinking Ethics in the Midst of Violence: A Feminist Approach to Freedom*, foreword by Claudia Card (Lanham, MD: Rowman and Littlefield, 1993), *passim*. For the classic statement on the subject in philosophy of existence, see Jean-Paul Sartre's *L'être et le néant*.

15. Think, for example, of black women who have been imprisoned for resisting white men's sexual advances and assaults. For discussions of the sexual exploitation of black women by the U.S. criminal justice system, see Calvin Hernton, Sex and Race in America (New York: Grove Press, 1965); Herbert G. Gutman, *The Black Family in Slavery and Freedom, 1750–1925* (New York: Vintage, 1976); and Gerald Horne, "On the Criminalization of a Race," *Political Affairs* 73, no. 2 (February 1994): 26–30.

16. See my discussion of Isaac Julien's *Frantz Fanon: "The Fact of Blackness"* in the penultimate chapter below for some implications of interracial homosexual liaisons. For interracial lesbian relationships, Audre Lorde provides many insights in *Sister Outsider* on the egalitarian project she and her lover Frances (a white woman) worked at developing.

17. Cf. *Peau noire*, p. 9/*Black Skin*, p. 12.

18. See *Fanon and the Crisis of European Man*, chap. 3, for discussion of typification. See also Maurice Natanson, *Anonymity: A Study in the Philosophy of Alfred Schutz* (Bloomington: Indiana University Press, 1986).

19. See *Bad Faith and Antiblack Racism*, Part IV.

20. See Merleau-Ponty's discussion in the preface, *Phénoménologie*, p. vi/*Phenomenology*, p. xii.

21. *Peau noire, masques blancs*, *Bad Faith and Antiblack Racism*, and *Existence in Black* address this dimension of theorizing about living in an antiblack/misogynist world. See also *Rethinking Ethics in the Midst of Violence* and Cynthia Willett's *Maternal Ethics and Other Slave Moralities* (New York and London: Routledge, 1995).

CHAPTER FIVE

USES AND ABUSES OF BLACKNESS: POSTMODERNISM, CONSERVATISM, IDEOLOGY

The first premise of all human history is, of course, the existence of living human individuals.

—*Karl Marx*, The German Ideology

We do not confuse exploitation or exploiters with the color of men's skins; we do not want any exploitation in our countries, not even by black people.

—*Almicar Cabral*, Revolution in New Guinea

Marxism exists in nineteenth-century thought like a fish in water: that is, it is unable to breathe anywhere else.

—*Michel Foucault*, The Order of Things

It is difficult to talk about human beings these days. It is not so much that the age-old problem of dealing with practical reason and human science persists, for at least that keeps the human being in sight. Instead, what we find is a form of preemption of the human in human subjects for the sake of, above all, pseudopolitical and pseudoethical concerns. I say *pseudo* because without such an adjective there may rest the illusion of commitment, which may be too much commitment to ascribe to the avowedly uncommitted and the chronically cynical.

In 1845, Marx wrote the following in *The German Ideology*:

> The Young Hegelian ideologists, in spite of their allegedly "world-shattering" statements, are the staunchest conservatives. The most recent of them have found the correct expression for their activity when they declare they are only fighting against *phrases*. They forget, however, that to these phrases they themselves are only opposing other phrases, and that they are in no way combating the real, existing world when they are merely combating the phrases of this world.[1]

He could easily have been describing the 1970s, the 1980s, and the first half of the 1990s. This period has been marked not only by the ascendence and hegemony of literary, cultural, and pseudopolitical postmodernism in the popular North American academy, but also by Reagan-Bush conservatism and subsequent Clinton Democratic conservatism in national politics. Although postmodernists may object to the association of their ascendence with conservatism—particularly yuppie conservatism—their objection requires an appeal to causal relationships that may not be, in the end, postmodern. For if postmodernism and conservatism are mere accidents, in what sense could such "accidents" be coherent without "coherence" in history, a notion that postmodernism of the antihistorical and anticoherence variety rejects?[2] Think, for instance, of Foucault's various schematizing of historical moments as *epistemes* and power/knowledge: How do their assessments as such work without an overarching, metahistorical, transcendental thesis? Although one possibility is to appeal to the practices of assessment that emerge, we must also consider the status of this appeal. Is it not a prepractical appeal?

The general rhetoric of postmodernism has been used in the service of a trenchant anti-Marxism, often ironically in the name of Marxism, in the final third of the twentieth century.[3] According to Brian Meeks:

> If the collapse of the Berlin Wall signalled the end of a certain model of "socialism" it also signalled an explosion in the debate on the relevance of Marxist analysis. Indeed, an earlier split from Marxism occurred in the seventies and eighties with the expansion of the feminist debate and the development of various postmodernist schools including Foucault's dissection of the sources of power and Lyotard's rejection of "grand narratives." Since then, the reemergence of the Hegelian version of the dialectic and, far more critically, the dramatic assertion of neoliberalism as a dominant ideological form in the 1980s have further served to bring into focus the relevance and usefulness of Marxist analysis and what one can consider as a central weakness in the historical materialist argument.[4]

The postmodernist goal has often been to take the economic dimension out of the interpretation of production and shift focus to other "sites" of production—for example, epistemic production, cultural production, or sexual production. Yet these shifts often present themselves as though they deal with antipathetic realities. Why should epistemic production and economic production be mutually exclusive? Why should sexual production and economic production be mutually exclusive? And racial production?

A distinction should be made between "postmodern" and "postmodernism." The former is a quality or epoch that may or may not be endorsed by those who exemplify it, whereas the latter is an ideological prescription of that quality. My concern is with postmodernism. To identify idealogues of postmodernism, I will use the term "postmodernist." My reason is simple: Not all postmoderns are postmodernists.

I have always felt that if one were to scratch the surface of postmodernism, one would find conservatism under guises of bourgeois aestheticism and existential stoicism. Both turns pose no challenge to systemic orders of production by virtue of not engaging them in action or thought, the consequence of which is to leave the powers that be to their Machiavellian techniques of self-preservation. This concern about postmodernism isn't new. The ascription of neoconservatism to postmodernism was a position Jean-François Lyotard attempted to refute in his famous postmodernist tract, *The Postmodern Condition: A Report on Knowledge.* [5]

I will lay claim less to "argument" and more to exploring various patterns I've seen surface now and then under the guise of postmodernism. My reason for doing so is straightforward: It is not clear where argument (and perhaps description) stands in a postmodernist's world (perhaps the futile modernist effort to present the unpresentable?). I may be simply wasting my time by advancing them. If the situation being addressed here is political, then the place of *proof* may be one of displacement to begin with.

So, perhaps the key political consideration to bear in mind is the shift in politics from speech to rhetoric and subsequently to "writing." The shift itself emerges from the ascendence of a dimension of forms of French poststructuralism that emphasize writing over speech, inscription over deed. The terrain has been rehearsed over the past three decades: Jacques Derrida's *Of Grammatology, Writing and Difference, The Margins of Philosophy*, and *Disseminations* and Foucault's *The Order of Things* and *The Archaeology of Knowledge* being the most influential instances. There, as in contemporary physics and mathematics, the invisible world of "deep structures" are "read" by the expert, but with a twist: Like Kurt Gödel's incompleteness theorem in mathematics, where any system sophisticated enough to refer to itself is demonstrated to be *logically* incomplete, poststructuralists such as Derrida and Foucault demonstrate the incompleteness and points of indecision in nearly every self-referential order of knowledge. By self-referential order of knowledge, I mean theory of theory, what philosophers call *metatheory*. With Derrida, particularly favored targets are metatheories that center speech and other forms of active experience over writing, especially with appeals to the supposed "authoritative" force of "presence."

Now, I regard political speech as action or praxis oriented.[6] Political
rhetoric, however, I regard as primarily stylistic and used for purposes of
persuasion. When theories of political rhetoric are such that *all* political
activity collapses into rhetoric, the consequence is linguistic idealism. Linguistic idealism is a reduction of the world to language. To be is to be
linguistic. In that world, everything, including "actors," are linguistic manifestations. Thus, it is not people who act in such a world, it is language
that enacts people.[7]

Political writing can manifest speech or simply be rhetorical. When
poststructural insights are taken to be the end-all of reality, political writing
loses force as speech, because speech, too, is here rhetorical in the end. A
consequence of centering political matters on rhetoric is the concealment
of political reality, because the political dimension of the political is rendered invisible by virtue of being regarded as purely performative—or, as
in more Foucaultian/Nietzschean articulations of this drama, purely manifestations of will to power.[8] *What* one performs is rendered immaterial.
Whatever "is" is simply a performance within a claustrophobic system of
signs (Derridianism) or power/knowledge (Foucaultism). Leveling out
emerges, the consequence of which is a predilection toward what I shall
call *political nihilism*. Political nihilism is the lack of faith not only in the
political as a means of social change, but also in the human ability to effect
social change. It is, in other words, a rejection of political solutions or
amelioration of human problems and the human ability to address those
problems. We find this phenomenon in the 1980s with the infamous "political correctness" charge. The charge is a perversion of the existential
observation that it is difficult to be a political actor without having dirty
hands.

It is a turn of irony that the charge of political correctness became the
rallying cry for conservatives during the 1980s and 1990s, for what is more
postmodernist than the rejection of a politically correct position? When
conservatives hurl charges of political correctness, they are letting loose a
Trojan horse upon reality. For political correctness as a charge is always
issued against the articulation of interests that deal with the powerless, usually by way of leveling out the perception of power into an equal-opportunity affair of "relative truths." Its epistemic core is a consciousness of limits-
skepticism and judgment-skepticism—judging judgment becomes the
order of the day, and denial of any politically legitimate position beyond
the denial of defending such a position is its consequence. When it comes
to addressing its ideological dimensions, however, one needs to ask: Who
benefits from a world in which politically correct positions are denied? If

judgments are judged untenable, then the powerful in effect both have their cake and can eat it too, for they can dominate and judge, without being judged.

A classic form of self-deception has emerged, wherein there is the ironic advancement of antijudgment, which carries the consequence of concealing judgment. An evasiveness permeates postmodernist self-presentations to the point of standing squarely in the realm of bad faith; it is never what one sees, hears, says, or identifies it to be. As Jean-François Lyotard sees it:

> The postmodern would be that which, in the modern, puts forward the unpresentable in presentation itself; that which denies itself the solace of good forms, the consensus of a taste that would make it possible to share collectively the nostalgia for the unattainable; that which searches for new presentations, not to enjoy them but to impart a stronger sense of the unpresentable (*The Postmodern Condition*, p. 81).

Thus, there are postmodernists who range from the identification of postmodernism as premodernism, to after-modernism, to even more-rigorous-modernism.[9] These identifications stand in persistently ironic ways, where they are advanced for the sake of being denied, denied for the sake of being advanced; even postmodernist identification of self-deception has been used in the interest of continued deception. Think, for example, of Derrida's poststructural-postmodernist use of the term *bad faith* when describing the "ill-tempered" speaker to, in effect, disarm criticism of deconstruction in his essay, "Force of Law: The 'Mystical Foundation of Authority' ":

> An ill-tempered speaker might say: I don't see the connection [between deconstruction and justice], no rhetoric could bend itself to such an exercise. . . . Such a speaker wouldn't merely be in a bad temper, he'd be in bad faith. . . . The "sufferance" of deconstruction, what makes it suffer and what makes those it torments suffer, is perhaps the absence of rules, of norms, and definitive criteria that would allow one to distinguish unequivocally between *droit* and justice.[10]

Given Derrida's well-known attacks on agency and consciousness, and given that bad faith is a form of self-deception, where is the lie to oneself located in this charge of bad faith? Is Derrida saying the ill-tempered speaker is aware of that which he denies?[11]

Political skepticism, which in "Continental" philosophical circles draws heavily on Paul Ricoeur's hermeneutics of suspicion, is a hallmark of post-modernism, but interestingly enough, we often find such skepticism fo-cused on the travails of the left. For, as Lyotard articulated rather clearly, two major quarries of postmodernism are the "totalizing" currents of liber-ation and enlightenment theory and politics.[12] On the left, this meant an attack on progressive and revolutionary politics on the one hand, and dem-ocratic universalism on the other. I always have found this focus to be disingenuous, not out of any absurd notion that the left should not be judged or criticized, but out of concern that those who now articulate such judgment stand bereft of anything to lose in any political order short of a régime that affects in any positive way the material conditions of the col-ored poor; and this consequence is because, even where such postmodern-ists are colored and may have once been poor, their political-economic reality is one of clear material enhancement by way of the benefits of acting as liaisons between the powerful and the powerless.[13] There is, as William James would say, cash value in a left persona with a conservative platform. On that matter, we need simply consult the array of popular publications that have emerged from "former radical left" intellectuals since the days of Richard Wright's public departure from the Communist Party USA. Such a tradition "sells" a left identity through rejecting many conditions for developing any coherent program of action from the standpoint of the left.[14] That is because the political skepticism that undergirds some of these writers has a negative impact on the very notion of political strategizing. They attack strategy as grand, teleological, and totalizing because it's a fu-ture-oriented activity.[15] What they prefer are forms of primarily linguistic tactics, which, for postmodernists of the hermeneutical, textual, or decon-structive vein, amount to rummaging through the refuse of political arti-facts through a glorification and centering on "writing," "reading," and aesthetic "play." Thus, without strategy, liberation itself becomes subordi-nated, and praxis, being fundamentally liberating activity, dies. As Edward Said states in the following criticism of Lyotard:

> The purpose of the intellectual's activity is to advance human free-dom and knowledge. This is still true, I believe, despite the often repeated charge that "grand narratives of emancipation and enlighten-ment," as the contemporary French philosopher Lyotard calls such heroic ambitions associated with the previous "modern" age, are pro-nounced as no longer having any currency in the era of postmodern-ism. According to this view, grand narratives have been replaced by local situations and language games; postmodern intellectuals now

prize competence, not universal values like truth or freedom. I've always thought that Lyotard and his followers are admitting their own lazy incapacities, perhaps even indifference, rather than giving a correct assessment of what remains for the intellectual a truly vast array of opportunities despite postmodernism. For in fact, governments still manifestly oppress people, grave miscarriages of justice still occur, the co-option and inclusion of intellectuals by power can still effectively quieten [sic] their voices, and the deviation of intellectuals from their vocation is still very often the case (*Representations of the Intellectual*, pp. 17–18).

So in the midst of the conservatives' attack on political correctness and the postmodernist attack on the notion of having a right position—an attack that is usually cloaked in rhetoric of "totalization," "essentialism," "centrism," "modernism," and even "terror"—much is eventually spoken, but little is actually said, which means that far less is actually done.

I say "rhetoric" because in this game we find the market tool of duping the consumer. The consumer is being duped because postmodernism has a lot to sell, and sell it does, but a great deal of its sales pitch rests on convincing the consumer that if she or he were only wise enough, she or he would then be able to "see" or, as the antiocular theorists prefer, "dance." And see or dance to what? That one should not bother to ask "what"? In the meantime, much is promised (often ironically through the play of denying making promises at all)—think of the many Derridians and Foucaultians who continue to keep vigil—whilst there remains a pauper with no clothes enamored of emperors who also, ultimately, have no clothes. As Callinicos puts it:

> Foucault, more democratic, asks why "everyone's life couldn't become a work of art?" The answer, of course, is that most peoples' lives are still . . . shaped by their lack of access to productive resources and their consequent need to sell their labour-power in order to live. To invite a hospital porter in Birmingham, a car-worker in Sao Paolo, a social security clerk in Chicago, a street child in Bombay to make a work of art of their lives would be an insult—unless linked to precisely the kind of strategy for global social change which . . . poststructuralism rejects (*Against Postmodernism*, pp. 90–91)

One danger in criticizing postmodernism is that it is often confused with poststructuralism. Although there are postmodernists who are poststructualists, we should bear in mind that there also are postmodernists who are not poststructuralists and poststructuralists who are not postmodernists. Marking these trajectories is a difficult task. For even the modern, against which postmodernism is nearly always contrasted, is difficult to articulate. Recall that, unlike most Western philosophers, who mark an epistemic beginning to modernity through the work of René Descartes, Enrique Dussel marks modernity in moments of a people's ability to enforce their conception of universality on the rest of the world, which for him was 1492. In Foucault's writings, the modern is much later, in the 19th century. And yet for others, it is the age of enlightement, in the 18th century. The postmodern moment represents, then, a rupture from designated modern moments. Still, there are others who see postmodernism in atemporal ways. Linda Martín Alcoff, for instance, sees postmodernism as a different way of thinking:

> Its [postmodernism's] originality lies, rather, in its large-scale attack on the borders and boundaries between philosophy and other enterprises of theoretical thinking. The autonomy and integrity of epistemology, for example—considered to be unique and separable from sociology, political theory, and psychology, among other disciplines—can no longer hold firm. The new theory understands that questions about the justification of belief require cross-disciplinary exploration, and that such forays cannot be restricted to the biological sciences or to artificial intelligence studies, as analytic philosophers seem to think. I realize many philosophers hold that sociology and related disciplines may tell us how beliefs *actually* attain justification, but that epistemology alone pursues the question how they *should* attain justification. But this border between the normative and the sociological is perhaps the most important border that needs to be crossed. . . . Let those of us working in the United States never forget that border control has no intrinsic value (*Real Knowing*, p. 4).

I don't agree with Alcoff that this is *postmodernism*'s originality. Theorists of color have been arguing this point since the 19th century.[16] European philosophers of existence, such as Gabriel Marcel, Jean-Paul Sartre, Albert Camus, and Simone de Beauvoir, have challenged similar borders. I think her point about the importance of this critique of disciplinary purity and border–integrity is right on target, however, which suggests that on the epistemological and disciplinary planes, people like me would fall under this description of postmodern theorists. Callinicos's criticism of the consumer dimension of postmodernism should, therefore, be considered in its uniquely political context: Late capitalism would like to depend less on the worker in the pursuit of profit. The worker must see him or herself less as a worker and more as a consumer. Thus, new tailors have come into town with magical fabrics for all to wear. More paupers are being asked to believe that their naked bodies are clothed. That the paupers have no clothes has enabled postmodernist sites of production, if we will, to produce themselves with unprecedented rapidity. In the midst of the hullabaloo, historical responsibility has been lost and the cat has been let out of the bag. As long as one has access to the means of epistemic production—which are peculiarly also economic in terms of being the media, expensive information-age technologies, publishing houses (with their related industries of paper manufacturing, typesetting, etc.), government grants, universities, etc., all of which are linked to their cultural expression in dominant ideologies—one can almost say anything once the avowal of postmodernism, and, ironically, even the antipostmodern form of postmodernist avowal, has been made. Anything can be said because, when it comes to historical responsibility and such ancient, medieval, and modernist commitments as truth and integrity, humanity and liberation, progress and revolution, postmodernist avowals function like empty sets in logic. They can generate anything.

Thus, in spite of valorized sexual creativity, suburban endorsements of what is simultaneously white male-centric and white female-centric, bourgeois multiculturalism, and marketably hip, designer fetishism, there is the gnawing other side: U.S. conservatives such as Rush Limbaugh, Newt Gingrich, and Dinesh D'Souza have, after all, spewed falsehoods to millions of people and have been held unaccountable precisely because many of those who continue to rebut them don't have access to such resources, and postmodernists who do have such access don't spend their time on responding with appeals to "facts" or, worse—"oppression" and "struggle."

Perhaps the best engagement with a postmodernist conservative I have come across in a popular medium is Bev Smith's encounter with D'Souza (who at times even claimed to be "deconstructing" the left) on her BET program *Our Voices* (September 1996). Smith is not a postmodernist by any stretch of the imagination. She represents a black voice, rooted in identifications with Africa and a key concern for progress in black communities. In her meeting with D'Souza, Smith brought facts to bear on his many misrepresentations of black people in the United States and his personal motivations behind his role in contemporary conservative race politics through *directly* confronting his published words and his biography: D'Souza not only claims that black people would have become civilized by prolonged slavery, but he also asks us to consider whether black people owe reparations to abolitionists for ending slavery. His biography is atypical: He came to the United States as an "exchange student" from India and, subsequently became a Dartmouth undergraduate and eventual mouth-piece for a conservative think tank.[17] His immigration experience marks the stark difference between his opportunities and the stratified black communities he viciously criticizes. Smith provided excerpts from D'Souza's writings and gave him ample opportunity to contextualize his claims. In each instance, Smith maintained her focus on oppression, struggle, and *truth*. The irony of it all is that BET, a cable network, airs the program on Sunday mornings, so most of those who needed to see that important encounter were either in church, out having breakfast, or simply asleep.

By contrast, Henry Louis Gates, Jr., noted neoliberal scholar in African American studies and a major proponent of postmodernist poststructural interpretations of African American studies, has published falsehoods on black communities in the *New York Times* (as well as through quite an array of prestigious academic publishing houses) about blacks and Jews and black scholarship and, because of his position, is presumed to be unchallenged or supported by black communities, in spite of the efforts of many black writers and community activists to respond to his misrepresentations.[18] For the most part, Molefi Asante is cited by popular media, with occasional references to Manning Marable, as though Gates's only critics are his Afrocentric rival at Temple University and his social democratic rival at Columbia University.[19] Most influential was Gates's caricature of black "nationalist" scholarship as anti-Jewish in his *New York Times* article, "Black Demagogues and Pseudo Scholars" (20 July 1992): There, he also issued an attack on black presses, particularly Third World Press, in an effort to devalue such important resources for the dissemination of black knowledge productions—resources that brought the lives of black people to other Americans long before the editors at Oxford (Gates's main press) ever took it upon themselves to realize that black people *think* and *read*.

In recent years, there has been a growing, ideological, pop-cultural form of black pseudo-scholarship that has borne the Oxford name as well; and one wonders what impact that array of scholarship, with its problematic, often antiblack "racial sobriety" standing nestled within the Trojan horse of anti(black)authenticity, will continue to have on representations of blackness in the future. In considering Gates's presentations of black nationalism as anathematic to Judaism, the reader also should see a text that a scholar of Gates's stature should have consulted to form some context for his discussion: Howard Brotz's *The Black Jews of Harlem*,[20] as well as the texts listed by Haki R. Madhubuti in "Blacks, Jews and Henry Louis Gates, Jr.," in *Black Books Bulletin* (p. 8). Perhaps what is most offensive about the recent opportunism of the U.S. "blacks and Jews" bandwagon is not only the erasure of black Jews (the largest American populations of which are in New York City and Bridgeport, CT), but also its failure to appreciate that the antagonistic Jewish and black communities in the most publicized region, Brooklyn, NY, are predominately *immigrant* populations: Eastern European Jews and *Caribbean* blacks.[21] (Many U.S.-born, second- and third-generation Jews and an even larger number of U.S.-born blacks do not live in New York City.)[22] The tale is familiar: Successful Jews are white and successful West Indians are West Indians. Victimized Jews are Jews and "bad" West Indians are blacks. U.S. blacks receive blame for this situation, although they have been nearly always absent from many of these controversial encounters.

We see here a typical case of saying anything against the powerless and the disenfranchised and being presented and commended as a brave individual "speaking out." To his credit, Gates has taken advantage of the "pecuniary" benefits of taking these kinds of stands against black communities ("$11 million for various black studies projects at Harvard") by organizing his version of the "talented tenth" and making plans for a doctoral program in Afro-American studies at Harvard.[23] In addition, Gates makes no pretense of concerns beyond his entrepreneurial spirit, elitist sensibilities, and postmodernist mixture of Euro-criticism and African American textual productions. The *moral* question—"At what price. . . ?"—is meaningless in this manifestation of capitalism. African American studies programs and departments with little money, like poor African Americans, don't count here. Media and dollars do. I recall a scene from *Ed Wood* (1994), where Bela Lugosi announced, "Bad press is still press!" Frank Matthews, publisher of *Black Issues in Higher Education* and a staunch Gates supporter, agrees when he declares: "I think the only bad publicity is no publicity." He adds: "Given the caliber of the intellectuals there [at Harvard], it bodes well for all the black studies programs around the country. We tend to overlook other programs, but that is not Harvard's fault. That is just the nature of being the no. 1 institution."[24] Liberalism suffers a well-known tension between the right and the good, where the former focuses on the means and the latter on the ends. It is clear which strand of liberalism is manifested here.

Although they may complain about the "cultural elites" (some of the most high-profiled of whom are postmodernists) on university campuses, the "open" conservatives commonly deploy postmodernist techniques to their advantage, as we have seen in Dinesh D'Souza. Because claim to a correct historical position carries the charge of being hegemonic about history, the open conservative can say anything, whether pro-hegemonic history or not, because his opponents are the left, and their resources, under an anti-Marxist "left" intelligentsia—Marxism, we must remember, is that peculiar 19th-century ideal—also are suspect because they *deny* having a hegemonic counterposition. For example, Harold Bloom complained in a *Charlie Rose* interview (29 December 1994) about the avalanche of leftism in the academy and how one need only be a Communist or person of color to get an academic job. Whatever Bloom's situation at Yale and New York University may have been, most of the academy remains persistently anti-left, especially anti-Communist and anticolored, if demographics in the *Chronicle of Higher Education* (Fall 1996) were correct. One still has nearly a 90 percent chance of getting a tenure-tracked position in the academy if one is white, male, and neoliberal (which is the "left" fringe of today's ultra-right conservatism) in one's views and scholarship, and even higher probabilities of receiving promotion and tenure as well.[25] Compare Angela Y. Davis's situation at the University of California at Santa Cruz, where a state senator contested her appointment as university professor and her grant for student research. The senator took it upon himself not only to see about blocking grants for faculty associated with the left, but also to demand review of departments in which scholars associated with the traditional left have written their doctoral dissertations. The old truism on the left returns: If one is radical left, one had better produce work of higher quality and greater quantity than even one's liberal counterparts. What is both disingenuous and bizarre is that a powerful figure like Bloom could advance the claim that somehow these groups exercise and wield the same level of power as he, if not more.

The "closet" conservative conceals himself in a different way. Although he has technique, his marketability rests on his being in left or at least liberal sheep's clothing. Thus, his foe becomes substance itself, and in that regard, modernity or the modern emerges as a substance to be rendered insubstantial. The problem is that we get much bad history out of this turn, because ultimately every idol to be broken seems suddenly to have emerged in the modern era, despite premodern texts that show otherwise. Think, for instance, of postmodernist criticism of mathematical and calculative reason, in spite of many mathematical systems having evolved in "premodern" and non-Western societies, as we see in algebra, which had its birth in India. Both turns are particularly egregious in cases of dealing with the United States' most unassimilable minority, who are the focus of this discussion—blacks.

I have had many encounters but shall here consider two that may illustrate the chimera of which I have been speaking. Because I am a black scholar, writer, and musician, these endeavors are rich with what I call the uses and abuses of blackness, in terms of what I am expected to perform in the service of mass delusion. The concept of "mass," José Ortega y Gasset has shown us, is not always egalitarian. Consider his observation that:

. . . the present-day writer, when he takes his pen in hand to treat a subject which he has studied deeply, has to bear in mind that the average reader, who has never concerned himself with this subject, if he reads does so with the view, not of learning something from the writer, but rather, of pronouncing judgment on him when he is not in agreement with the commonplaces that the said reader carries in his head. If the individuals who make up the mass believed themselves specially qualified, it would be a case merely of personal error, not a sociological subversion. *The characteristic of the hour is that the commonplace mind, knowing itself to be commonplace, has the assurance to proclaim the rights of the commonplace and to impose them wherever it will.* As they say in the United States: "to be different is to be indecent." [Contemporary valorizations of difference collapses into pressured conformism.] The mass crushes beneath it everything that is different, everything that is excellent, individual, qualified and select. Anybody who is not like everybody, who does not think like everybody, runs the risk of being eliminated. And it is clear, of course, that this "everybody" is not "everybody." "Everybody" was normally the complex unity of the mass and the divergent, specialized minorities. Nowadays, "everybody" is the mass alone. Here we have the formidable fact of our times, described without any concealment of the brutality of its features.[26]

At the 1994 conference of the Society for Phenomenological and Existential Philosophy (SPEP), I had the opportunity to present a paper during a symposium on continental and African American philosophy and to attend the presentation of three papers on Jacques Derrida's *Specters of Marx*.[27] In the symposium, I found myself wedged between two gifted African American colleagues whom the audience clearly identified as postmodernist intellectuals. Perhaps most striking was their effort to distance themselves from any hint of a classical left position. Although not their intent, their dissatisfaction with articulating the roles of economic modes of production and spiritual emancipation (particularly in terms of a working class and liberation), as well as questions of scientific rigor, signaled a message of safety to the bourgeois, postmodernist whites in the audience. By the same token, my unceasing resistance to such declarations made me more palatable to the audience's critical modernist and, yes, bourgeois left elements.

The major difference between the two factions of the white audience, however, was that the bourgeois critical left modernists recognized their bourgeois status as a relevant category of emancipatory critique. When one of my fellow panelists kept referring to W.E.B. Du Bois's critique of modernity in terms of the enslavement of people of color for the interests of profit, I found myself having to intervene with the reminder that a critique of capitalism is not identical to a critique of modernity, and that to imply that Du Bois was an antimodernist is absurd given not only his advocacy of socialism (and, depending on which period in his life, his high-modern scientism), but also his membership in the Communist Party USA. When the colleague retorted by emphasizing the importance of focusing on cultural production, I said that doesn't preclude economic and other forms of productions. All that focus on cultural production proves is that to be more rigorous, one must analyze both, but such a full account of the issues, being identical with the search for rigor, hardly stands as postmodernist, does it?

Blackness was here being abused in the same way that Marxism, feminism, liberation theology, and other forms of liberation theorizing have been misrepresented. For before me stood two black theorists who were postmodernists only in presentation, not in content. The appearance-content dualism evident, bad historicizing (ideological genealogical poststructuralism) and crude standpoint epistemology as textual reductionism (ideological textual poststructuralism) had seeped into the very concept of the speaker, and as such, *what* these theorists were actually saying was not generally being heard except by a small portion of the audience. In the end, it is not clear that these two theorists regarded themselves as postmodernists at all. It was as if, like a kiss on the ring, a rhetorical allegiance to postmodernism had to be made. Similarly, my critical stand on postmodernist criticisms of liberation theory raised concerns about my being a pawn. After all, it is absurd to place me or any other black (and "peripheral") theorist neatly on the modern/antimodern divide. For I am not so much antimodern as I am anti-Eurocentrism. There are elements of modernity that I avow and elements that I reject. To reject Eurocentrism is not identical to rejecting European civilization *in toto* or rejecting modernity, and it is a seriously racist form of reasoning that would make white people the only bearers of a modern consciousness.[28] One would have to conclude, in effect, that black people are incapable of being modern or developing their own forms of modernity or alternatives *beyond* premodernity, modernity, and postmodernity. What is to be made of the work of Sylvia Wynter, for example, which is a form of poststructuralism that is not postmodern? If modernism can be seen as an effort to decenter European hegemony over the past through the development of an alternative future, then Wynter's effort to develop a semiotic order that is neither modern European nor postmodern European, but instead Africana critical modernism, is a modern project indeed. For Wynter, the poststructural encounter with knowledge raises the possibility of our struggling for new modes of knowledge and, in effect, new forms of life. She writes;

> Frantz Fanon has pointed out—in his book *Black Skins, White Masks*—that Freud oversaw the fact that the level of human life, the organic process of ontogenesis, is always accompanied by the culturally instituted processes of sociogenesis. It is this rupture with the purely organic processes of ontogenesis and its correlation with the always culture-systemic processes of sociogenesis that can be defined as the first emergence. For this was a process by which all human forms of life, and their language living systems, can now be seen to have come into being only on the basis of their rupture with the genetically regulated circuits of organic life, therefore, for the narratively instituted symbolic circuits that were to orient our socialized modes of subjectivity and of interaltruistic symbolic conspecificity, or non-genetically determined variant forms of "kin" recognition and misrecognition that are defining of human "forms of life."[29]

A similar question applies to Paul Gilroy, whose aim in *Black Atlantic* is to state the complexities of a transatlantic "modern" culture(s) that resists reductive, linear readings of modernity. Consider also the work of Edouard Glissant and the many contributions of Wilson Harris.[30] And beyond Africana studies, there is kindred spirit in Enrique Dussel's declaration:

> Latin America is neither pre-, anti-, nor post-modern; and, for that reason, we cannot "realize" fully an incomplete modernity (as Jürgen Habermas suggests optimistically), because as the slave (before the "Lord" of slavery) we have "paid" with our misery, with our "non-Being" (since 1492 as colonial world, first, and since 1810 as neocolonial world); for "Being," the primitive accumulation and successive supercession of the "happy" capitalism of the center, and even of those who are so-called delayed (the "developmentalist" notion of *Spätkapitalismus*, conceals the "exploited capitalism," and because of that the underdevelopment of the periphery) (*Underride of Modernity*, pp. 3–4).

So, back to the panel on continental philosophy and African American thought; in a way, what I thought on the matter was irrelevant to some extent, for the trajectory I represented and the trajectory my purportedly postmodernist black colleagues represented stood, writ large, as black extensions of a white battle in a white world. While we may have seen ourselves as Du Boisian, Fanonian, (C.L.R.) Jamesian, or simply ourselves, the audience saw us as derivatives of Western icons: Derridian, Foucaultian, Sartrean, or Marxian.[31]

Must this have been so?

Part of the problem relates to two competing interests over the black woman and black man's soul. On the one hand, there is the historic interest of orthodox Marxism, where the memorable phrase "nothing to lose but chains" found a logical niche in descendants of slaves. On the other hand, there is, specifically, poststructuralism, both textual and genealogical, where the glorification of marginality and claims of breaking constructed idols through alternative sites of deconstructive interpretations found a logical niche in descendants of people who were, as Fanon once described them, slaves of their appearance. At first glance, there is no intrinsic reason why these two interests should be antithetical, for both engage in ideological critique. Yet as we have seen thus far, outside the sphere of blackness they seem to be at least hostile to each other. So what happens when they confront each other over the black prize?

In the *Specters of Marx* discussion, Martin Matuštík advanced the claim that in the text-mania of Derridanism, there was a general failure to see the faces that stood behind texts and textualization. As an example, he offered Frederick Douglass's classic "text," his first *Slave Narrative*, to illustrate the existential and liberatory significance of an ex-slave's perspective. Given the concomitant margin-mania of Derridanism, and several other forms of poststructuralism, Matuštík's effort seemed at first on safe ground.[32]

A member of the audience stood up, however, and unleashed what she regarded as a form of "speaking out" or "corrective intervention" or, better yet, "writing out loud": "I am offended," she declared, "by your use of Frederick Douglass's *Narrative* without regard to the large number of African American critics' positions on that text." She continued, "And what's wrong with texts anyway? I prefer to read black writers' knowledge productions than black writers and black people. Why should I be concerned with faces behind texts?"

There it was: the ideological framework for blackness, multiculturality, and racial justice on bookshelves instead of in classrooms and neighborhoods. There it was, a defense of representative tokenism that signaled not only the safety of "reading" but the safety of what constitutes reading. After all, Matuštík's reading of Frederick Douglass's *Narrative* was held suspect without African American critics' writings on that narrative; Matustík was, in fact, being assailed for reading Frederick Douglass without a translator—without a black guide on a safari through the apparent jungle of black literary expression ("Here is what Douglass meant, *Bwana!*")—even though Frederick Douglass clearly wrote that text for a predominately white and sometimes black abolitionist audience.[33]

Still, the market function was violated, for black critics have products to sell, too, and the hegemony of the critic's role in the uncovering of deeper meanings was here challenged. But having something to sell isn't enough, for as is now well-known, being a black critic isn't enough. One must be a black critic who stands in a position like that of Booker T. Washington's Tuskegee Machine to be anointed Hermes to white gods of approbation and, thereby, have, in a word, "being." Thus, an appeal to black critics is really an appeal to certain black individuals and certain conceptions of politics to begin with: Blacks who assure everyone that because they sit—representatively though it may be—at the table and no longer bounce around for crumbs that may fall, there is no reason to worry about those blacks who do not. The irony of the postmodernist turn is that the task of *writing* black lives has led to the project of focusing that writing on those who can properly *decenter* the lives of black folk—the black critic. It is no wonder that the hottest site of recent scholarship has been the critics themselves under the rubric of "public intellectuals." Focus on the critic leads, however, to a slippery slope to the point of centering the supposedly most distant critic—white critic—of black reality.[34]

I have mentioned earlier that the product is sold by concealing the naked truth from the pauper; the pauper is also deluded into thinking she or he is an emperor by virtue of the prevailing market conception of democracy manifested in the consumer as the locus of persuasion. What is being concealed from black consumers—especially when, for the most part, theoretical production treats black consumers as irrelevant? The black consumer in this context is the black student and the black theorist and critic who seek an equal place in the theoretical dining halls of white theorists and critics, for after all, these texts are hardly food for thought for black populations who are still locked within the dictates of an industrial society of structural unemployment and a social status well below a managerial élite's.[35] These texts are indicative of the growing, global relations that every human being has with university systems in economies that can no longer sustain unskilled labor. Black theorists are being shown a game to play as a rite of passage, and if they play it well, their price need only be named (provided black inclusion remains scarce) and they can play their part in helping the powerful hide from themselves behind their own growing power. After all, it's a game that white theorists and critics also have had to play. Black critics can attack affirmative action as unjust, for instance, as if convincing blacks of its justice or injustice is of any relevance to how affirmative action functions in a society in which administrative and bureaucratic resources—especially those that deal with hiring and firing, and the distribution of investment—remain in predominately white hands.[36]

That the pauper is being sold a seriously flawed product is evident in the place of writing itself in the postmodernist enterprise. Although writing and reading can be construed very broadly, to the point even of being vague, where they can apply to what is produced through uses of pens and keyboards to assembly meetings and machine guns (that is, manufactured products of a supposedly postindustrial society) and the roads, neighborhoods, and cities that are "written" across the earth's landscape, it so happens that the postmodernist writings and readings that one persistently encounters always turn out to be the ones that emerge from pens and keyboards and printing presses; they are, in short, texts that are found on shelves and computer monitors. They are, in the end, bodies of literature. These texts are notorious for their stylistic inaccessibility, their exaggerated rhetoric, and their tendency to be primarily understood by, and even be the sole concern of, a self-referential élite. In this regard, postmodernist knowledge productions function no differently than any other élite, professional products in the modern market: They demand purchase of their productions for the sake of attempting to understand previously purchased productions. It is irrelevant that they actually say nothing (or persistently reproduce what they already have said) since by the time that is figured out, all the accolades for supposedly having said something have been bestowed upon them.

A typical response that I have encountered in trying to articulate the impact of postmodernism in Africana philosophy has been the denial of there being *postmodernists* in the first place. "Who are these postmodernists anyway?" is a question that nearly always emerges from my postmodernist colleagues whenever someone refers to postmodernism. They demand names. I often have found that meeting their request is nearly impossible, because no matter who or how many are advanced, that person or group of persons stands, nominalistically, by itself. One can refer, for social thought in general, to Stanley Aronowitz, Homi Bhabha, Jean-François Baudrillard, Drucilla Cornell, Gilles Deleuze, Jacques Derrida, Michel Foucault, Henry Louis Gates, Jr., Félix Guattari, François Lyotard, Gayatri Spivak, and (early) Cornel West (just to "name a few" who have either referred to themselves thus or are often identified as such), but all one would have, from such critics' point of view, are twelve individual standpoints thrown together—in a word, a *totalization* of separate and distinct positions.

Yet those same critics know where to go and who to consult when they seek out postmodernists, and they know how to identify postmodernist performances. If asked, they could easily assemble a set of authors for a course entitled "Postmodernism," especially if a prestigious chair were offered at a prestigious university for such a field. In spite of their denial of a form of postmodernist canon, a purported expert in postmodern studies would be held suspect if he or she were not aware of the twelve theorists I have just mentioned, even though Derrida, Spivak, and West pose serious challenges to such an identity. That theorist would be expected to know a great deal about several individuals and disciplines—for example, the influence of architecture and film and popular culture on postmodernist thought. It is this required breadth of knowledge, by the way, that places me in an ambivalent relation, in the end, to the *academic* importance of contemporary postmodernist sites of intellectual focus: poststructuralism, psychoanalysis, and neopragmatism. There is a level of freedom afforded the academic in the aestheticization of the process of inquiry.[37] There is something to be said for *reading* blackness once it is understood that such reading should not foreclose alternative forms of political praxis.

I should like at this point to close with an observation on the political that I find emerging time and time again. In his critique of Cornel West's *The American Evasion of Philosophy*, Robert Gooding-Williams found himself making similar reminders on W.E.B. Du Bois as I did in the panel discussion on Continental and African American philosophy.[38] In West's effort to make Du Bois a pragmatist, he presented Du Bois's thought as though the author of *Black Reconstruction* or *The Autobiography of W.E.B. Du Bois: A Soliloquy on Viewing My Life from the Last Decade of Its First Century* was motivated solely by pragmatic "moral" concerns premised on both Emersonian transcendentalism and Jamesian "cash-value" practicality, instead of the phenomenological complexities of double-consciousness and the revolutionary demands of class struggle.[39]

It is fitting that Marx's observations on the Young Hegelians apply so well today. After all, postmodernism, particularly in its poststructural incarnation, has two conservative, antihumanist German idols—Nietzsche (by way of Foucault) and Heidegger (by way of Derrida). I don't think Nietzsche or Heidegger would be disappointed with an antiblack legacy, although they would be disgusted by some glorifications of black cultural

productions that emerged from their postmodernist heirs, given their dis-
taste for black cultural productions as well. But for the attack on correct
political positions to hold, one finds oneself at odds with Marx's eleventh
thesis on Feuerbach when one's theoretical tools leave one in a place of
tactics without strategy. For the historical nihilism that stands opposed to
historical materialism is also a form of antihistorical-antihumanism.[40] How
could the political be formulated, then, beyond the positivism of tactics
and procedures? Could postmodernisms step beyond mere *ex post facto* relations to the political world? To his credit, West identifies this problem
well when he identifies Foucaultian politics' "naiveté about social conflict,
struggle, and insurgency—a naiveté primarily caused by the rejection of
any form of utopianism and any positing of a telos."[41] Yet conservatives
know that the writing is on the wall, as the following right-wing postmodernist, A.M.C. Waterman, attests:

> The events of the last ten years or so, from disillusion with the welfare
> state to the fall of the Soviet empire, have undermined the socialist
> foundations of modern liberation theory. Many true believers are still
> so dazed by cognitive dissonance as to have made no response at
> all. Those economists who still describe themselves as Marxist have
> abandoned virtually every distinct feature of Marx's own economic
> analysis. Social-Democratic governments in capitalist countries vie
> with one another in their zeal for "market forces," privatization, and
> deficit-reduction. The New Feminism of the 1980s has hit upon the
> brilliant idea of lumping Marx in with the Enlightenment, so discred-
> iting both. For "liberation," as I remarked at the outset, is an Enlight-
> enment idea, a predominantly male (if not "masculinist") notion of
> "abstract, universal freedom," which women embrace at their peril.
> Female liberation from the mental constraint of "Enlightenment
> myth" is now variously believed to be available from literary, cultural,
> and discourse studies, as well as from psychoanalysis, post structural-
> ism, semiology, deconstruction, genealogy, and post-Marxist critical
> theory. Though I have no evidence, I would conjecture that a some-
> what similar rejection of the Enlightenment myth of "liberation"
> might be chosen by black and aboriginal groups seeking cultural self-
> determination in our Western, rational, capitalist, ex-Christian, male-
> constructed world.[42]

Within black studies, similar language has emerged. Black studies of
blackness have a rich history of simultaneously addressing the question of
human liberation, the question of social identity, and the question of rigor

in the study of human beings. Postmodernist (anti)black studies of blackness, however, attempt to reject the first and the third of these dimensions
of black studies of blackness. In the midst of all this, they carry the onus
of demonstrating that black theorizing will somehow have advanced by
accepting such a position, a position that in effect rejects the very notion
of advancement or progress. We have heard such rhetoric before. Zeno of
Elea tried to achieve something about 2,400 years ago by showing that one
can never get anywhere. Nevertheless, as the cliché puts it so well, life goes
on.

Notes

1. *The Marx-Engels Reader*, 2nd ed., ed. by Robert C. Tucker (New York:
W.W. Norton & Company, 1978), p. 149 (this trans. of *The German Ideology* by S.
Ryazanskaya).

2. For discussion of postmodern criticisms of coherence, see Linda Martín
Alcoff, *Real Knowing: New Versions of the Coherence Theory* (Ithaca: Cornell University Press, 1996), esp. chaps. 4–7.

3. The work of François Lyotard, Stanley Aronowitz, and Cornel West are
some instances of this tendency. Although the first two are more conspicuously
so, West may seem a questionable case to some. If so, I suggest reading West's
autobiographical ruminations in bell hooks and Cornel West, *Breaking Bread: Insurgent Black Intellectual Life* (Boston: South End Press, 1991). That West openly identified himself as a Marxist throughout the 1980s complicates his postmodernist
identity. West's political and academic work also raises a challenge to this avowed
identity. In the end, West may be a very modern postmodern intellectual. See our
discussion of West in chap. 11, below.

4. Brian Meeks, *Radical Caribbean: From Black Power to Abu Bakr*, with a foreword by Rupert Lewis (Kingston, JA: The University Press of the West Indies,
1996), pp. 104–5.

5. François Lyotard, *The Postmodern Condition: A Report on Knowledge*, trans.
by Geoff Bennington and Brian Massumi, foreword by Fredric Jameson (Minneapolis: University of Minnesota Press, 1984), especially the Appendix.

6. For discussion of this view of speech, see Hannah Arendt, *The Human
Condition* (Chicago and London: University of Chicago Press, 1958), and for a
critique of Arendt's conception of speech (with its association of speech with
power), see Jürgen Habermas, *Philosophical Profiles*, trans. by Frederick G. Law-
rence (Cambridge, MA: MIT Press, 1983), pp. 171–188. Among Habermas's criticisms of Arendt is that she failed to appreciate the significance of instrumental
power. Arendt's concerns were, however, more with matters of policy than imple-

mentation. I don't think she would reject the view that states have to be managed, and there are times when *who* manages them and *how* they are managed make all the difference in the world, as has certainly become clear in those states that suffered Republican control in 1995.

7. In deconstruction, there is another step: Language is enacted by a system of differing/defering signs, the result of which is a more radical articulation of fields of action. For discussion, see the various essays in *Communicating Differences: Essays in Philosophy and Communicative Praxis*, ed. with an intro. by Jacqueline Martinez and Lewis R. Gordon (Lanham: Rowman and Littlefield, 1998).

8. Michel Foucault was, without doubt, among the best by way of theorists that postmodernism has offered, although his status as a postmodernist may be questionable given the transcendental and metanarrative possibilities of his notion of an *episteme*, a notion for which he is most known. The link to postmodernism emerges, however, in the relationship of his notion of power/knowledge and Nietzsche's will to power. See Foucault's *Nietzsche* (Paris: Minuit, 1967), *Discipline and Punish: The Birth of the Prison*, trans. by Alan Sheridan (New York: Vintage, 1979); *Power/Knowledge*, ed. by C. Gordon, trans. by C. Gordon, L. Marshall, J. Mehpam, and K. Soper (New York: Pantheon Books, 1980), and Nietzsche's *Will to Power*, trans. by Walter Kaufmann and R. J. Hollingdale (New York: Vintage Books, 1968). And for a critique, particularly against the appropriation of Foucault/Nietzsche in the name of political "resistance," see Alex Callinicos, *Against Postmodernism: A Marxist Critique* (Oxford: Blackwell/Polity, 1989), pp. 62–91, and William Preston's provocative essay, "Nietzsche on Blacks." See also Cynthia Willett's *Maternal Ethics and Other Slave Moralities* for discussion of Foucault's turn to stoicism in his later thought.

9. For recent discussion that runs the course of this trajectory, see Drucilla Cornell's *Philosophy of the Limit* (New York: Routledge, 1992), "Introduction: What Is Postmodernity Anyway?" For discussion of postmodernism as premodernism and more rigorous modernism, see Lyotard's appendix to *The Postmodern Condition*, and for discussions of postmodernism in art theory, see *Art in Theory (1900–1990): An Anthology of Changing Ideas*, ed. by Charles Harrison and Paul Wood (Oxford: Blackwell, 1992), especially part VIII. For discussion of modernism as secularism and postmodernism as recognition of the inconsistencies of dogmatic secularism, see Victor Anderson's *Beyond Ontological Blackness: An Essay on African American Religious and Cultural Criticism* (New York: Continuum, 1995). And for discussion of postmodernism in black literary studies, see Sandra Adell's *Double-Consciousness/Double Bind: Theoretical Issues in Twentieth-Century Black Literature* (Urbana and Chicago: University of Illinois Press, 1994), especially chap. 5: "The Crisis in Black American Literary Criticism and the Postmodern Cures of Houston A. Baker, Jr., and Henry Louis Gates, Jr."

10. In Drucilla Cornell, Michel Rosenfeld, and David Gray Carlson, eds., *Deconstruction and the Possibility of Justice* (New York: Routledge, 1992), pp. 3–4.

11. Derrida's attacks on consciousness are multitude, but see especially his various discussions in *The Margins of Philosophy*, trans. by Alan Bass (Chicago: University of Chicago Press, 1982). His addendum about indecisionism is in the afterword to *Limited Inc.*, "Toward an Ethic of Discussion" (Evanston, IL: Northwestern University Press, 1988). For discussion of bad faith, including the impact of its intersection with deconstruction, see *Bad Faith and Antiblack Racism*, chap. 25. For discussion on poststructuralism and phenomenology, which relates to these categories of consciousness and politics, see Lewis R. Gordon, "Identity and Liberation: A Phenomenological Approach" in *Phenomenology of the Political*, ed. by Kevin Thompson and Lester Embree (Dordrecht: Kluwer Academic Publishers, fortchoming). I should like to say here that I do not consider Derrida to be a postmodernist but instead an intellectual theorizing in a postmodern environment (see also my discussion in chap. 9, below). It is in the United States that Derrida has been primarily received as a postmodernist. For discussion, see Clevis Headley's depiction of "Yankee deconstruction" in his essay, "Postmodernism, Deconstruction, and the Question of the Black Subject" in *Black Texts and Textuality*.

12. See also Fredrick Jameson's critical foreword to Lyotard's *The Postmodern Condition* (p. xiv), where at least the question of a morally flawed working class is shown to be a misguided critique because it conflates the "mood" of a class with its function.

13. For discussion of this demographic makeup, see Aijaz Ahmad, *In Theory: Classes, Nations, Literatures* (London and New York: Verso, 1992), and Callinicos's *Against Postmodernism*. Think also of Fanon's observation, in the first chapter of *Peau noire*, of black *petit-officers* in colonial armies functioning primarily as translators and his discussion of the national bourgeoisie in *Les damnés* as having nothing but "political" capital between the former metropoles and the contemporary neo-colonized Third World nations.

14. For discussion of this phenomenon, see Edward Said's *Representations of the Intellectual* (New York: Vintage, 1996), chap. VI.

15. "Progress" is a much-hated term in postmodernist politics. For recent discussion of this form of attack on praxis, see my critique of recent anti-Fanon literature in *Fanon and the Crisis of European Man*, chap. 5.

16. See *Existence in Black*. In the 20th century, the works of W.E.B. Du Bois, Frantz Fanon, C.L.R. James, and Sylvia Wynter are among those that take a similar stand outside of postmodernism.

17. Dinesh D'Souza, *The End of Racism* (New York: The Free Press, 1995). In addition to Bev Smith's interview, also see David Theo Goldberg's *Racial Subjects: Writing on Race in America* (New York and London: Routledge, 1997), chap. 10: "Wedded to Dixie: Dinesh D'Souza and the New Segregationism."

18. On this matter, see "Blacks, Jews, and Henry Louis Gates, Jr.: A Response," *Black Books Bulletin: WordsWork* 16, nos. 1 & 2 (1993–1994): 3–31.

19. Instances abound, but see the most recent example: Peter Applebome's "Harvard's Black Studies Powerhouse," *The New York Times Educational Life*, Section 4A (November 3, 1996), pp. 22–8.

20. Howard M. Brotz, *The Black Jews of Harlem: Negro Nationalism and the Dilemmas of Negro Leadership* (New York: Schocken, 1970).

21. For discussion of the unique demographics of Brooklyn, NY, see Philip Kasinitz, *Caribbean New York: Black Immigrants and the Politics of Race* (Ithaca: Cornell University Press, 1992). For a discussion of black-Jewish relations that is sensitive to the existence of black Jews, see David Theo Goldberg, *Racial Subjects: Writing on Race in America* (New York and London: Routledge, 1997), chap. 7: "Between Blacks and Jews."

22. Think, for instance, of Houston, where there are large Jewish communities and the South in general, where most U.S. blacks live.

23. "Harvard's Black Studies Powerhouse," p. 24. The article does not mention the sources of these funds. That Harvard's alumni include wealthy people of color suggests that the endowment emerged from diverse funding sources.

24. Quoted in "Harvard's Black Studies Powerhouse," p. 38.

25. For a chronicle of these realities, see Derrick Bell's *Confronting Authority: Reflections of an Ardent Protester* (New York: Beacon Press, 1994). See also his poignant *Faces at the Bottom of the Well*.

26. José Ortega y Gasset, *The Revolt of the Masses*, trans. anonymous and "authorized" (New York: W.W. Norton, 1932), p. 18. Emphasis in the original.

27. Jacques Derrida, *Specters of Marx: The State of the Debt, the Work of Mourning, and the New International*, trans. by Peggy Kamuf, intro. by Bernd Magnus and Stephen Cullenberg (New York and London: Routledge, 1994).

28. For discussion of the convergence of black people as "modern," see Orlando Patterson, "Toward a Future That Has No Past: Reflections on the Fate of Blacks in the Americas," *The Public Interest*, no. 27 (Spring 1972): 60–1; Frank M. Kirkland, "Modernity and Intellectual Life in Black," *Philosophical Forum* XXIV, no. 1–3 (Fall-Spring 1992–93): 136–63; and Paul Gilroy's *Black Atlantic*.

29. "Is 'Development' a Purely Empirical Concept or Also Teleological?," p. 310. See also, among Wynter's many provocative essays, "On Disenchanting Discourse: 'Minority' Literary Criticism and Beyond," *Cultural Critique* 7 (Fall 1987); "Beyond the Categories of the Master Conception" in *C.L.R. James' Caribbean*, ed. by Paget Henry and Paul Buhle (Durham, NC: Duke University Press, 1992); "Rethinking 'Aesthetics': Notes Towards a Deciphering Practice" in *Ex-Iles: Es-*

says on Caribbean Cinema, ed. by Mbye B. Cham (Trenton, NJ: Africa World Press, 1992); 'The Pope Must Have Been Drunk, the King of Castile a Madman': Culture as Actuality, and the Caribbean Rethinking 'Modernity' " in *The Reordering of Culture: Latin-America, the Caribbean, and Canada*, ed. by Alvina Ruprecht and Cecilia Taiana (Ottawa: Carleton University Press, 1995); and "Africa, the West, and the Analogy of Culture: The Cinematic Text, after *Man*" in *Africa and the History of Cinematic Ideas*, ed. by June Giovanni (London: British Film Institute, forthcoming).

30. See especially Edouard Glissant's *Les discours antillais* (Paris: Les Editions du Seuil, 1981); *Caribbean Discourse: Selected Essays*, trans. with an intro. by J. Michael Dash (Charlottesville: University Press of Virginia, 1992) and Wilson Harris's *History, Fable and Myth* (Wellesley, MA: Calaloux Publications, 1995).

31. To their credit, neither Derrida, Foucault, nor Sartre endorses such readings of black intellectual productions. I don't know how this concern will relate to Marx, for he has the disadvantage of being rooted in the 19th century, whereas the others are firmly rooted in the 20th.

32. Foucault's genealogical poststructuralism comes to mind among others, but see also the work of Homi Bhabha, Henry Louis Gates, Jr., Gayatri Spivak, and Cornel West for examples situated in the realm of "color."

33. I say "sometimes" because black audiences were, for the most part, irrelevant as far as those white audiences were concerned. Note, however, the voice that emerged in Douglass's second autobiography in opposition to Garissonian abolitionists' tendency to reject black interpretations of their reality: *My Bondage and My Freedom*, ed. with an intro. by Willam L. Andrews (Urbana and Chicago: University of Illinois Press, 1987). *My Bondage and My Freedom* stands as a poignant moment of a black political thinker's effort to forge his identity beyond the narrowly defined parameters set out for him by whites on both the "right" and the "left." For discussion of the differences between the two narratives, see Bernard R. Boxill, "The Fight with Covey" in *Existence in Black* and Cynthia Willett's discussion of Douglass in *Maternal Ethics and Other Slave Moralities*. Finally, there is irony behind the castigation Matustík received. The observation on Frederick Douglass's copyright was not his. He got it from me, a black theorist, during a coffee discussion on existentialism the previous year, in which we outlined two political works on existentialism to present at the 1994 meeting of the Pacific Division of the American Philosophical Association.

36. For discussion of this phenomenon, see Lewis R. Gordon, "Black Texts and Black Textuality" in *Black Texts and Textuality*. See also Adell's *Double-Consciousness/Double Bind* for discussion of the black critic.

35. Here we find a limitation in one of the most influential postmodernist motifs, Daniel Bell's *The Coming of Post-Industrial Society* (New York: Basic Books,

1973) and *The Cultural Contradictions of Capitalism* (New York: Basic Books, 1976), where, as the title of the former attests, industry and, by implication, the industrial worker are deemed *passé*. Their alternative? Managerial, information-age élites who "produce" knowledge services. Meanwhile, there is a rise in the number of so-called "obsolete" or "unworking" people in one region while labor is exploited in other regions. What is often missing in these analyses is the mobility of industrial capital. Information and service economies *see* only their kind because their industrial resources are often produced elsewhere, in countries where labor is cheap and governments are subordinated by First World foreign and economic policies. Local labor without resources of movement becomes obsolete. Those who are migratory become "cheap." Meanwhile, global capitalism profits from cheaper labor gained from the impact of the, in some cases permanently, unemployed. These arguments depend on absolutizing the economic system, which makes it normative and invisible. When one has to fix people instead of changing systems while denying that people effect and affect systems, systems take on godlike qualities. The effect is theodicean. People who do not benefit from such systems are blamed for their condition. Something is "wrong" with them.

36. For discussion of those academic, administrative, and bureaucratic dynamics, see Joe R. Feagin, Hernán Vera, and Nikitah Imani, *The Agony of Education: Black Students at White Colleges and Universities* (New York and London: Routledge, 1996).

37. I return to this point on the aestheticization of thought in the penultimate chapter of these sketches.

38. Robert Gooding-Williams, "Evading Narrative Myth, Evading Prophetic Pragmatism: Cornel West's *The American Evasion of Philosophy*," *The Massachusetts Review: A Quarterly of Literature, the Arts, and Public Affairs* (Winter 1991–1992): 517–542.

39. For excellent, detailed discussions of double-consciousness, see Sandra Adell's *Double-Consciousness/Double Bind* and Ernest Allen, Jr., "On the Reading of Riddles: Rethinking Du Boisian Double-Consciousness" in *Existence in Black*.

40. See the foreword to Joy Ann James's *Transcending the Talented Tenth*.

41. Cornel West, *Keeping Faith: Philosophy and Race in America* (New York and London: Routledge, 1993), p. 84.

42. A.M.C. Waterman, "Liberation Movements and the Market Economy," *The Intercollegiate Review: A Journal of Scholarship & Opinion* 29, no. 2 (Spring 1994): 33–4.

Chapter Six

In a Black Antiblack Philosophy

The habit of considering racism as a mental quirk, a psychological flaw, must be abandoned. . . . The racist in a culture with racism is normal. He has achieved a perfect harmony of economic relations and ideology.

—Fanon, "Racisme et culture"

At the corner I turned into a drugstore and took a seat at the counter. . . . The counterman came over.

"I've got something good for you," he said, placing a glass of water before me. "How about the special?"

"What's the special?"

"Pork chops, grits, one egg, hot biscuits and coffee!" He leaned over the counter with a look that seemed to say, There, that ought to excite you, boy. Could everyone see that I was southern?

"I'll have orange juice, toast and coffee," I said coldly.

He shook his head. "You fooled me," he said, slamming two pieces of bread into the toaster. "I could have sworn you were a pork chop man. Is that juice large or small?"

"Make it large," I said.

I looked silently at the back of his head as he sliced an orange, thinking, I should order the special and get up and walk out. Who does he think he is?

[Later. . . .] Is it an insult when one of us tips one of them? I looked for the counterman, seeing him serving a plate of pork chops and grits to a man with a pale blond mustache, and stared; then I slapped the dime on the counter and left, annoyed that the dime did not ring as loud as a fifty-cent piece.

—Ralph Ellison, Invisible Man

The midpoint of the millennium's final decade has left historians of American and African race politics with material worthy of their attention: Fascist militia assaults on federal structures; polarized responses to both OJ Simpson verdicts;[1] the Million-Man March on Washington, D.C.;[2] the devastating number of blacks who were incarcerated; the disproportionate number of dark-skinned people around the world who were starving; and the genocidal expeditions cropping up world-wide, with ironic black-antiblack racial manifestations, as emerged in countries like Burundi and Nigeria. If there continued to be intellectual historians and historians of philosophy among them—even historians of African philosophy and critical race theory—they might find themselves perplexed by the succession of events saturated with phenomena declared passé by influential thinkers of a mere few years ago. How could individuals with such wonderful intellectual training, who both studied and stood in these prevalent phenomena, be so blinded to their reality?

Perhaps such investigators would rummage through intellectual material from mid-century thoughts on the matter and encounter one of Fanon's astute injunctions that "It is necessary to analyze, patiently and lucidly, each reaction of the colonized, and every time we do not understand, we must tell ourselves that we are at the heart of the drama—that of the impossibility of finding a meeting ground in any colonial situation."[3] Fanon does not here mean that there cannot be instances of friendship, as his "Letter to a Frenchman" in *Pour la révolution africaine* demonstrates. Instead, his point is that colonialism is a "systematized de-humanization," a circumstance molded by structural asymmetric relations.

Today's neocolonized stand in a bewildering morass of misinformation resulting from a failure to articulate the extent to which vestiges of the colonial order remain in this supposed postcolonial moment. The tall tales and evasions are many, but I shall here focus on one of the most influential voices in current philosophical and "critical" race theory: Kwame Anthony Appiah.[4]

It is often difficult to determine the significance of a moment while living it, but it can be safely said that many influential theorists in the field take a circumspect stand on race issues. Race, their story goes, is a social construction (*pace* the redundancy of such a notion) and must therefore be understood, as in the work of Michael Omi and Howard Winant, as expressions of interests that generate such social formations.[5] Race theorists are then encouraged, given the circumstances, to approach their task as an archaeological inquiry into the formation of certain "unifying stories" of racial formations and race thinking. This route could have led in many directions, but the ideological underpinning of such an approach had already laid down a path by determining an *obstacle* to that approach in the first place: black-centered discourses of race and racial oppression. The consequence has been, as one might expect, a vigorous assault on concepts of race whose opaque reference is the black or, more pointedly, *the Negro*. The attack on race often took anti-Negro form. This attack culminated in what I shall call *black antiblack scholarship,* with a specific focus on what Kwame Anthony Appiah has characterized as "New World Blacks."[6] Black spokespersons against black folks is not a new phenomenon. In North America, the black immigrant is used to downgrade the North American-born black population; in Europe, the North American black is used to downgrade the black European and African and Caribbean permanent residents there. Each instance allows the dominating populations to conceal their racism by appealing to a worse racism elsewhere and by castigating the resident population for failing to excel under the *status quo*. How often have I heard American blacks speak of how wonderfully they were treated in Europe![7] My experience—perhaps due to my looking *too* African in Brussels or *too* black in Prague—is that European whites are not particularly different from U.S. whites when they think the black is one of their "own," which ironically includes the type of immigrants they are used to. West Indian immigrants, as we have seen in our brief examination of the dynamics of blacks and Jews in Brooklyn, are noble savages when they are good and plain old black ones when they are bad. They represent the familiar type of black immigrant in the United States. Black Britts are, however, another variety. They function in the Americas as African Americans do in Europe, and at times, in Southern Africa. The popularity of Kwame Anthony Appiah's *In My Father's House: Africa in the Philosophy of Culture* is a continuation of this racial/immigrant dynamic.

The subtext of Appiah's book is the unenlightened New World black, whose crass, egotistic ways have set a totalizing trail of "authenticity" on the black diaspora ultimately by constructing the very notion of a black diaspora whose homeland is the African continent. The politics at work here are familiar: they emerge in contemporary outcries of "black antisemitism," "black homophobia," "black misogyny," as if there would have been any concern for Semites (even Jews), homosexuals, and women (of any racial-ethnic-religious-class-sexual orientation) without these discourses of black pathology. Beyond that, we should ask ourselves about the political value of focusing our critical gaze on hatred expressed by groups who lack the institutional power to order that hatred systematically or structurally. Is it politically relevant that there are blacks, Native Americans, and Australian aboriginal peoples who hate whites? Perhaps ultimately in an ideology bent on making those who cry racism quiet down, cease—in other words, shut up. It's safer to criticize the powerless.

I begin with these remarks primarily as an exploration into the underlying disappointment I experienced in my first reading of Kwame Anthony Appiah's important book, *In My Father's House*; I criticized his stand on race in *Bad Faith and Antiblack Racism*, and I found problems in subsequent readings. My judgment is not against the literary accomplishment of the text. Nor is it a judgment regarding the wealth of philosophical, scientific (and pseudoscientific), and literary resources drawn upon by its author. After all, it accomplishes its logocentric, neopositivist agenda well. So what is it about this book that bothers me and—as I have gleaned from numerous conversations—many other black scholars in both the "Old" and "New" worlds?

In My Father's House has an ostensible thesis—that Pan-Africanism, the ideology that undergirds the invention of Africa as supposedly a monolithic, unanimistic point in the pseudobiblical narrative of a black exodus, suffers from the fictional narrative designed to organize the whole schema, and that narrative is, in a word, *race*. There is, however, also a subtext that can be read as follows: The people of the African continent lived and would continue to live free of racial strife with Europeans but for the intrusive, racist antics of New World blacks and their cognitively impaired attachment to nineteenth-century racial concepts. If we connect the subtext to the overt text, we find the following argument: the African-American obsession with race led to a racist construction of their supposed origins—Africa. That racist construction, epitomized in the nation-building activities of Alexander Crummell, Martin Delany, and Edward Blyden and best represented in its pseudo-social-scientific and ultimately racist clothing by W.E.B. Du Bois (without reference to Anna Julia Cooper, who co-organized the 1903 Pan-African Congress), led to a totalizing articulation of the people who live on that continent. To free the descendants of the cancer that accompanies that ideology—namely, racism—calls for the abandonment of the concept that undergirds the confusing construction. In a moment of candor, Appiah's postcolonial dreams are revealed: ". . . there are bases for common action in our shared situation: the Organization of African Unity can survive the demise of the Negro race" (p. 20).

Appiah provides scores of autobiographical material in this work, yet leaves out quite a bit of ultimately relevant stuff as well. Ordinarily, biographical material may be considered irrelevant, but it is precisely Appiah's use of such material that makes more biographical information about him relevant. He speaks of "our shared situation," for instance, but Appiah's situation is shared by a modicum of the people who live in Africa (and most of Europe) and by a small percentage of those who theorize about such a reality. For his situation is intruded upon by his abased Negro, whereas the situation of many intellectuals of African descent is the realization of *being* that Negro. Cases in point are his references to his father's jotting off to Europe and returning with a white wife, of a childhood of returning regularly to Europe (he was born in London and for the most part *visited* Africa but *lived* in Europe), of traveling around the European and African continents *for leisurely purposes*. Nearly all of his tales provide a portrait of convenient identity: African enough to be exotic and sell Africa to white companions who participate in a complex game of racial exceptionalism. Do the black aristocracy and pseudobourgeoisie who undergird Appiah's text *really* receive an accurate portrait of whites whom, for all intended purposes, they can buy?

I recall attending Appiah's George A. Miller Lecture at the University of Illinois-Urbana (1995). He began his lecture with a story about having to fill out Immigration and Naturalization Service (INS) forms for permanent residence to the United States, given his position as a permanent faculty member in Afro-American Studies and Philosophy at Harvard. At a certain point, the questionnaire had boxes for racial designation. He walked over to an official and told her he didn't know what to fill in. She asked where he was born. He told her London. She said, "Then check white."

Appiah then looked at the audience and quipped, "One should not argue with the INS."

I wondered what he would have done if the official had looked at him and said, "Then check black."

Appiah is correct that some type of African unity can survive the demise of the Negro race—with all the genocidal connotations that such an offensive remark suggests—but that would be both a different kind of Africa and a different basis for unity. We might as well consider, as Anna Julia Cooper pointed out near the end of the nineteenth century, the racist's *fait accompli*: a world without blacks.[8] As I have argued elsewhere, however, such reasoning simply evades the problem instead of addressing it; a world without blacks is hardly a solution to the challenge of treating blacks with moral respect. Who says an Africa without Negroes would be an Africa without Caucasions? There is the disturbing subtext that emerges by such an imaginative act in *our world*, for in our world the only racially neutral, "normative" positioning available is white. Appiah's counsel, although not necessarily his intent, is for a *white*, multiethnic Africa.

Many of the arguments of *In My Father's House* have been discussed without criticism in far too many journals of philosophy and literature to list here. The work ironically has garnered a secure place for the author in the world of contemporary elite *black* scholarship, which for the most part is determined by elite *white* scholarship and media outlets, particularly in the spheres of liberal political thought and postmodern cultural studies. I say ironic because, had Appiah been white and had not been in a crucial moment in the development of *U.S.* black studies (when Houston Baker and Henry Louis Gates, Jr. achieved eminence), I am not sure how his work would have been received. Think, for instance, of David Theo Goldberg, whose *Racist Culture* is influential for its sophistication and nuanced discussion of neocolonialism in Africa and racism in Britain and the United States, but is hardly ever evoked as a benchmark text. Goldberg is white and Jewish and was born and raised on the African continent. Appiah is black (to his chagrin) and British and was born of aristocratic black Ghanian and aristocratic white English parents in Europe. Yet the *interest* in Appiah's text is a product of the racism it deplores: It is a text in what readers are misled to believe is a black African perspective and, worse, a *typical* enough black African perspective to be experientially and philosophically informative when mixed with the author's professional expertise. Although Appiah dismisses appeals to cultural or racial authenticity, the irony of the presentation of *In My Father's House*, and the enthusiasm generated by the author's biography, is that the text's success in part emerged from many reader's assessment of the author's cultural and racial authenticity.[9]

I mentioned elite black scholarly endorsements of *In My Father's House*. The black academic elite is, fortunately, not monolithic. Criticisms have been voiced. Paget Henry's "African Philosophy in the Mirror of Logicisms," where the errors of Appiah's logicism—which rest on a form of neopositivism—is one instance.[10] Lucius Outlaw and Robert Gooding-Williams have written criticisms of Appiah's misguided interpretations of W.E.B. Du Bois.[11] The reader also is encouraged to read Tommy Lott's "Du Bois on the Invention of Race" for an interpretation of Du Bois that is not precluded by the type of neopositivism we find in Appiah's work while preserving a constructivist account. Kwame Gyekye's *An Essay on African Philosophical Thought*, Revised Edition, takes Appiah to task for his notion of "invention" in the African context.[12] Nkiru Nzegwu's "Questions of Identity and Inheritance" is an essential discussion of Appiah's subordination of West African cultural norms and views of matrilineality.[13] And I have already stated most of my criticisms of his notions of intrinsic and extrinsic racism, as well as his basis for rejecting racism (that is, his neo-Kantianism), in *Bad Faith and Antiblack Racism*. There is, therefore, no point in repeating covered terrain. So I should like here to turn to a dimension that has been informally discussed by many critics but not put to print: the antiblack dimensions of Appiah's thought.

First, a serious flaw with Appiah's conception of racism is evident from the remark I made earlier about power. Like many liberal thinkers, who proffer a theoretical standpoint of equal-opportunity or "mass" racism, Appiah ascribes racism as freely to blacks as to whites.[14] He differs from Fanon, for instance, who argues that *Le Nègre, Le Noir*, and antiblack racism cannot emerge without asymmetrical, sociogenic factors. Although Appiah's critique of bad science is an appeal to the sociogenic reality of scientists' impact on what Foucault, echoing Lucretius, calls "the order of things"—where they have constructed race as modernity has constructed "man" who will one day be "erased, like a face drawn in the sand at the edge of the sea"—his formal account of racism is more analytically determined.[15]

Appiah's philosophical argument is well situated in what has become known as the linguistic turn in Anglo-analytical philosophy. He argues that racism must be rejected because it stands on a false concept, the notion of "race." Race is a problematic concept because it fails to meet criteria of what he repeats in a more recent work as both ideational and referential accounts of meaning.[16] The ideational account focuses on people's beliefs about race. There, race fails to achieve consensus needed for univocality of meaning. Race also fails on the referential account because (1) natural (especially genetic) scientific support is lacking and (2) no cultural configuration meets the strict criteria of identity and relevant distinctions needed for such reference. Race is thus philosophically meaningless and fictional. This conclusion does not, however, entail our getting rid of identities formed by how we relate to race. We could consider these identity formations, especially where critical, "authentic" identities, although we should recognize their limitations, their fundamental incompleteness. In *Color Conscious*, he counsels us that ". . . the identities we need will have to recognize *both* the centrality of difference within human identity *and* the fundamental moral unity of humanity" (p. 105).

Commendable though his humanistic conclusion may be, there are some serious problems with the arguments taken along its way. Could *any* generalization or social categorization meet the ideational and referential criteria of meaning? Would not the objections about race on the basis of failed consensus and reference also apply to such concepts as "love," "community," "sociality," "humanity"—or, perhaps worse for Appiah, "science," "logic," and "reason"? Further, the rejection of race on the basis of its being a meaningless concept depends on a *semantic* or terminological analysis. Whether ideational or referential, isn't the presumption that a semantic discussion will determine the validity of anthropological and social claims fallacious? What is the status of "existence" in the challenge raised here? Must phenomena, in order to exist, have an isomorphic relation to the terms that designate them? On a *syntactical* account, which focuses on the grammar of our conceptual schemes, the *practices* of racialization and racism adapt to semantic developments, which accounts for the semantic resilience of race and similar anthropological concepts.[17] A crucial consideration is therefore missing in Appiah's clearly neopositivist account of race and racism: Scientific fiction does not entail social fiction, and semantic fiction does not entail syntactical invalidity.

In both *My Father's House* and *Color Conscious*, Appiah provides a history of the concept of race that takes him back and forth across the Atlantic, from North America to Europe and Africa. The account is a tale from natural history to natural science and theories of civilization. We could say that history serves as the "grammar" for the semantic presentation of race, but there is no advance of this sort of poststructural motif in Appiah's thought. In the end, the continued appeal is to the semantic, not the syntactical or grammatical, failure, which amounts to appealing to the meaninglessness of racial concepts. Again, race is, in other words, the advancement of a false idea on humankind. Its rejection is a matter, then, of truth, where truth draws its legitimacy from natural science and formal logic.

I mentioned that Appiah's discussion of the sociogenic impact of scientific practice suggests some affinity with Fanon. Fanon's point is, however, more than an appeal to a social-systemic factor. His point is an appeal to context. That is why Fanon finds sociogeny between phylogeny and ontogeny.[18] For Fanon, the lived-reality of blacks is the *objective,* intersubjective reality of racial ideology. To put it differently, any black who attempts to believe in black superiority is in serious conflict with modern (and postmodern) reality. Racism, we should remember, is also a structural imposition on identity formation. For the transition into racism—conviction of his racial and, as a consequence, his race's superiority—the black literally needs *another world*. The existential ontological reality emerges, then, at the core of reason and truth. What is, after all, more reasonable and more truthful than to believe *that which is the case*? When Appiah discusses Hitler (p. 18), for instance, he fails to account for a crucial aspect of Hitler's argument in *Mein Kampf*—that if value is collapsed into facts, then one's superiority and another's inferiority become factual affairs, and what is more reasonable than to acknowledge the fact of who rules? This question emerges equally when science rules, as the history of biomedical science's relation to blacks in the United States and Jews in Europe attests. How relevant are individual attitudes in a racist *episteme*?[19]

Although the obvious question is what of the superior race when it no longer rules, the obvious, cold-logic response is that such a group will at that point no longer be the superior race. Hitler's conception of race was, in effect, like the analytic philosopher Nelson Goodman's *grue*, which is green by day and blue by night: It was conveniently adaptable.[20] Appiah identifies Hitler, and would no doubt identify this example as a case of what he calls extrinsic racism (that is, racism with the effort to advance evidence—"rational racism," if we will), but what it fails to account for is how specifically blacks emerge in such a discussion. For it has been the case not only for Hitler but also for generations of his predecessors over the span of a millennium that blacks are indeed a special case. It is not simply that they are inferior, but that they *must be* inferior. In Fanonian language, they *are* inferiority. Such an indictment cannot work according to the extrinsic/intrinsic model, for Appiah has set up the extrinsic model as other-directed on the one hand and intrinsic racism as self-referential on the other. The extrinsic racist needs to be convinced of *others'* equality, whereas the intrinsic racist needs to be convinced that he and his group aren't superior to others. Appiah has, in other words, placed the cart before the horse. He has confused what Paul Gilroy has called "raciality" with "racialogy." Raciality pertains to the sorts of beings designated by the racialogical (scientific) rationalizations of race.[21] For many whites, it is not a matter of being loyal to any race. It is simply that blacks are inferior. The loyalty issue, the intrinsic solidarity issue, is one that emerges primarily for oppressed groups, and it is no accident that Appiah develops such a schema in texts where he wants to debunk what is ultimately a basis for black commonality and solidarity.

J.L.A. Garcia shares my concerns about commonality and solidarity in a recent article in which he voices disagreement with both my theory of racism as a form of bad faith and Appiah's view of racism as intrinsic or extrinsic appeals to a meaningless concept of humankind. He writes:

> Appiah's view of racism and its types commits him to the implausible claim that efforts among oppressed races to advance racial solidarity or promote racial loyalty are not just ill-advised or troublesome but themselves racist, even if they encourage no racial hostility and avoid claims of racial superiority. . . . Lewis Gordon confusedly identifies racism both with a certain kind of choice and with a certain kind of belief. Moreover, his claim that "the racist believes either that one's own race is the only race qualified to be considered human or . . . is

superior to other races," if taken (as the context suggests) as a commitment to the superiority of one's race or *all* other races, seems,
implausibly, both: (i) to exonerate from racism a race-hater who sees
her race as superior to some others but not to all, and (ii) to exclude
any possibility that someone might internalize ambient racism to the
extent of becoming a racist against her own group.[22]

Garcia here commits a gross misrepresentation of my position and quotes
me in a rather strange way. The context did *not* suggest that the racist
considers his own race superior to *all* other races. I simply wrote "other
races," to signify a general claim.[23] Garcia's position on racism is also curious. He argues that racism is a form of "ill will." *Ill will?* How does one
nonvoluntaristically *will* anything? What's more, Garcia's position cannot
account for exoticism, the form of racism that appeals to a supposed "love"
for other races (meant here as "not all other races") over one's own. It
strikes me, however, that Garcia doesn't understand the concept of bad
faith, which is an *ontological* claim about the conditions that enable even ill
will to become manifest, and Appiah's position, which appeals to evidential
criteria in the extrinsic instance. Like sociogeny, bad faith stands between
the phylogenic and the ontological: The concept is a convergence of
agency and social reality, where the person in bad faith may deny the social
world or his or her involvement in that world. That is why bad faith is also
described as an effort to evade one's humanity, and it is so at times paradoxically through perverse or ironic assertions of one's humanity—that is, one's
humanity as what it is not. In *Bad Faith and Antiblack Racism,* criticized
above by Garcia, there also is discussion of black antiblackness (where some
blacks valorize whites) and exoticism as instances of human erasure. Moreover, in that work I present a long phenomenological description of the
relation between choice and belief. The problem is old and akratic: Does
Garcia consider it confused to claim that people often choose what they
believe and often choose to believe what they claim to believe? Garcia
provides no reasons for why this is a supposed confusion, and this problem
of agency cannot be treated with justice here.[24]

Returning, then, to Appiah's depiction of intraracial solidarity as racist,
it so happens that the rejection of black nationalism on the basis of race
isn't new. Fanon has already pointed out the limitations of this view in *Peau
noire, masques blancs,* in his discussion of Antilleans and Africans in *Pour la
révolution africaine,* and in his discussion of the misadventures of national
consciousness in *Les damnés de la terre.* Fanon pointed out the complex
social forces associated with Africa, where one expects to find the supposed

"blackest blacks." But what Appiah fails to consider is that for many Europeans, this means that most of Africa was a "peopleless" place save for European presence here and there. Fanon has stressed this point in *Les damnés de la terre*, that the French saw themselves taking over land, not people. The (black) African literally represented, and to some extent still represents, a point *below the Other*—a point of *no one*. As Arnold Toynbee observed:

> When we Westerners call people "Natives," we implicitly take the cultural colour out of our perceptions of them. We see them as trees walking, or as wild animals infesting the country in which we happen to come across them. In fact, we see them as part of the local flora and fauna, and not as men of like passions with ourselves, and seeing them thus as something infra-human, we feel entitled to treat them as though they did not possess ordinary human rights. They are merely natives of the lands which they occupy; and no term of occupancy can be long enough to confer any prescriptive rights. Their tenure is as provisional and precarious as the forest trees which the Western pioneer fells or that of the big game which he shoots down. And how shall the "civilized" Lords of Creation treat the human game, when in their own good time they come to take possession of the land which, by right of eminent domain, is indefeasibly their own? Shall they treat these "Natives" as vermin to be exterminated, or as domesticable animals to be turned into hewers of wood and drawers of water? No other alternative need be considered, if "niggers have no souls." All this is implicit in the word "Natives" as we have come to use it in the English language in our time.[25]

Discourses on moral contact with the Other are therefore fine and dandy for many purposes of philosophical ethics, but they are limited in that they fail to address the main problem with racism, the dimension that makes some individuals lose themselves in a frenzied attack on the concept of race itself as a means of escaping that problem. Racism *dehumanizes*. The term *human* is here metaphorical, since dehumanization emerges in the plots we craft in science fiction as well. It refers to a point of dignity, the refusal of which constitutes denigration and degradation. The discourse on the Other is different. Implicit in the Other is a human minimum. Thus, in spite of the struggles that may accompany self-Other relations, at least in such instances the Other is considered human—albeit often an unequally treated human being.

Appiah goes to great lengths to jettison the notion of Africa as a homeland for blacks. What he fails to address, however, is the complex history around such identification. When New World blacks identify with Africa, there are at least two dynamics at work. The first is cultural. Although European cultures function as dominant and colonizing political influences in the Americas, much of the cultural formations from Africa south of the Sahara have survived in "traditional" black communities in the New World. Many of my colleagues from Nigeria and Ghana, for instance, often have to look twice as they travel through the Southern United States and the Caribbean; they look twice to make sure they are not in a market or countryside community of Nigeria and Ghana. Once the cultural link is recognized, then realities peculiar to traditional African communities on the continent need be considered. Archaeological and anthropological data show that migratory and linguistic patterns have been such that cultural connections similar to the so-called Indo-Europeans of the north exist in Africa.[26] Many languages have evolved with cognates from a small set of languages in regions that are today the Sudan, Kenya, Ethiopia, and Tanzania.

The second dynamic is that it isn't a fantasy on their part that millions of individuals identified by Europeans as Negroes were kidnapped and brought to different parts of the world. It is also no fantasy on their part to address the ethical issues raised not only by their being descendants of those people but also by imagining what would constitute those people not having died in vain. However much of European humanity permeates the gene pool and cultural resources of those descendants, the narrative that dominates their existence, as a narrative that is different from the European's, is one that haunts the European's existence as well.

There is a reason why the European, the Euro-American, and the Euro-Australian prefer a world of selective memory, a world that is ultimately theodicean, Manichæan, and eschatological: When all is said and done, something good, perhaps even "ordained," has to come out of it, but such validation is not forthcoming.[27] However much some people of African descent may also attempt to identify with their European ancestry (which, in my view is strained by redundancy since that is nearly all they learn to do any way), the matter of those ancestors recognizing them betrays radical asymmetry. It was not slaves who rejected their descendants. New World black families have always known about the whites from whom they also descended, but it is white families who often cleanse their genealogy. One could imagine meeting one's white ancestral spirits. Recognition? Possibly, but unlikely: "He does not see her, because for him there is nothing to see. . . . She looks up at him and sees the vacuum where curiosity ought to lodge. A something more. The total absence of human recognition—the glazed separateness."[28]

Is there a unique relation to one's African ancestry? The slave trade, like genocide in the Americas, has left us with a world of angry, ancestral spirits, with a haunted present. Nearly all West and Southeast African communities speak of ancestral obligations. To expect New World blacks to turn their back on those who died to bring them here is not only unethical, but also, ironically, not African. It is to deny the existence of their African heritage by virtue of their manifesting it. The uniqueness of this relationship does not mean that there may not be other unique relations. One's ancestry could also be Native American, where a similar "hauntology" would emerge. Or one's ancestry also could have emerged from Armenians fleeing Turkish programs of genocide or Jews fleeing the Nazis' final solution. These portraits have a link with what it means to be what was not meant to be: to survive a systematic effort to extinguish one's potential to contribute to the ongoing instantiation of humankind. No white person can substantiate the slave's claim for survival. It is a unique onus. The same applies to every effort to substantiate the survival claims of groups targeted for genocide: Only their descendants, however "mixed," can take that place.[29]

But now we hear that proverbial voice rolling down the corridors of history: the point is to change the current condition, which raises the instrumental question, What is to be done?

Appiah is no revolutionary, but interestingly his liberalism rejects a significant site of black revolutionary activity. Could a liberation project emerge for blacks without, in a word, *blacks*?

Appiah's criticisms of black nationalism offer the same array of criticisms we find in most valorizations of color-blindness and postmodern rejections of "totalizing discourses" and "man"; they cleverly protect the most relevant totalization—the one that can muster the force and power to render itself normative and, therefore, invisible: whiteness. We find a form of double-standard throughout Appiah's rejections and acceptances: Totalizations—as in Zionism and even Europeanism—save those premised upon race (even though Zionism is rarely ever *not* racial) are fine. He points out that the cultural diversity of Africans militates against the efficacy of a nationalist program, whereas Zionism can be satisfied by the existence of a single state (p. 43). For both Pan-Africanism and Zionism, Appiah calls for unions without the factor of race, and he adds that he finds it odd that such "victims of racism, endorsed racialist theories." He calls Crummell racist in spite of Crummell's *Christian* imperialism being the main factor in Crummell's negative attitude toward traditional African religions and customs.[30]

In the end, Crummell didn't particularly care what *race* any one was as long as one was an English-speaking Christian. For him, the problem with Africa is that most of the continent was not Christian and was, therefore, living in sin (paganism) and, thus, risked exclusion from "salvation." The errors of Crummell's position are obvious to those of us who argue against cultural imperialism today. Ironically, given the Judeo-Christian dimensions of cosmopolitan liberalism, the same criticism could be applied to Appiah's hopes for liberalism in Africa. There is a Jewish state that espouses liberalism. There are Christian states that espouse liberalism. As Asian states became more liberal, their citizens became more Christian. The Shah of Iran had attempted to make Iran a liberal Muslim state. The *theological* response has a well-known legacy. Liberalism, like missionaries of old, has its historic specificity in Judeo-Christianity. Whether Crummell's frank admission or Appiah's oblique reference, the consequence is the same: The project of making Africa more liberal amounts to making Africa more Christian—ironically, even in cases where the appeal is to *secular* liberalism, for it should be obvious here that the history of secularism is peculiarly *culturally* Christian.[31]

Appiah's claim that contemporary Zionism can work without appeal to a Jewish "race" is highly questionable. Whatever he may know about Judaism, the fact of the matter is that for most Jews, Judaism hardly stands as a *cultural* marker but a racial one.[32] Conjoined with gender, these concerns are obvious when one thinks of the *racial* significance of matrilineality in contemporary Judaism.[33] Appiah considers a uniquely racialized view of *blacks* to be the correlate of this view. So we find remarks like this one:

> But black philosophy must be rejected, for its defense depends on the essentially racist presuppositions of the white philosophy whose antithesis it is (p. 92).

I don't see how a presupposition of there being a white philosophy entails there being a black philosophy that mirrors it. Nor do I see why "black" *must* signify a racist presupposition.[34] Why couldn't a black philosophy be one that actively resists being a white one? How about a black philosophy that emerges from the rejection of a white supremacist one? Why not a black philosophy that addresses *antiblackness* (which is not identical with white supremacy)? Or a black philosophy that is antiracist? Doesn't, in similar fashion, feminism presuppose patriarchy as an adversary? Does this presupposition render feminism philosophically bankrupt?

Moreover, couldn't black and Africana philosophies simply be understood metaphilosophically as identities for themselves? Kwame Gyekye discusses this in *An Essay on African Philosophy*, as do D.A. Masolo in *African Philosophy in Search of Identity*, Lucius Outlaw in *On Race and Philosophy*, and Paget Henry in his series of articles on African and Afro-Caribbean philosophy.[35] Couldn't there be African, Africana, and black philosophies in the same way that there are European philosophies—philosophies that, if we consider the divide between the *Anglo*-Analytical gangs and the *Continental* gangs, are distinct yet common?[36] When Husserl wrote the *Crisis*, he noted that *Europe* was not a geographical affair but a "spiritual" one.[37] It could not be defined lexicographically nor in its *essence*, but it was "seen," lived, and understood in a multitude of ways. One might as well define it as blacks are often defined by *rhythm*.

What can be learned from raising the question of African, Africana, and black philosophies is the critique of the scope of philosophy itself. The *Geist* war, or war of the spirit, if we will, has presented a conception of Western philosophy that rejects the necessity of examining conceptual schemes beyond itself. The constant presence of Western philosophy as a context for contemporary African philosophy, as Appiah's and many other texts demonstrate, already challenges the borders of philosophy through its constant awareness of *metaphilosophical* possibilities. So when Appiah declares that "if the argument for an African philosophy is not to be racist, then some claim must be substantiated to the effect that there are important problems of morals or epistemology or ontology that are common in the situation of those on the African continent," he begs the question, creates a false dilemma, and sets up a straw man. He begs the question by presupposing a limited selection of questions as philosophical questions (questions that philosophy is supposed to determine, not questions that are supposed to determine philosophy), which leads him to a false dilemma, because not even Western philosophy limits itself solely to the set of concerns he has chosen. And even if we accept Appiah's set of questions as the scope of our philosophical concerns, I don't see how there *isn't* a unique set of moral, epistemological, and ontological questions posed by the cultural-historical specificity of African communities south of the Sahara. Those groups relate to their antiquity in a different way than Europeans do since the European continent has only experienced *religious* imperialism (Christianity), whereas the African continent has experienced every imaginable kind. It is perhaps because of these fallacies that Appiah fails to consider the body of texts in African philosophy that not only considers the set of problems he has outlined, but also created a set of problems of their own.

In Gyekye's work, for instance, there is an innovative organization of African philosophy into classical periods (philosophical sages), middle periods (critical documentation and philosophical engagement with the sages and their ideas in a vein similar to Plato's *written* encounter with Socrates' thought), and contemporary, academic professional periods (which are contextualized by the first two stages). Gyekye takes issue with other contemporary African philosophers, especially Appiah and John Mbiti, for either their misrepresentations or inconsistencies or failure to account for similarities and differences where relevant. For instance, beyond the defining impact of colonialism, there are lively debates on problems of time and ethical responsibility in African philosophy—especially given the importance of ancestral obligation and predestiny in African cosmologies and metaphysics.[38] Gyekye addresses, in other words, the ambiguity of Appiah's use of the word *common*. Common situations do not mean identical situations, and all that is needed for the philosophical project at hand is sufficient similarity for the formulation of philosophical context. Europeans can pretend that European philosophy isn't racialized because European hegemony has rendered European racial identity normative and thus invisible as a supposedly racially neutral term. European commonality is hidden by an appeal to (European) universality.

So what is Appiah up to in this stage of his argument? His theories on race and racism are the culprits here. His construction of racism is such that he is able to articulate a straw-man conception of black philosophy as racist by virtue of its use of the concept of race. On that matter, we need only point out that antiblack reality can persist without having to make a single appeal to the concept of race, and people who bear the brunt of that reality can certainly develop a philosophical praxis of criticism that also does not make a single reference to the concept of race but is, nevertheless, black. Ironically, to turn Appiah on his head, black philosophy can survive without ever making a single reference to the *concept* of race and, hence, Appiah's argument.

What, then, is to be achieved by arguments that appeal to postracial realities as postracist ones? I don't think this question can be fruitfully broached as a future affair. We will have to ask about whom it speaks in the present. For those who live in a world in which race and blackness function as intrusions into an otherwise *kalipolis* (beautiful city-state, just political order), a postracial reality would have achieved the eradication of a nuisance. But for others, the lived-reality of blackness in the *kakapolis* (ugly, unjust state) and the otherwise *kalipolis* is still a matter of survival.[39]

Notes

1. Much of this polarization was antiblack. See Alexander Cockburn's "White Rage: The Press and the Verdict," *The Nation* (October 30, 1995), which catalogs

monolithic condemnations and placements of blame on black communities ranging from demanding apologies, equating whites with reason and technology and
blacks with emotion and superstition/divination, to threats of a reasserted (redundant, no?) white power. Writes Cockburn (on responses to the murder trial), "The
last rung on the racist ladder was the expectation by white commentators that each
black must represent all blacks. Each must apologize for Simpson and for any black
person who cheered the verdict. Turn here to the ever-reliable [Gloria] Steinem,
who told [Charlie] Rose of a touching encounter that made her realize she could
get past the pain of the verdict after all: 'An older black man stopped me in the
airport, and he said, 'I'm sorry. I just want you to know that not all of us feel
this way.' And I—you know, I mean, I, I think we have to trust our human
encounters.'

"I wonder if Steinem felt compelled to walk up to black strangers in 1992 to
apologize after her hero Bill Clinton put Rickey Ray Rector to death to improve
his numbers in New Hampshire" (p. 292). See also "Race & Racism in the Last
Quarter of '95: The OJ & Post-OJ Trial & the Million Man March—a Symposium," ed. by Lewis R. Gordon, *The Black Scholar* 25, no. 4 (Fall 1995): 37–59.
Responses to the civil trial vary. BET had a call-in with Johnny Cochran on February 6, 1997. The general discussion of audiences, white, black, and brown, was
marked by a failure to realize that a civil suit only calls for a "proponderance of
the evidence" instead of the establishement of guilt "beyond a reasonable doubt."

2. See "Million Man March," *The Black Scholar* 25, no. 4 (Fall 1995).

3. Frantz Fanon, *Sociologie d'une révolution* (Paris: Maspero, 1978), p. 111;
translated into English by Haakon Chevalier, with an intro. by Adolfo Gilly, as *A
Dying Colonialism* (New York: Grove Press, 1965), p. 125. Originally published in
1959 as *L'An V de la révolution algérienne*.

4. Most of these texts are diatribes against affirmative action and black authenticity, spanning a new wave of black "conservative" literature—think, for example,
of Shelbey Steele's, Ron Carter's, and Glenn Loury's work. A body of literature
has emerged from the academic "left," who are often more "right" of left than
their readers imagine, that warrants consideration here as well. These texts usually
take the form of villifying a black activist scholar as racist, sexist, or homophobic.
I have been touching on this literature throughout this volume. Targets of such
vilification are Martin Delany (Gilroy's *Black Atlantic*), Alexander Crummell (Appiah's *In My Father's House*), Ida B. Wells-Barnett (Alice Walker and Valerie
Smith—see penultimate chap. of this volume), W.E.B. Du Bois (Appiah), and
Fanon (Gates). Gilroy's text is socially and historically rich, however, in a way that
would not receive justice in this work without an imbalance in the project of
philosophical *sketches*, and, with the exception of his views on "masculinism," his
discussion is primarily descriptive, articulating the complexities of a modern culture of cross-cultural mixture on both sides of the Atlantic Ocean. For a discussion

of that work's importance for race theory, see Linda Martín Alcoff, "Philosophy and Racial Identity," *Radical Philosophy* (Spring 1996).

5. I provided some discussion of Omi and Winant's views in the earlier discussion of biracial and mixed-racial formations in chapter 3. For my discussion of the redundancy of "social construction," see chapter 3 of *Fanon and the Crisis of European Man* and my essay, "Communicative Bases of Social Reality in Light of Deconstructive Appeals to Difference" in *Communicating Differences*.

6. My focus is Appiah's *In My Father's House*, which situates Alexander Crummell's and W.E.B. Du Bois' thought as racist. Similar texts are Paul Gilroy's *Black Atlantic*, which presents Martin Delany as failing to meet criteria of contemporary feminist politics. For discussion of Delany, his views toward women, and criticisms of Gilroy's depiction, see Maya Rockeymore's "Black Nationalism and Democratic Theory: Exploring the Political Contributions of Martin Robison Delany" in *Key Figures in African American Thought*, ed. by Lewis R. Gordon (Oxford: Blackwell, forthcoming). Rockeymore points out that Delany in fact argued *for* active political and economic participation of black female citizens, and forums in whose organizing he played significant part had female voting rights for which he had vehemently argued. Other ninteenth-century figures who carry the shame of not meeting criteria of contemporary gender politics are Edward Blyden and Ida B. Wells-Barnett. Nineteenth-century black liberation figures seem to be fertile ground for a certain brand of cultural critique at the end of the twentieth century. The underlying question is, How do black intellectuals at the end of the twentieth-century compare with those in the nineteenth? We will return to this question in the course of our subsequent discussions of the political configurations of the late 1990s.

7. Although not all instances are marked by exotic racism, black American academics, artists, and political activists are well aware of the type of racism manifested by European fascination with U.S. blackness. For discussion of this type of racism, see my chapter, "Exoticism," in *Bad Faith and Antiblack Racism*. And for a brilliant development of this thesis through an explanation of the aesthetics of exotic judgment, see Darrell Moore's "Critique of Exotic Judgment," *Radical Philosophy Review* 1, no. 2 (1998).

8. See Cooper's essay, "What Are We Worth?" in her *A Voice from the South*, intro. by Mary Helen Washington and foreword by Henry Louis Gates, Jr. (New York and London: Oxford University Press, 1988).

9. *In My Father's House* focuses on the authenticity of the African writer: "Yet, and here is the crux, for European writers these others who define the problem are 'my people,' and they can feel that they know who these people are, what they are worth. For African writers the answer is not so easy. They are Asante, Yoruba, Kikuyu, but what does this now mean? They are Ghanaian, Nigerian, Kenyan,

but does this yet mean anything? They are black, and what is the worth of the black person? . . . So that though the European may feel that the problem of who he or she is can be a private problem, the African asks always not 'who am I?' but 'who are we?' and 'my' problem is not mine alone but 'ours' " (p. 76). By 1996, his thought on authenticity is mediated by admiration for and criticisms of Charles Taylor's *Multiculturalism and "The Politics of Recognition,"* ed. by Amy Gutmann, with commentary by Gutmann, Steven C. Rockefeller, Michael Walzer, and Susan Wolf (Princeton, NJ: Princeton University Press, 1992). Appiah's recent criticism is ironically existential: Both racial and cultural (even multicultural) authenticity fail to appreciate individual projects of the self; see his "Race, Culture, Identity: Misunderstood Connections" in *Color Conscious.*

10. Paget Henry, "African Philosophy in the Mirror of Logicisms: A Review/ Essay," *The C.L.R. James Journal* 4, no. 1 (Winter 1993).

11. See their contributions to *The Critique of Custom: W.E.B. Du Bois and Philosophical Questions*, ed. by Bernard Bell, Emily Groscholz, and James Stewart (New York and London: Routledge, 1997). See also Outlaw's *On Race and Philosophy.*

12. Kwame Gyekye, *An Essay on African Philosophy: The Akan Conceptual Scheme*, Revised Edition (Philadelphia: Temple University Press, 1995).

13. Nkiru Nzegwu, "Questions of Identity and Inheritance: A Critical Review of Kwame Anthony Appiah's *In My Father's House*," *Hypatia* 11, no. 1 (Winter 1996).

14. The silly opposition to Appiah denies the possibility of black racists. I have argued that black antiblack racists exist, but black antiwhite racists require believing in the superiority of blacks without slipping into bad faith. Such a belief requires promethean denial of social reality. Could such a belief be sustained without slipping into psychosis? For discussion, see *Bad Faith and Antiblack Racism*, part III, especially pp. 104–123. See also our return to this issue in this chapter, below.

15. The quote is from Michel Foucault's *The Order of Things*, trans. by anonymous (New York: Vintage, 1994), p. 387.

16. "Race, Culture, Identity: Misunderstood Connections" in *Color Conscious.*

17. We find here the wisdom of Derrida's turn to grammatology, Foucault's turn to epistemes, and Sylvia Wynter's turn to liminality. These poststructural approaches focus on the practices of meaning. In phenomenology, a similar point could be said with regards to Alfred Schutz, who focuses on meaning constitution in the natural attitude.

18. See our discussion of sociogeny in chap. 2, above.

19. Although this matter is central for trials and moral condemnation by those

who are in a position to *judge* the actors of a racist episteme, the objective of a racist episteme is to render its own moral condemnation impossible. The thickness of social reality is that the complex of reasons behind people's actions belie absolute conclusions on many deeds. The victimizer may, for instance, continue to victimize in the hope of intervening forces coming into play, while those intervening forces may stand at bay in the hope that the victimizer's moral agency will win the day, the consequence of which is a circumstance of things going too far. The political history of mass slaughter—whether micro or macro—reveals such tales of contingent, though not accidental, brutality.

20. For discussion of *grue*, see Nelson Goodman's *Fact, Fiction and Forecast*, 4th Edition (Cambridge, MA: Harvard University Press, 1983). For discussion of Hitler's "logic," see C.W. Cassinelli, *Total Revolution*. For a discussion of race theory in Germany during the 1920s, see Marianne Sawicki, "Edith Stein on the State" in *Phenomenology of the Political*.

21. This distinction, which Gilroy brilliantly developed from Part II of *Bad Faith and Antiblack Racism*, "Logic of Racism, Racist Logic," was made in his paper, "Modernity, 'Race' and Historicality" presented at *Modern Culture and Modernity Today*, a conference at Brown University (March 14, 1997).

22. J.L. Garcia, "Racism as a Model for Understanding Sexism" in *Race/Sex*, p. 57, n. 17.

23. Here is what I wrote: "The terms 'racism' and 'race' will unfold in their peculiarities in the course of our investigation. Preliminary formulations of my use of these terms are as follows. By racism I mean the self-deceiving choice to believe either that one's race is the only race qualified to be considered human or that one's race is superior to other races," *Bad Faith*, p. 2.

24. Readers interested in my position on choice and belief are encouraged to consult *Bad Faith*, especially pp. 10–13. The problem of the status of belief permeates much of modern philosophy since the Cartesian moment of centering epistemology as first philosophy. There, the status of one's belief is crucial for the divide between simply believing and knowing. In my work, I reject this turn, since it requires an external factor of the form, ". . . and in fact knowing." The status of "in fact" is external to the belief condition. It is an ontological appeal.

25. Arnold Toynbee, *A Study in History*, vol. 1 (London: Oxford University Press, 1934), pp. 152–3. I thank Robert Westley for providing me with this quotation.

26. See *The African Frontier: The Reproduction of Traditional African Societies*, ed. by Igor Kopytoff (Bloomington: Indiana University Press, 1987) and *The Archaeology of Africa: Food, Metals and Towns*, ed. by Thurstan Shaw, Paul Sinclair, Bassey Andah, and Alex Okpoko (London and New York: Routledge, 1993). See also

African History and Culture, ed. by Richard Olaniyan (Lagos, Nigeria & Essex, UK: Longman, 1982).

27. For a discussion of the tendancy of slave-owners and early Pan-African Christians to appeal to theodicean understandings of slavery, see Josiah Young, *A Pan-African Theology* (Trenton, NJ: Africa World Press, 1992), Parts I and II.

28. *The Bluest Eye*, p. 42. These remarks on rejected recognition do not pertain to children of biracial marriages, however, since the complexities of recognition here could go either way. The parents may offer their different cultural heritage and racial experiences to their offspring, which is a complex dynamic of recognition. This is not to say that the child is necessarily recognized in these instances. There are cases of parental denial in many communities for other than racial reasons.

29. We could regard memorials as an effort to take such responsibility on the part of outside groups. Memorials make "memory" the instantiation of the group's survival. But such memory has a simultaneous danger of becoming a trophy. A live dodo will forever change the meaning of dodo as an extinct species. Memory of the dodo is, after all, also a wicked affirmation of the bird as an inferior species: It is remembered as stupid, delicious, and extinct.

30. This is not to say that Crummell did not believe that there were "races." See, for instance, his "The Destined Superiority of the Negro" in *Destiny and Race: Selected Writings (1840–1898)*, ed. with an intro. by Wilson Jeremiah Moses (Amherst, MA: The Univerity of Massachusetts Press, 1992), pp. 194–205. For discussion of the Christian imperialism manifested in Crummell's thoughts on Africa, see Josiah Young's *A Pan-African Theology*, part II.

31. A conversation on this matter emerged in a law and religion conference in April 1995 at Brown University. In her commentary on Martha Nussbaum's presentation, "Women and Human Rights," Carol Weisbrod appealed not only to the complexity of women's relation to legal systems, but also to the peculiarly Christian-centric conceptions of sex and family that emerge in liberal articulations of law. Why couldn't polygamy, for instance, be permitted without appeal to religious freedom? Couldn't polygamy be defended on "secular" grounds? A collapse of secularity into monogomy is fallacious, but the historical fact remains: secular systems do not endorse polygomy as a *secular* option. Empirical study should be conducted on the relationship between secular hegemony and conversions to Christianity in Northeast Asia and much of Africa. I suspect the findings will bear out this hypothesis. Even avowed atheists seem in the end to endorse Christian cultural motifs, which raises the Hegelian question of whether non-Christian cultural alternatives are possible in a liberal society. For discussion of Hegel on liberalism, with attention to its Christological dimensions, see Steven Smith's *Hegel's Critique of Liberalism: Rights in Context* (Chicago: University of Chicago Press,

1989) and "Hegel on Slavery and Domination," *Review of Metaphysics* 46, no. 1 (1992): 97–124.

32. Which raises the question of whether the black-Jewish debate over Afro-centrism and traditional European classicism also has another racial threat: If Greece and Egypt are blackened, and enslaved Hebrews in antiquated Egypt were nearly indistinguishable from their Egyptian slave masters, the conclusion of an Africanized Hebrew population returning to Canaan is around the corner. The subtext of Lefkowitz's *Not Out of Africa* (New York: Basic Books, 1995) may be a smokescreen for a tale of another nation. Although Abraham is purported to be from Ur (in contemporary Iraq), the populations who greeted fellow Hebrews in Canaan had to *prove* that their god was the god of Abraham. For discussion of the origins of Judaism and the legitimation challenge faced by the Hebrews who came out of Egypt, see Karen Armstrong, *A History of God: The 4,000-Year Quest of Judaism, Christianity, and Islam* (New York: Ballantine Books, 1993), chaps. 1 and 2.

33. For explorations of the complexity of these considerations, see *Judaism Since Gender*, ed. by Miriam Peskowitz and Laura Levitt (New York and London: Routledge, 1997). The reader may wonder how religious conversion works here. A man who converts to Judaism will need to have children with a Jewish birth-mother to father Jewish children. If he doesn't have children with a Jewish birth-mother, then his children will have to go through conversion, not to remain Jewish, but *to be* Jewish. A woman who converts to Judaism does not have this problem. Since her children will now *racially* be Jewish, one could argue that her conversion resulted in an ontological transformation as well. See also David Goldberg's "Between Blacks and Jews" in *Racial Subjects*.

34. I am not alone. Amy Guttman takes a similar position in "Responding to Racial Injustice," her contribution to *Color Conscious*. She argues that color discrimination could exist without an appeal to the concept of race, and that color-blindness makes the error of presenting a just ideal under less-than-ideal circumstances, the result of which is a rejection of implementing policies toward realistic social change.

35. D.A. Masolo, *African Philosophy in Search of Identity* (Bloomington: Indiana University Press, 1994; and London: Edinburgh University Press, 1994), and for Paget Henry's work, see his "Afro-Caribbean Philosophy: An Introduction" and "CLR James, African and Afro-Caribbean Philosophy," both in *The CLR James Journal* 4, no. 1 (Winter 1993), "Fanon, African, and Afro-Caribbean Philosophy," in *Fanon: A Critical Reader*, and "African and Afro-Caribbean Existential Philosophies" in *Existence in Black*.

36. See, for instance, Lucius Outlaw's "African, African American, Africana Philosophy," in *On Race and Philosophy*; see also *I Am Because We Are: Readings in Black Philosophy*, ed. by Fred Lee Hord (Mzee Lasana Okpara) and Jonathan Scott Lee (Amherst: University of Massachusetts Press, 1995), introduction. For those

who wonder why I use the terms *gangs* to describe these divisions, it is because they are marked more by philosophical bullying and clan membership than by the problems of philosophy themselves. Those in doubt may wish to consult F.C.S. Schiller's June 9, 1903, letter to William James, in which he offers his "table of countraries":

1. *The Good and Finite*	vs.	*The Evil and Infinite*
2. Humanism		Scholasticism
3. Pragmatism		Verbalism
4. Personal Idealism		Naturalism
5. Pluralism		Absolutism
6. radical Empiricism		Apriorism
7. Voluntarism		Intellectualism
8. Anthropomorphism		Amorphism
9. Briticism		Germanism
10. Witticism		Barbarism

Schiller adds: "That is comprehensive enough, don't you think? . . . It appears to me . . . that the thick of the fight (once we get to close quarters) is going to be about the indetermination of truth and reality prior to experiment." Quoted from Ralph Barton Perry, *The Thought and Character of William James* (New York: George Braziller, 1954), p. 302.

There are, of course, exceptions: "The historians of twentieth-century philosophy have already secured a niche for Gilbert Ryle as a leading representative of twentieth-century analytical philosophy. What tends to be overlooked, however, is his role in the critical reception of continental philosophy by the Anglo-American philosophical world. He was one of the first of his profession to write a review of Martin Heidegger's epoch-making *Sein und Zeit* shortly after its publication," Calvin Schrag, *The Self After Postmodernity* (New Haven and London: Yale University Press, 1997), p. xi. The same could be said for J. L. Austin's role in bringing Husserl's ideas across the British channel.

37. Edmund Husserl, *The Crisis of European Sciences and Transcendental Phenomenology: An Introduction to Phenomenological Philosophy*, trans. with an intro. by David Carr (Evanston: Northwestern University Press, 1970), p. 273.

38. For discussion, see Gyekye's criticisms of Mbiti's *African Religions and Philosophy* (New York: Anchor Books, 1970) in *An Essay on African Philosophy*, chap. 11. See also chap. 7. In addition, Paget Henry's "African and Afro-Caribbean Existential Philosophies" provide discussion on predestiny across a number of Africana communities. The impact of ancestral obligation in Africana thought can be found in suprising places. Anna Julia Cooper's argument, that each individual achieves maturity in "debt" to the generations who raised and preceded them and must contribute enough beyond that debt to be of value, is one instance. In my course, Black Existentialism, one of my students, Jessica Purdy, offered an ingenius

response to the problem of ancestral debt: If one incurs a burden through raising children, then our children can alleviate a good portion of that debt by raising children of their own.

39. Another translation of *kakapolís*, by the way, is the "shitty state."

CHAPTER SEVEN

AFRICAN PHILOSOPHY'S SEARCH
FOR IDENTITY: EXISTENTIAL
CONSIDERATIONS OF A
RECENT EFFORT

These times are unprecedented in the history of Africana thought in the American academy. There are more texts written on Africana philosophical thought than ever before, the effect of which is a shift in climate for young scholars interested in working in the field. I have had the good fortune, for instance, to have examined a candidate who wrote a comparative dissertation on Luo, Japanese, and cyberspace communitarianism.[1] This period of production warrants a moment's pause to evaluate the circumstances that have led to it. Such a task is complicated primarily because to raise the question of the African, which for the most part entails the subtext of what Fanon calls *le Noir* (*the black*), is to uncover complex practices, whose fundamental leitmotif is of a humanity divided into contradictory "species."

I recall an exercise from a course I taught on Africana philosophy. I asked my students to think of images of Europe, of Asia, of Central America, of North America. For Europe, they imagined old, magnificent buildings; glorious art work; double-decker buses in London; the Queen's guards; the Eiffel Tower and cafés in Paris; the Vatican in Rome; and so on. In Asia, the Great Wall of China came to mind; the Taj Mahal in India; millions of people in Tokyo; accrobats; and other splendors for the imagination. In North America, when the students were asked to think of the indigenous populations, they came up with "spirituality" (a naturalism straight out of Rousseau's romantic speculations on "noble savagery"). In Central America and South America, they thought of pyramids built by the Aztecs and the Incas. Then I asked them to think of Africa. The imagination took them to the savannah and to jungles, to wild animals, to many, many animals. I asked my students why they didn't think of people. Or if not of people themselves, of human artifacts—buildings, bridges, roads, etc.?

This is a classroom's tale, true, but a tale that pertains directly to the awesome task taken on by D.A. Masolo in his *African Philosophy in Search of Identity*. Masolo shows that it takes much patience to be an Africana philosopher examining the history of African philosophy. One must work through a morass of racial insult and dehumanizing narrative. In a way, he undertakes a task that, by the prevailing racist ideology, *he* as a man of African descent is supposed to be incapable of doing. The text, therefore, has a tragic subtext of authorship, in that the author himself is the contradiction of many theses that he meticulously, patiently, articulates and evaluates. The book thus has the effect of rolling pebbles growing into a full-scale landslide.

Masolo's avowed thesis is that "the contestation over the definition of and claim over reason is an important center of the discourse on African philosophy" (p. 180). In one sense, then, Masolo's project is historical: to present a narrative of the contestation over the definition of and claim over reason in African philosophy. The deck is already stacked on Masolo's side, however, because the presumption here is that, in articulating African reason, he also will articulate the identity of African philosophy. In other words, African philosophy's search for identity is also *Africans'* search for identity. At first sight, the battle over reason may seem misguided, since there is an implied problematic in the conjunction of the *African* with *reason*. Therein is the source of the problem—the subtext of the black, the savage, the primitive, the thing that steps in the door, as Fanon says, and constantly finds Reason walking out. Masolo's text, therefore, has an underlying project, one that comes to the fore in a powerful discussion in the penultimate chapter and conclusion: What is the role of reason in African philosophy and how does African philosophy articulate its own identity when part of its identity is a critique of reason as historically constituted? Given my objections to Appiah's assessment of an African, much more a black, philosophy, Masolo's text, one of the most ambitious attempts at a counterargument to date, warrants my attention here.

One more set of preliminary remarks. It is not my view that philosophy should be resuscitated at all cost. Philosophy is for the most part in a state of crisis, where most of its avowed practioners are comfortable engaging in a form of professional banality—more like attorneys filing memoranda and briefs than theorists probing the limits of thought. The thought of revolutionary thinking in philosophy has become such a thing of the past that those of us who expect no less are often greeted by raised eyebrows or condescending laughter.[2] That philosophy requires critique in addition to other areas of disciplinary production suggests that our times call for radical thinking or theorizing that is ironically beyond philosophy in one sense and yet being so lends itself to being domesticated by philosophy in another sense: It is, after all, difficult to go beyond philosophy without being philosophical. But whether one's theoretical commitment is philosophical or not must be suspended in order properly to issue a critique of philosophy. That is why I have appreciated the spirit behind the phenomenological method. In *Fanon and the Crisis of European Man*, part of the crisis is Western philosophy's continued effort to be the center of rationality while closing off radical resources of self assessment.[3] For me, Western philosophy is but one among many struggles in the human quest to understand itself and reality. In our age, its quest has taken the ironic form of a secular religion, and great priests and theologians of the past have now been replaced by new counsels on faith and Being. (Contemporary theologians attempt to legitimate their positions *philosophically*.) Although most of humanity's great philosophers (Western and otherwise) were not academics, the academy's contemporary hegemony over knowledge has been such that the academic philosopher has gained primacy over what we should believe and how we should believe it. With such primacy emerges a stultification of creativity and gall, the result of which is a culture of production that maintains its sense of security by virtue of regulation and predictability; that is why, in many areas of philosophy, no more can be said since the resources of genuine speech and thinking have been exhausted. The result is theoretical decadence, where one's disciplinary perspective takes on ontological characteristics. Theoretically decadent theorists criticize other disciplines for not meeting criteria along the assumed "theoretically correct" discipline. That is why many areas of philosophy suffer from more than a problem of technical proficiency and new combinations from its axioms of thought. They suffer from what many of them know is their true folly: boredom. They are not capable of speaking their "truths" to others. Philosophical energy must now be drawn from elsewhere. That said, let us move on to Masolo.

In spite of all the nuances of Masolo's readings, the underlying motif is the dialectic between the binary of the rational and the irrational. This dialectic is traced through the various efforts to articulate both descriptions of and prescriptions for African reality by way of the philosophical resources available to thinkers who have raised the question of African philosophy. The inauguration of modern dialectics is ignominiously embodied, as we have seen, in Hegel's dismissal of *Geist* and, consequently, world history in what is called "black Africa" today. Recall Hegel's conclusion to the section on Africa in the introduction to his *Philosophy of History*:

At this point we leave Africa, not to mention it again. For it is no historical part of the World; it has no movement or development to exhibit. Historical movements in it—that is in its northern part— belong to the Asiatic or European World. Carthage displayed there an important transitionary phase of civilization; but, as a Phoenician colony, it belongs to Asia. Egypt will be considered in reference to the passage of the human mind from its Eastern to its Western phase, but it does not belong to the African Spirit. What we properly understand by Africa, is the Unhistorical, Undeveloped Spirit, still involved in the conditions of mere nature, and which had to be presented here only as on the threshold of the World's History (p. 99; cf. also 91-8).

The problem already is situated by the racist occlusion of human presence from Western conceptions of the African continent, the vestiges of which continue to this day, as my experiment with my students attests. The binary situates Reason, rationality, self, "here" (meaning of Western kind) as opposed to "nature," "irrationality," and supposedly "other"—"there" (meaning not of Western kind). I say "supposedly" because what both my experiment with my students and the Hegelian (as well as Nietzschean) sentiment suggest is not that it is the European's *other* that is located in Africa but, as we have seen in our discussion of Fanon and philosophy of racism, *no-one*, nothing.[4]

Masolo discusses the many African and Africana responses to the Hegelian occlusion, many of which ironically deploy Hegelian modes of argumentation against Hegel himself. The discussion is rich and it will, unfortunately, be impossible to convey the many roads trod in Masolo's painstaking, critical discussion from negritude through ethnophilosophy through antiethnophilosophy and sage philosophy through contemporary modern, postmodern, and analytical positioning; from Marxism and phenomenology (philosophical and "religious") and existentialism to textual and genealogical poststructuralism and neopragmatism; to the persistent problem of the question of the African as the threat of relativism. Guided by the two most influential questions at the heart of Africana existential reality—what I shall call the teleological and the ontological questions—the text's argument is as follows.

The teleological question focuses on the *purpose* of African philosophy, which Masolo correctly shows is rooted in a sentiment that is unavoidably linked to Marx's eleventh thesis on Feuerbach, where the goal is to change the current condition of a dominated Africa (in all senses of domination).

The ontological question emerges from the *identity* question, where Masolo focuses on the African world-view(s) and African identity. *Africans*, as is now well-known through the work of V.Y. Mudimbe, though I would argue that its origin is in the work of Fanon and Sartre, is an organizing identity imposed upon the multitude of peoples/cultures who live on the continent known through the lens of European modernity as *Africa*.[5]

After spending the greater part of the book examining the tension between the teleological and ontological divide, the strengths and shortcomings of nearly every effort to articulate (prescriptively) what Africans should be doing when they do philosophy, Masolo concludes:

> [T]here is no single philosophical tradition that was tailor-made and produced like an industrial product. There is no justifiable reason, therefore, why one individual or group should try to tailor-make African philosophy by prescribing what ought to be its content, method of reasoning, and standards of truth (p. 251).

He then adds:

> Like other philosophical systems and traditions, African philosophy must also be born out of its own peculiar cultural circumstances combined with a living and constructive zeal among individual African intellectuals to understand and explain the world around them. . . . Debate and the desire to get our concepts properly understood are two vehicles of intellectual inquiry that have helped in the establishment of philosophy as a special intellectual activity; and we have no reason to exempt African philosophy from them.

I will return to Masolo's conclusion. But first, some additional remarks.

A major difficulty of developing texts in intellectual history of any kind is the array of resources one has to deploy. The disciplines and techniques are vast, and without question, the intellectual historian has the problem of having not only to articulate a theory but to articulate it both in the form of its purpose and its translation. The philosophical skill with which Masolo works his way through African philosophers as diverse as Pauline Hountondji, Kwasi Wiredu, and the late Oderu Oruka, as well as Euro-philosophers such as Peter Winch and W.V.O. Quine and Noam Chomsky is commendable. It is understandable, however, that with such a vast range of thinkers, dimensions of their thought that may be relevant may be put aside in the development of the architectural scheme.

Instead of addressing such instances one by one, let us instead focus on those that pertain to the dimension of Masolo's text that relate to Fanon, because Fanon, as should now be obvious, is the voice behind all of our philosophical sketches thus far.

Masolo focuses on Fanon as an existential-Marxist. Such an ascription to Fanon is not entirely inaccurate. Fanon took many Marxist stands, but he also took stands that were not Marxist, except in the sense that Marxism can be understood in its *existential* and *philosophical* focus on change. But what is missing from Masolo's discussion is another dimension of Fanon's thought, one that pertains directly to the theme of the book. Fanon argued early in his career that one cannot construct a human science that articulates the lived-experience of the black without an appeal to sociohistorical reality—in a word, *sociogenesis*. The point about sociogeny was that, whenever the black is considered, historical and cultural forces come into play. This insight is at the heart of black existential philosophy. Central existential concepts like anxiety, dread, and despair carry *historical* urgency in black existential thought.[6] This is so for good reason: Without recognizing historical and cultural factors in our theorizing, blacks would disappear. The ahistorical and the acultural are the historical and cultural impositions of whiteness. Now at first glance, this insight may seem relative only to black existence, but instead there is another turn. Fanon argued that the European practice of science was such that to achieve objectivity it often denied the existence of the black in its construction of the human being. Universality was, therefore, a door available only through the exclusion of blacks. The obvious problem, however, is that the exclusion of blacks signified a de facto failure of universality; it signaled an artificial structuring of one branch of humanity into a species above another. This circumstance was an inhuman relationship, in which there were those who were below the realm of human being and, consequently, another group "above" humanity—in other words, as we have seen in our discussion of Pico Della Mirandola's cosmology, a world of gods and animals.[7]

I do not wish here to examine the ethical significance of such a construction. Instead, we should note that the artificial situating of the African outside of the universal leads to a particular conception of the "scope" of reality. We see it in the discourse that emerges over African philosophy. African philosophy is treated by many theorists as a type of suppressed prime. One has the Western logos and its logos-prime, its logos-other, or logos-exterior. Yet in practice, one often speaks of the former without reference to the latter, whereas the latter always evokes the former. The white/Western philosophical reality becomes the "governing fiction," as Fanon would say, over the discourse that Africans and others have on African philosophy. Now although this governing fiction suggests at first that "real philosophy" is Western, there is a logic that can show that African philosophy is broader in scope than Western philosophy because it includes the Western in its self-articulation.[8] In *practice*, Western philosophy may be a subset of African philosophy. The suppressed prime may be the set with a larger domain.

A problem with such a view, however, is that it does not account for why a subset has more hegemonic weight than the set of which it is a part. Why is Western philosophy hegemonic when it excludes other philosophies, yet African philosophy, which includes Western philosophy, lacks such influence? Fanon's argument is that such an account always requires an appeal to an *external* consideration of the system or set. For the African, it is the absence of normative weight, the appeal that renders an "outside" invisible, that conditions its identity as a subset or, in less polite language, a "subspecies," of Western practices. For Fanon, this question required a critique of the tendency to center European reality and to treat realities of color as derivative realities.

What Masolo shows, in his reading of nearly every influential twentieth-century African philosopher, is that the legitimacy of the African has been articulated in a way that makes one wonder if the African-prime, *formally speaking*, is relevant to its own reality. The content of V.Y. Mudimbe's thought, for instance, is that Africa is invented; but the form of his thought is genealogical poststructuralism—in a word, *Foucaultian*.[9]

Herein lies the irony. The African resources, read as non-European, appear located in the past, but the impetus for seeking out those resources is a concern for a restructured future. The Akan Sankofa bird stands behind the African's head, who looks into a mirror in which Foucault, Derrida, Sartre, Heidegger, Husserl, Marx, and Hegel smile back.

What is the "identity" sought here? In a concrete sense, it can be according to the taxonomy developed by Odera Oruka, correlates of which are ethnophilosophical identity, professional identity, political-ideological identity, and sagacious identity. But in another sense, the identity project is existentially problematic to begin with, because it calls for the project to "catch up with itself," to become one with a supposed essence, which Masolo rightly rejects as a closure that could only maintain itself at the expense of the discipline.

Our existential ascription emerges in many ways. This dimension is not immediately apparent, because Masolo wrongly situates existentialism in the "irrational." I have argued in *Bad Faith and Antiblack Racism* that existence raises the possibility of the *non*rational, which stands between irrationality and rationality—a claim that Masolo recognizes only in John

Dewey's thought. This distinction comes into focus in chapter six of Masolo's text, where he discusses what is in effect linguistic transcendentalism, where what he describes as Winch's relativism can also be regarded as the thesis that one cannot articulate meaning outside of a language, which raises a challenge to the centering of any language as an ideal *metalanguage*.[10] The transcendental turn here is an ironic one in that it undermines the very notion of a suprastructural language that takes the concrete form of any one closed system over another—in the case of Masolo's discussion, it is the problem of "magic" versus "natural science" for the claim of "reason." But the existential turn, which undergirds even Wiredu's appeals in spite of his supposed pragmatism, has to be such that perhaps it cannot even concede reason as the goal but instead that which, among other items of consideration, must be evaluated by the activity itself. If that is so, then implicit in the existential turn in the various inquiries is more than the question of critique and dialogue, but also the question of *radical* critique and dialogue. If that is so, then the following observation, where Masolo criticizes Hountondji's rejection of ethnophilosophy in place of philosophy as a body of critical literature, is rendered problematic:

> And Hountondji [has a limited position] because, in trying to shatter this ontological mythologization [of ethnophilosophy], he creates another myth in its place: the scientific establishment of philosophical activity, *the restoration of philosophy as a rigorous science* (p. 203, emphasis added).[11]

Although Hountondji's neo-Marxist scientism and Derridian focus on writing fall prey to the error of theoretical decadence, where the ultimate point of criticizing other theories is that they are not the theory that one is espousing (in other words, the presumed validity of one's form of theorizing as Theorizing-in-itself—philosophy supposedly *is* literature), I don't see how rejecting the aim of philosophy as rigorous science works as a critique here. For in effect, Masolo accuses Hountondji of not being rigorous by pursuing rigor. Recall our critique of the notion of European philosophy as *the* universal. At the heart of the critique is the European tradition's failure to embody its own goals, which included a universal description of reality. Any effort to describe reality by excluding key segments of it is a de facto fallacious application of itself. It is, in a word, not rigorous.

Although "rigor" as a goal of philosophical inquiry isn't fashionable these days, we should be careful not to confuse absence of rigor with the impossibility of rigor or definitions of rigor premised on limited or closed systems.[12] Philosophical rigor may depend on an open-ended practice that is similar to what Masolo advocates at the end of *African Philosophy in Search of Identity*. Philosophical rigor may be contextually hermeneutical because, as many metaphilosophers—including Husserl, with his appeal to radicality, and Fanon, with his appeal to radical constructing of new concepts—have realized, it is sufficiently reflective and self-reflective to nihilate itself, to displace, that is, its own identity. I suspect that is what Masolo may be admitting in the end, when he says, "So while we say yes to African personality, we ought to say yes to technological modernism; yes to the African conscience, but also yes to universal science." This seems to be an appeal to rigor in African philosophy.

African decentering of Europe should not, then, involve a failure to address the implications of its own practice. It is its mission, as perhaps it is the mission of all philosophies, always to consider that which is often hidden from thought on the most profound levels, levels that are often also invisibly familiar.

Notes

1. Samuel Oluoch Imbo, "Inadequacy of Individualistic Conceptions of Moral Responsibility" (West Lafayette, IN: Philosophy Department doctoral dissertation, Purdue University, 1995). Imbo has also written an essay on teaching recent literature in African philosophy. See his "African Philosophy in 1997," *APA Newsletter on Philosophy and the Black Experience* 96, no. 2 (Spring, 1997).

2. On this matter, see my essay "Identity and Liberation" in *Phenomenology of the Political*.

3. For a discussion of the phenomenological significance of the argument in *Fanon and the Crisis of European Man*, see Marilyn Nissim-Sabat's "Globalism from Below: An Appreciation of the Philosophy of Lewis Gordon," *The C.L.R. James Journal* 5, no. 1 (1997).

4. See Fanon's discussion of Self-Other relations in *Peau noire* and *Les damnés* (esp. the penultimate chapter), and discussions of those relations in *Bad Faith and Antiblack Racism*, *Fanon and the Crisis of European Man*, and various sections of this volume, especially chap. 4 above. See also William Preston's "Nietzsche on Blacks."

5. See especially Fanon's "Antillais et Africains" and Sartre's essay "Black Presence" in *The Writings of Jean-Paul Sartre*, vol. 2, *Selected Prose*, trans. by Richard McCleary and ed. by Michel Contat and Michel Rybalka (Evanston, IL: Northwestern University Press, 1974).

6. For a collection of voices on black existential philosophy, see *Existence in Black*. See also *Fanon: A Critical Reader*.

7. See chap. 3, above.

8. For a philosopher who argues that African philosophy is not "real philosophy," see Robin Horton's "African Traditional Thought and the Emerging African Philosophy Department: A Comment on the Current Debate," *Second Order: An African Journal of Philosphy* 7, no. 1 (January 1977) and "African Traditional Thought and Western Science" in *Rationality*, ed. by Bryan R. Wilson (Oxford: Blackwell, 1974). See Gyekye's *Essay on African Philosophy*, chap. 1 for criticisms of Horton's views. For a collection of a number of influential contributions to the debate on this issue, see Tsenay Serequeberhan, *African Philosophy: The Essential Writings*, ed. by Tsenay Serequeberhan (New York: Paragon, 1991).

9. See V.Y. Mudimbe's *The Invention of Africa* (Bloomington: Indiana University Press, 1988).

10. For an informative discussion of linguistic transcendentalism, see Karl Otto Apel's "Is Intentionality More Basic than Linguistic Meaning?" in *John Searle and His Critics*, ed. by Lepore and Van Gulick (Oxford: Blackwell Publishers, 1991), pp. 31–56.

11. For Pauline Hountondji's position, see *African Philosphy: Myth and Reality*, trans. by Henri Evans, with the collaboration of Johnathan Rée (London: Hutchinson University Library for Africa, 1983; Bloomington: Indiana University Press, 1983).

12. Cf. *Fanon and the Crisis of European Man*, chaps. 3 and 5.

PART II

THE INTELLECTUALS

CHAPTER EIGHT

LORRAINE HANSBERRY'S TRAGIC SEARCH FOR POSTCOLONIALITY: *LES BLANCS*

It's an old problem, really . . . Orestes . . . Hamlet . . . the rest of them . . . We've really got so many things we'd rather be doing.
—*Tshembe, from Lorraine Hansberry's* Les Blancs

In 1961, Lorraine Hansberry wrote a scathing review of Jean Genet's *The Blacks*.[1] The context of the review itself is a complex tale of translations and mistranslations, interpretations and misinterpretations. After all, *The Blacks* is an English translation of the French *Les Nègres*, which means both Negroes and "niggers." *The Negroes? "Niggers"*? Genet himself claimed that the play, which was originally titled *Foot-Ball*, was not written "*for* Blacks but *against* Whites," against whites' flawed images of blacks.[2] According to Edmund White in his award-winning biography of Genet, Genet was inspired by three things to write *Les Nègres*. The first was public reaction to Jean Rouch's film *Les Maîtres-Fous* (1954), which was about the black "urban proletariat of Accra who go into the bush and celebrate a ritual, enter into a trance, and perform a sort of exorcism" (*Genet*, p. 426). Genet was struck by French viewers' ready acceptance of the film's misrepresenting iconography. The second inspiration was an elaborate music box. Genet's words are worth a lengthy quote:

> The point of departure, the trigger, was given me by a music box in which the mechanical figures were four Blacks dressed in livery bowing before a little princess in white porcelain. This charming *bibelot* is from the eighteenth century. In our day, without irony, would one

imagine a response to it: four white valets bowing to a Black princess? Nothing has changed. What then goes on in the soul of these obscure characters that our civilization has accepted into its imagery, but always under the lightly foolish appearance of a caryatid holding up a coffee table, of a train-bearer or a costumed servant bearing a coffee pot? They are made of fabric, they do not have a soul. If they had one, they would dream of eating the princess.

When we see Blacks, do we see something other than the precise and sombre phantoms born of our own desire? But what do these phantoms think of us then? What game do they play?[3]

His slippage into the European association of blacks with cannibalism aside, it is clear that Genet was struck by the mundanity of antiblack racism, the familiar acceptance of its normative dimension that renders it almost invisible in daily life. Genet's third source of inspiration was the commissioning of the play by Raymond Rouleau, who, according to White, had been asked by a black actor for a play that could be performed by blacks (p. 428). It would seem, given these circumstances, that Genet's good intentions were on safe ground.[4]

In her review, however, Hansberry accused Genet of taking the easy way out by writing a play that elicits white *guilt* instead of addressing the question of action. Genet attempted his project by way of an exoticized blackness which, in Hansberry's assessment, placed what W.E.B. Du Bois, Richard Wright, Frantz Fanon, and even Jean-Paul Sartre called "the white problem" out of focus: If *white* misrepresentation of blacks were the issue, why didn't Genet simply title his play, *Les Blancs* (*The Whites*)? *Les Nègres* represents a complex form of signification, because it at once refers and is displaced in its reference. In the title, the third-person reference signifies a white first-person plural pronoun; " 'we,' the whites, have distorted images of 'them,' the blacks." So although blacks are mentioned in the title, the title supposedly signifies whites. Yet double-references aren't always understood. One expects a play entitled *The Blacks* to be one about blacks, no? And given that nearly all literature was at that time ultimately written to whites, there appears to be redundancy in Genet's declaration that it was a play for white edification (or perhaps chastisement?): Ironically, in spite of its all-black cast, *Les Nègres* is a play without blacks. Blacks are here absent in spite of their presence. They are visibly invisible. Given Hansberry's logic, if Genet wanted to address the white problem, *The Whites* would have been a good start.

After her review, Hansberry decided to transform a work in progress into such a play. Composition of her play, *Les Blancs*, had in fact begun in 1959.[5] It addressed a topic she was struggling with, ironically, at a time when her contemporary Frantz Fanon was fully steeped in the actual practice of its reality: the question of violence in a liberation struggle. I mention Fanon because of the ironic similarities between Fanon and Hansberry, and because it is my work on Fanon that led me to this examination of Hansberry's work. Although the two were six years apart in age and individuals from very different cultures, both were heavily influenced in their early adult years by direct engagement with the revolutionary black voices in their communities: Fanon with Aimé Césaire; Hansberry with Paul Robeson and Du Bois. Both produced their first major work in their twenties: Fanon, *Peau noire, masques blancs*, at age 26; Hansberry, *A Raisin in the Sun*, at age 28. Both works were complex explorations of black subjectivity in the face of attempting a dialectical relationship with the White World. (Nearly all of the themes in *Peau noire* emerge in *Raisin*, including the complex relation with negritude that marks a defensive strategy in the struggle for black liberation.) Both delivered important speeches on the role of the black writer in 1959.[6] Both devoted a portion of their last works to the question of violence in a liberation struggle. Both had white spouses who played crucial roles in their literary production. Both were revolutionary humanists. And, as is well-known, both died very young.

In *Fanon and the Crisis of European Man*, I advanced an argument that led to this encounter with Hansberry's thought on the subject. I argued that revolutionary thinkers like Fanon and C.L.R. James had developed a special type of tragic text for the colonial and neocolonial ages.[7] These texts explore classic themes of moral conflict among powers that affect entire communities, the consequence of which is a form of meta-ethical understanding of the contemporary situation of humankind. This meta-ethical understanding, marked by paradox, irony, and pathos, displaces Western ethics by setting it up for transvaluative assessment. Tragedy, in this context, raises questions of *audience*, *purpose*, and *relevance*. When Fanon, for instance, concludes *Les damnés de la terre* with the encomium of developing new values, values that are not dependent on a centered European standpoint on the world, he also raises the complex question of Europe's *relevance*. In the style of classical tragedy, "good" kings and queens are beside the point in a polluted city. Things need to be set right, but this setting of things right has terrible consequences. Tragedy is the adult realization of the idiocy of, as Freud had so many times observed, our childhood fantasies and penchant for happy endings. In adult life, we find that there is often violence where we allow ourselves to remain blind and comfortably wrapped in the security of the mundane. Under the shield of everyday morality, we are able to maintain, often righteously, the conditions of systemic violence.

As a consequence, I argued that most pleas for so-called nonviolent solutions to problems of systemic oppression fail, ultimately, to make a proper case for their own relevance. In an oppressive régime, bent upon its own theodicean preservation—where evil can only be accounted for through the existence of bad *individuals* or *groups*, not the system—*any* effort toward systemic change will be regarded as violent. Consequently, to meet the system's criteria for nonviolence, one must ensure preservation of the system itself. The only forms of "resistance" that a colonial régime will accept as nonviolent are those that either preserve colonialism or transform it into a form of neocolonialism. Because the discourse on "violence" and "nonviolence" is not dictated in such cases by the oppressed group's interpretation of these phenomena (otherwise, their many cries for relief would have been heard and acted upon), then the discourse on nonviolence issued against people who suffer systemic violence becomes a naive exercise in irrelevance and hypocrisy: Like Genet's play, it sets, as its mission, the salvation of oppressive souls.

I have mentioned Hansberry's similarities to Fanon. Her differences—her being a U.S.-American black woman and her not having engaged directly in a national liberation struggle—raise the question of whether her position on the question of violence in the struggle for national liberation would be any different from Fanon's. I must confess, I had hoped to find something different, something *very* different, if but for the sake of gaining a new insight into the questions raised by Fanon, James, Cabral, et al. What I found, however, is that her position, at least on the tragic text of revolutionary violence, is identical to theirs. Unlike their texts, however, which were not traditional tragic texts in form except by virtue of their *subtext* of addressing a Third World audience's understanding of its situation, Hansberry's text is a tragic text in traditional form and content. On classical tragedy, Eva Figes has written that it is

> the sad story of an ancestral protagonist who, either deliberately or by accident, offends against the most fundamental laws of the society, those laws which are so basic as to be considered divine. . . . In tragedy a community can see . . . the central protagonist who has polluted his environment, bringing disruption on himself and the community within which he lives, is eliminated, whereupon peace and order are restored. Whether the protagonist intended to break the divine social laws or not is beside the point.[8]

I have related elsewhere the various interpretations of tragedy that have been offered over the ages since Aristotle's classic definition of it as a serious play that arouses *pathos* and a *cathartic* effect from the calamities that befall a person of high social standing and character.[9] Aristotle related a lot of other "particulars" that help elicit the desired effect, such as plots with deeds of parricide, matricide, and fratricide. In that regard, *Les Blancs* meets most criteria. Let us now turn to examining the play itself.

First, the characters themselves raise some questions. They are The Woman, African Villagers (and Warriors), Dr. Marta Gotterling, African Child, Peter, Charlie Morris, Ngago, Dr. Willy DeKoven, Maj. George Rice, Soldiers, Prisoner, Madame Neilsen, Eric, Tshembe Matoseh, and Abioseh Matoseh. In this play, written by a black female playwright, there are no black female characters "present" in the sense of being human beings represented by actors on a stage, although there are black female "characters." The Woman, for instance, is a symbolic, ancestral figure who dances through the minds and hearts of the African warriors. The only other black female character is known through her *absence*: she is the dead mother of Eric, Tshembe, and Abioseh. Three other characters who are present through their absence are Abioseh Senior (also dead), the Reverend Neilson, and Kumalo (a Martin Luther King/later Mandela figure who is attempting dialogue with the colonial government). Tshembe is the prodigal son, returning for his father's funeral. He has wandered through Europe and North America. He is now married to a plain European woman and has a son. He claims, through most of the play, to have made London his home. Then there is his brother Abioseh, who has taken vows to become a Catholic priest. He plans to change his name to Paul Augustus. Dr. Marta Gotterling is a blond, blue-eyed missionary physician who, throughout the play, is a paradigmatic example of care-giving racism. Peter is the servant at the missionary hospital. His character is familiar in black protest literature: He plays Sambo by day, while he organizes revolution by night. Although his name is listed as Peter, the name he uses when he is organizing is Ntali. Charlie Morris is a white journalist from the United States. His arrival marks the beginning of the play. Dr. Willy DeKoven is a disillusioned missionary physician who slips gifts to Eric, who is a biracial product of rape. Maj. George Rice is the typical military official who oversees "security" in the region.

Now already names and naming play important roles in the drama. Peter, for instance, is an obvious biblical reference. That he goes by Ntali when he is organizing signals the revolutionary significance of the consciousness raised by that name. Double-consciousness here takes on double naming:

Peter addresses whites as *Bwana*; his body is sealed under what Frantz Fanon calls an epidermal schema, a schema of surfaces in which he is denied the lived-reality of possessing an "other side":

PETER (*Singsongy*): You wait here, Bwana. You sit, make self cool. Doctor be with you soon (p. 43).

As Ntali, however, he relates the moral of the play, through a West African folktale:

I "understand," cousin—that such men have forgotten the tale of Modingo, the wise hyena who lived between the lands of the elephants and the hyenas. Tshembe, hear me. (*What follows is not merely told but acted out vividly in the tradition of oral folk art*) A friend to both, Modingo understood each side of their quarrel. The elephants said they needed more space because of their size, and the hyenas because they had been *first* in that part of the jungle and were accustomed to running free. And so, when the hyenas came to him, Modingo counseled (PETER *rises to become the "wise hyena"*): "yes, brothers. True. We were first in this land. But they *do* need space—any fool can see that elephants are very *large!* And because I was born with the mark of reason on my brow—on which account I am called Modingo, 'One Who Thinks Carefully Before he Acts'—I cannot join you on our side while there is also justice on the other. But let me think on it." (*He sits, brow furrowed, chin in hand*) And thereupon Modingo thought. And thought. And thought. And the hyenas sat and waited. And seeing this, the elephants gathered their herds and moved at once—and drove them from the jungle altogether! (*Turning to TSHEMBE*) That is why the hyena laughs until this day and with it is such terrible laughter: because it was such a bitter joke that was played upon them while they "reasoned." (*There is silence for a moment, and then he leans forward to place his hand upon TSHEMBE's*) Tshembe Matoseh, we have waited a thousand seasons for these "guests" to leave us. Your people need you (p. 95).

Peter/Ntali here identifies another "character" in the play. At various points, there is the laughter of a hyena. The laughter is a signifier of the argument brought forth by the tale; it is paradoxically a reasonable subversion of reason, as laughter often turns out to be.

Charlie Morris is, of course, Mr. Charlie. Mr. Charlie is an African-American expression for White Man and Power. The irony is that the name Charles means common man. The choice of Charles as a name for an uncommon amount of power suggests the banality of that power. Mr. Charlie never sees himself as powerful, and it is this blindness that makes him insist on the "both sides" affair that conceals the fact that he is an elephant in these games of negotiation. Charlie's role in the events is therefore indicative of the Habermasian Man in search of ideal speech situations and dialogue.[10] He constantly seeks opportunities to establish dialogue with Tshembe and the white missionaries. Tshembe, however, constantly subverts Charlie's efforts, ironically, through dialogue. He brings forth the tragic dimension of their relationship through identifying Charlie's efforts, efforts typical of Western engagements with "ethics," as an easy way out:

> TSHEMBE: . . . Why do you all *need* it so?! This absolute *lo-o-onging* for my hatred! (*A sad smile plays across his lips*) I shall be honest with you, Mr. Morris. I do not "hate" all white men—but I desperately wish that I did (p. 78).

Marta Gotterling's name need only be pronounced. She presents the argument of "sacrifice," and in that regard becomes a *martyr* in the gutter and a fledgling goddess. In a crucial moment in the play, her colleague, Dr. Dekoven, demystifies the romantic dimensions of her role as a "saint" and savior with regard to the "native" situation:

> DEKOVEN: Mr. Morris, there is a hospital for Europeans only seventy-five miles from here. Entirely modern. Here things are lashed together with vines from the jungle. Surely you must have wondered why.

> CHARLIE: Well, I assumed I knew why—that it was obvious . . .

> DEKOVEN: Is it? Electric lines between here and Zatembe could be laid within weeks, a road in six months. The money exists. All over the world people donate to Missions like this. It is not obvious, not obvious at all.

> CHARLIE: But I thought the Africans wouldn't come if it were different. Marta—

> DEKOVEN (*With a gentle smile*): Marta is two things, Mr. Morris: a very competent surgeon and a saint; but she questions nothing very deeply. One of the first things that the new African nations have done is to set up modern hospitals when they can. The Africans go to them so freely that they are severely overcrowded, so something is wrong with Marta's quaint explanation, don't you think? . . . Mr. Morris,

the struggle here has not been to push the African into the Twentieth Century—but at all costs to keep him *away* from it! We do not look down on the black because we really think he is lazy, we look down on him because he is wise enough to resent working for us. The problem, therefore, has been how *not* to educate him at all and—at the same time—teach him just enough to turn a dial and know which mining lever to raise. It has been as precise as that—and that much a failure. Because, of course, it is impossible! When a man knows that the abstraction *ten* exists—nothing on earth can stop him from looking for the fact of *eleven*. That is part of what is happening here. . . . But only part (pp. 113–14).

Willy Dekoven explains the whites well to Charlie. He explains that Eric is not the Reverend's son, as Charlie suspects, but Major Rice's. The rape dimension of conquest is thereby placed into focus: The rape itself is more than violation; it is the telos of the colonial project. Not only does Eric's mother die during childbirth (symbolizing the death of ancestral Africa through the spawning of the current generation of conquest), but Rice (a name that signifies a *seed*) has literally effected his project of planting his seed into the soil of Africa and declaring it *his home*. Says Rice:

I do not enjoy my present role. I am not by temperament an adventurous sort. Or a harsh one. I have become a military man only because the times demand it. (*a curious, urgent and almost sad defensiveness*) This is my country, you see. I came here when I was a boy. I worked hard. I married here. I have two lovely daughters and, if I may presume an immodesty, a most charming and devoted wife. At some other time I should have liked to have had you out to our farm. This is our *home*, Mr. Morris. Men like myself had the ambition, the energy and the ability to come here and make this country into something. . . . *They* had it for centuries and did nothing with it. It isn't a question of empire, you see. It is our home: the right to bring up our children with culture and grace, a bit of music after dinner and a glass of decent wine; the right to watch the sun go down over our beautiful hills. And they *are* beautiful, aren't they? We wish the blacks no ill. But . . . —it is our home, Mr. Morris (p. 71).

Rice's remarks make it clear that his conception of his and the other settlers' relation to the land is one of "right." With both Rice's view of his group's right to the land and the Kwi's ancestral rights to the land, the tragic stage is set in terms of what Fanon has called "two species of men":

National liberation, national renaissance, the restoration of nation-
hood to the people, commonwealth: Whatever may be the headings
used or the new formulas introduced, decolonization is always a violent phenomenon. At whatever level we study it—relationships between individuals, new names for sports clubs, the human admixture
at cocktail parties, in the police, on the directing boards of national
or private banks—decolonization is quite simply the replacing of a
certain "species" of men by another "species" of men. Without any
period of transition, there is a total, complete, and absolute substitu-
tion. . . . Its unusual importance is that it constitutes, from the very
first day, the minimum demands of the colonized. To tell the truth,
the proof of success lies in a whole social structure being changed
from the bottom up. The extraordinary importance of this change is
that it is willed, called for, demanded. . . . But the possibility of this
change is equally experienced in the form of a terrifying future in the
consciousness of another "species" of men [and women]: the colonizers (*Les Damnés*, pp. 65–6).

For these two species of humanity, the violence around them takes on
different meanings: For the settlers and their lackeys, it is the "terror" (p.
59), for the Kwi, it is the "resistance." A resolution of this conflict cannot
be made under the assumption of equal sides in the drama. The side chosen
determines the meaning of terror or resistance. The context of this face-off
is exacerbated, moreover, by the accompanying racist ideology of colonial
conquest. Speaking through Tshembe, Hansberry provides her view of race
and racism, a view that parallels Fanon's position in *Peau noire*, that although the black is a white construction, the lived-experience of the black
is nevertheless a reality of overdetermined existence:

TSHEMBE: I said racism is a device that, of itself, explains nothing.
It is simply a means. An invention to justify the rule of some men
over others.

CHARLIE (*Pleased to have found common ground*): But I agree with you
entirely! Race hasn't a thing to do with it actually.

TSHEMBE: Ah—but it *has!*

CHARLIE (*Throwing up his hands*): Oh, come on, Matoseh. Stop
playing games! Which is it, my friend?

TSHEMBE: I am not playing games. . . . I am simply saying that a
device *is* a device, but that it also has consequences: once invented it

takes on a life, a reality of its own. So, in one century, men invoke the device of religion to cloak their conquests. In another, race. Now, in both cases you and I may recognize the fraudulence of the device, but the fact remains that a man who has a sword run through him because he refuses to become a Moslem or a Christian—or who is shot in Zatembe or Mississippi because he is black—is suffering the utter *reality* of the device. And it is pointless to pretend that it doesn't *exist*—merely because it is a *lie!* (p. 92).

Here, Tshembe challenges the fantasy ethics formation of Charlie and the Settlers. For them, something that is a lie must be nonexistent, even though many of them continue to live lies that carry enormous consequences. The categorical imperative of Kant, for instance, with its idealized kingdom of ends, may be a form of truth, but it is a form of truth that, if used as a model in the struggle for national liberation, boils down to a truth that does not exist. In the words of Major Rice: "I know, for instance, that authority in this colony has always depended on the sacredness of a white life—and once that authority is undermined—well, if four million blacks should ever take it into their heads to start killing white men . . ." (p. 100).

The objective condition of social practice, where black life is less valuable than white life, is the limit of ordinary ethical practice. Whether Kantian or Christian, the consequence of an appeal to an abstract rejection of violence is the same: maintenance of the status quo and continued violence upon the blacks. In the play, this situation comes to a head in the conflicted values of the two brothers, Tshembe and Abioseh. Abioseh's Christian sentiments and his views of the settlers are such that he regards the resistance forces as terrorists. It becomes his duty to provide whatever information he can against their advance. Upon discovering that Peter/Ntali is a major organizer, he promptly reports him to the settler authorities. Peter's identity and his demise are brought forth, ironically, through Rice's use of Peter's warrior *name*:

RICE: Peter—I think we can all use a drink. . . . Thank you, Peter . . . Yes, two hundred blacks and it looks like just the beginning. They don't stand a chance, of course. At dawn we begin a new coordinated offensive . . . fresh troops, helicopters, jets, the whole bloody works . . . (PETER *starts to leave*) Don't go, Peter. (PETER *halts and* RICE *motions that he'd like another drink*) Within three weeks the mopping up will be over, I can promise you that. (*Looking up as jets rocket overhead and into the distance*) Just listen, Mr. Morris: the sound we've been waiting for! (*As* PETER *approaches*) No spear on earth will bring one of those down—isn't that so, Peter?

PETER: Yes, Bwana.

RICE (*Takes the drink*): Thank you—*Ntali* . . . *!* (PETER *drops the tray and runs and, in split-second succession, the* SOLDIERS *and* RICE *open fire. He falls, jerks—and lies dead at* TSHEMBE'*s feet*) . . . (p. 117).

By this time, Kumalo, the chief spokesman of dialogue, has been arrested. The two incidents bring into focus the path that Tshembe will take. At the end of the play, after the final hyena's laughter, Tshembe returns to the mission site with other warriors, whereupon he kills his brother Abioseh, and Madame Neilson is killed in the crossfire.

Quite a bit can be said about this play. The role of names and naming, as we've seen, is a central motif. Black characters take on the names given to them by their black mothers when they are ready to fight. The biracial character Eric, for instance, takes on the name Ngedi. He announces his name at a point in the play when his brothers struggle over who will take him to his version of Europe: Tshembe, to his London; Abioseh, to the Catholic church. Both versions of Europe are embodied in a notion of the fatherland. Eric's announcement, as a biracial offspring of a European invader and a native mother, signals his existential and spiritual decision to identify with his dead mother. His choice, in effect, brings her alive through the liberating decision to fight the colonizers at all cost. At the moment that decision is made, it is irrelevant whether they will win or lose the battle. And Hansberry, in fact, leaves it open, since the play ends only with symbolic matricide (the killing of Madame is the killing of an adopted mother) and literal fratricide (the killing of Abioseh), which signals the end of the battle but not of the war.

The play itself can be regarded as a battle, at first, over semiotic resources available through the cultural, economic, and racial conflict that mark the context of the play. The patriarchal, Eurocentric discourse marks the conquered population as "natives," "savages," "terrorists." The matrilineal, Afrocentric discourse of the indigenous people marks the European settlers as "invaders," "violent," "exploiters," and the indigenous people as "Kwi," "revolutionaries," "resistance forces." At one point, when Abioseh appears at a resistance meeting, he is stopped at the door and not permitted to enter on the grounds that no "Europeans" are allowed. Abioseh, we must remember, has not only accepted a Europeanized version of a Middle Eastern religion, but also has chosen the names of Paul, who sealed the religion's Roman fate, and Augustus, a Roman emperor.

Then there is Hansberry's title itself. After all, since Genet's play was in fact *"Niggers,"* something was lost in the English translator's choice of *The Blacks*. Here is what White reports on the translator Frechtman's struggle with the title:

> Frechtman, in a letter to Charles Monteith, an editor at Faber and Faber in England, wrote that *The Negroes* as a title was "too polite and flabby" and loftily liberal-sounding, whereas *The Blacks*, the title he preferred, had "bite." He recalled the appalled reaction of Tennessee Williams to the possibility that the play might be called *The Niggers*, which, he said, would be "suicidal" (*Genet*, p. 435).

Had Hansberry responded to Genet's title, would a derogatory term for "whites" have been appropriate? *The "Honkies"*? *The "Crackers"*? *The "Pale Faces"*?[11] That Hansberry chose a French title for a play entirely written in English raises additional questions. What French words would have been appropriate for the pejorative references to whites? But there is more. In the effort to forge a response to colonizing language, Hansberry finds herself in a circumstance similar to that of many black poststructuralists, especially those who theorize about colonialism. The ongoing leitmotif is Shakespeare's *Tempest*, with its tale of Prospero and Caliban. In an insightful discussion of this theme, Paget Henry and Paul Buhle (1992) summarize the problem thus: "[The] inscription of Caliban's identity in the discourses of Prospero raises the question of Caliban's ability to project independent self-images and to imagine new social alternatives" (p. 113). The problem of imagining and *articulating* alternative identity formations leads to the question of structural resources beyond the current condition—in a word, *post*structural resources. Write Henry and Buhle:

> From the poststructural point of view, anticolonial discourses often achieve their deconstructive goals by means that are effective primarily on the semantic level. These include such strategies as (1) the discursive inverting of the colonial order of things; (2) revalorizing precolonial traditions; (3) renaming people, places, and events; and (4) delegitimating the arguments for colonial rule (p. 114).

Our portrait of Hansberry's text should have demonstrated by this point that she deploys all of these strategies. Yet there are some ironies in their deployment. For instance, if Hansberry is regarded as a Caliban responding to Prospero, the question emerges, *Which* Prospero? After all, the Prospero of the play and of Hansberry's experience is the British Empire and its American derivative. *Les Blancs* is a title that would have resonance to the

French Prospero. But then, why not a play in French? Ironically, the Prospero intended here is the English-speaking Prospero, which makes the title itself misleading. Or does it? After all, the white audiences who went to the play's 1966 performance *knew* what *Les Blancs* meant. Yet, one wonders what the response would have been to a play entitled *The Whites*? In effect, the American white audiences were, like Charlie, willing to see as long as the scene suggested a tale of race and racism set *elsewhere*.

The theme of Prospero and Caliban takes on a different form, however, if we consider the question of the play's protagonist. Although the *dialogue* begins with Charlie's arrival at the mission site, which locates the play at first in the Euro-modernist scheme of white male traveler (think, for instance, of some of Joseph Conrad's novels), the dialogue is taken over more and more by Kwi characters until, at the end, it is clear that the protagonist is Tshembe, whose spiritual subtextual identity is Mother Africa. An announced story of Prospero becomes Caliban's tale.

It is, however, in Caliban's tale that the limits of the poststructural dimension also emerge. At first, the limits are metasemiotic. The hyena's laughter is a sign, but it is not a sign in Prospero's language. The hyena laughs at all moments in which *talk* or *dialogue* is issued as an appeal. It is a sign that denies the resources of sign. Laughter leaves no room for argument. With laughter, the spotlight is shone; it declares, "You should know better. Why do you continue to play the fool?" Prospero/the Settlers offer a heavy world of talk, a world in which, as Tshembe observes, there is only pretense of listening to the colonized and of being concerned. In a world where the life of the colonized is not equal to that of the colonizer, the dialogical exercise is pointless. By the end of the play, only Abioseh and Madame speak. When the resistance forces enter, there are no words. The "text," if you will, is no longer verbal. The final signs are two: an "animal-like cry of grief" and the appearance of The Woman.

It is evident that Hansberry's efforts to state both a position on race and the role of violence in decolonization raise further questions of *audience*. Who, ultimately, is she trying to persuade? The audiences who tended to occupy the seats of Broadway also tended to be The Whites. But the catharsis, the tragic moment, the edifying realization of there being something *right* about the ending of the play is Antigone, Medea, Shylock, Caliban, and the Kwi's world. Can The Whites qua *whites* "see" or "know" The Woman in the play? Hansberry suggests, through the death of Madame Neilson, that the price is extraordinarily high, indeed, because the identity of European humanity is heavily invested in the status quo. The Whites must be made irrelevant.

Notes

1. Lorraine Hansberry, "Review of Jean Genet's *The Blacks*," *The Village Voice* (June 21, 1961). For Genet's play, see Jean Genet, *Les Nègres* (Isère, France: Decines, 1958); and, for the English translation, see *The Blacks: A Clown Show*, trans. by Bernard Frechtman (New York: Grove Press, 1960).

2. Quoted from Edmund White, *Genet: A Biography* (New York: Vintage, 1994), p. 429. Hereafter cited as *Genet*.

3. Quoted in *Genet*, p. 429. For a study of images of blacks in white popular culture, see Jan Nederveen Pieterse, *White on Black: Images of Africa and Blacks in Western Popular Culture* (New Haven: Yale University Press, 1992).

4. I should like to add that Genet on race, particularly with regards to Arabs and blacks, is a complex matter that may lead one, ultimately, to appeal to the existential credo that the character of a man is ultimately a function of his actions. Genet was a staunch supporter of Palestinian, African-American, and Afro-French rights from the 1950s to his death in 1986. With contemporary attacks on black nationalists as "homophobic," readers are encouraged to read White's discussion of Genet's involvement with the Black Panthers, which he did as an "out" homosexual before its contemporary vogue (*Genet*, pp. 521–40).

5. *Les Blancs* is included in the collection of her last plays, *"Les Blancs," "The Drinking Gourd," "What Use Are Flowers"*: *The Collected Last Plays by Lorraine Hansberry*, ed., with a critical backgrounds, by Robert Nemiroff, foreword by Jewell Handy Gresham Nemiroff, and intro. by Margaret B. Wilkerson (New York: Vintage, 1994).

6. Fanon's presentation in Tunis at "The Congress of Black Writers" in 1959 became his discussion on national culture in *Les damnés*; Hansberry's talk was delivered at a conference entitled "The Negro Writer and His Roots" at Howard University in March 1959, two months before the opening of *A Raisin in the Sun*.

7. See also chap. 9 of this volume (below) and my "Fanon's Tragic Revolutionary Violence" in *Fanon: A Critical Reader*.

8. Eva Figes, *Tragedy and Social Evolution* (New York: Persea Books, 1976), p. 12.

9. See *Fanon and the Crisis of European Man*, chap. 4.

10. See Jürgen Habermas's *The Theory of Communicative Action*, vol. 1, *Reason and the Rationalization of Society*, trans. by Thomas McCarthy (Boston: Beacon Press, 1984), and vol. 2, *Lifeworld and System: A Critique of Functionalist Reason* (Boston: Beacon, 1987). Cf. also our discussion of academic activism in chap. 11 of this volume (below).

11. I extend appreciation here to Burt Foster, Jr., for suggesting this third possibility.

Chapter Nine

Tragic Intellectuals on the Neocolonial–Postcolonial Divide

O town of my fathers in Thebes' land,
O gods of our house.
I am led away at last.
Look, leaders of Thebes,
I am last of your royal line.
Look what I suffer, at whose command,
because I respected the right.

—*Sophocles'* Antigone

Mr. Smith said to his interpreter: "Tell them to go away from here. This is the
house of God and I will not live to see it desecrated."
Okeke interpreted wisely to the spirits and leaders of Umuofia: "The white man
says he is happy you have come to him with your grievances, like friends. He will
be happy if you leave the matter in his hands."
"We cannot leave the matter in his hands because he does not understand our
customs, just as we do not understand his. We say he is foolish because he does not
know our ways, and perhaps he says we are foolish because we do not now his. Let
him go away."

—*Chinua Achebe's* Things Fall Apart

When I search for man in European technique and style, I see a succession of
negations of man, an avalanche of murders.

—*Frantz Fanon,* Les damnés de la terre

Among the phenomena that mark the present age is the advent of First
World postcolonial studies. In the midst of such study, there is the added
question of Africana philosophy, under whose umbrella as we have seen
are African, African American, and African Caribbean thought. This philosophy, whose central figures are now predominately located on American

terrain (with occasional excursions through Europe), faces postcoloniality as a question of location in the proverbial belly of the beast. However the question of cultural *Angst* may be formulated, as in Kwame Anthony Appiah's problematic of the Europeanized African, the North American reality is one of stringent, stratified political-economic domination that is so aptly phrased today as "global capitalism." For global reality today is such that there is no viable cultural, economic, or military opposition to the hegemonic weight of the current "World Order."[1] For example, by sheer force of its utility, the U.S. dollar has become the primary currency of the world. Even in former enclaves, such as socialist Cuba, there is a direct correlation between access to U.S. dollars and access to a higher standard of living. Such hegemony hardly signals a *post*, in the sense of former, past, or passed, colonial relation, but instead a new or properly *neo*colonial relation. This neocolonialism, bolstered not only by the fall of its Eastern European opposition, but also by years of successful political, economic, and military destabilization of Third World sites of resistance, finds itself facing the classical theodicean problem of legitimacy that has plagued many a previous imperial order: How can it legitimate its conquest without depending on conquest itself as its source of legitimation? In other words, "Now that we have conquered our opposition," it can be asked, "how do we assure that our victory isn't more than a case of might makes right?" The heart of the new régime must be demonstrated to be pure, to be good, in the midst of its contradictions. Its plight is a familiar performance of ideological legitimation. Its hopes are familiar hopes, signaled by familiar politics of absorption, extermination, and pathology; is there any longer a place for the miscreants, the outcasts, the anomalies, the sites of contradictions, sites regarded as problematic terrain?

The current situation is tragic. It is marked by tragedy because of the classic, paradoxical conflicts of unjust justice and just injustice that emerge from its various relations of power. Unjust justice is the lived condition of people under the ideological weight of a system whose legitimation is attained through the absence of a better system. Like John Rawls's differential principle, their disadvantages are ultimately offered as ironically beneficial to them.[2] Africana philosophy, in the midst of the unjust justice of hegemonic capitalism, faces the question of formulating a just justice in a system that offers no alternative but a just injustice—a justice whose only claim to legitimacy is the supposed absence of any better alternative. The question of *formulating* a just justice, which is a just injustice to those who reap the benefits of the current world order because of what they stand to *lose* in a just justice, is made particularly acute in the situation of the intellectual of African descent:

> Essentially consumers during the period of tyranny, the intelligentsia becomes productive. Its literature is at first willingly confined to the poetic and tragic genres. Then they go to novels, short stories, and essays. It seems to be a sort of internal organization, a law of expression, which wills that poetic expression diminishes in proportion to the precise objectives and methods of the struggle for liberation. Themes are fundamentally renovated. In fact, there is found less and less bitter and hopeless recrimination, [less and less of] that blooming and sonorous violence, which, on the whole, reassures the occupiers. The colonialists, in earlier times, encouraged these efforts, facilitated their existence. Sharp denunciations, slackened misery, expressed passions are, in effect, assimilated by the occupiers into a cathartic process. To facilitate such processes is, in a sense, to avoid dramatization, to loosen the atmosphere (*Les damnés*, 287).

Although Fanon is critical of the "tragic" and the "poetic" style, it is an ironic feature of his thought that his dramatization of colonial and neocolonial reality takes definite tragic forms in the violent face-off that he articulates.[3] Fanon here points to a fundamental contradiction in an intelligentsia whose work brings about a catharsis in hegemonic instead of colonized communities: The tragic stage, or *skene*, has been turned over in such cases, the consequence of which is a preserved unjust justice—an order of justice for the few.[4] It is a dramatic tale in which Sophocles' King Creon is left assured of the rightness of his sentencing Antigone to her death.[5] The intellectual, then, faces more than the urgent need "to build up his nation" (p. 247). The intellectual also faces the question of producing intellectual work that properly *dramatizes* the articulation of that need. It is the intellectual's role to help set the stage, as it were, for the characters to unfold in their peculiarities.

I argue, in what follows, that key features of classical tragedy suggest that there is a global political and spiritual context for tragedy in the contemporary world, and that role is one that centers liberatory texts like those of Frantz Fanon, Lorraine Hansberry, and C.L.R. James as contemporary loci of tragic literature. In that regard, in response to literary theorists such as Henry Louis Gates, Jr., Homi Bhabha, and Gayatri Spivak, as well as to a philosopher like Kwame Anthony Appiah, who have argued against both liberatory and global theoretical descriptions of and prescriptions for the times, we will see that the present age is global, and indeed all-too-global, in a tragic way. Recall Aristotle's definition of tragedy: "The representation of an action that is serious and, also, as having magnitude, complete in itself; . . . with incidents arousing *pathos* and fear, wherewith to accomplish its *catharsis* of such emotions" (149b24–28, emphasis added).[6] He writes this after announcing that the context of tragedy is a conflict between virtue and vice, which divides "all of mankind." In pathos, one suffers from and with another's suffering; and in identifying the achievement of catharsis, which in ancient times (in both the Mediterranean and the Nile) referred to the medicinal activity of purgation and cleansing, we can see that tragedy presents actions to the community that elicit communal suffering. The tragic lesson is that setting things "right" or "just," and thereby setting the community right, often calls for horrible interventions. We find in these tragic interventions, with their historic resonance, the terror and possibilities of what has been ironically identified by both Kierkegaard and the more Marxist Sartre as a dialectic of "mediations."[7]

The terrifying, cathartic dimension of mediation signals the audience's role in tragic presentation, a role that has been the subject of considerable debate for over two millennia. It is the question of audience that has in fact raised the skeptical claim of whether tragedies are still possible, given the absence of both the audience and the social conditions that they were designed to address. Oliver Taplin has pointed out, however, in his *Greek Tragedy in Action*, that much of that debate is mired in fallacies of decontextualized aesthetic claims.[8] A particularly egregious fallacy is to reduce the tragic setting to any one of its elements. Thus, it is important to respect what happens "on stage," as it were, as well as what happens in the audience. For matters of textual determination, understanding what happens on stage is vital. But to make it communicable requires understanding of what it is meant to achieve through what it is trying to say. Thus, the cathartic dimension of tragedy, placed in a contemporary context, presumes its relevance to contemporary audiences.

According to such European philosophers as G.W.F. Hegel and Arthur Schopenhauer, classical tragedy holds themes that are of great relevance to modern audiences. For Hegel, the fundamental theme emerged through a performance of conflicting right, where two characters face each other in the midst of a just injustice. In *Antigone*, for instance, tragedy emerges as King Creon's (the state's) rightful condemnation of a traitor and Antigone's (the household's) rightful efforts to provide a proper burial for her brother, who, in spite of his act of treason, remained her brother to the end. Hegel's claim raises a question, however, of the accuracy of his egalitarian moral face-off, for the Greek (and even the Elizabethan) audiences had, after all, a definite *right* that was to be exemplified by the characters in the drama.[9] Although a just injustice elicits pathos, there was nevertheless a teleological context, *dikê* (order of the cosmos), which suggests a just justice in the dramatic unfolding of events.

Schopenhauer, on the other hand, presents tragedy as an indirect bringing to consciousness of that which we carefully attempt to avoid, and that is the failure of existence itself and the fall of the just and the innocent, a conclusion that hardly embraces the modern taste for fairness and happy endings. Schopenhauer adds:

> What gives to all tragedy, in whatever form it may appear, the peculiar tendency towards the sublime is the awakening of the knowledge that the world, life, can afford us no true pleasure, and consequently is not worthy of our attachment. In this consists the tragic spirit: it therefore leads to resignation.[10]

Schopenhauer's description of tragedy aptly fits the colonial, pseudo-bourgeois mentality that Fanon was criticizing earlier. It is that type of tragedy that signals the pessimistic, resentful, antiliberatory productions of an impotent élite. On the other hand, Schopenhauer's conclusion of quietude, resentment, and pessimism destroys the dynamism of tragedy as a *human* and *political* presentation, and in that regard, we can view Schopenhauer as perhaps the first *postmodern* theorist of tragedy. For, like Lyotard (and, for that matter, Gates and Appiah), he rejects both humancentrism and the politics of liberation within the material sphere (the place governed by what Schopenhauer called the *principle of individuation*).[11] What Schopenhauer fails to see, however, is that by ultimately making life itself tragic, not only would Greek audiences not recognize his pessimistic message but neither would we: Pessimism is neither a *goal* nor an ally of tragedy, but a condition of which tragedy is supposed to be an adversary.

The etymology of the word *tragedy* offers an alternative picture. From the Greek words *tragos* (meaning goat) and *idê* (meaning song), tragedy is clearly linked to the proverbial burden-carrier itself: the scapegoat. On this basis, Eva Figes, in her *Tragedy and Social Evolution*, advances the following theory:

> The origin of the word "tragedy" is thought to lie in the Greek word for a goat, and though the ritual associations are obscure one inevitably thinks of the Israelite scapegoat, which Aron was required to send into the wilderness with the sins of the community on its back. The

rituals of cleansing and atonement did in fact require two goats, the second one being sacrificed for a sin-offering. We know that animal sacrifices were made at the start of drama festivals in Athens, as at other important public gatherings, such as the political assembly (p. 11).

Taplin has been rather critical of at least the "ritual" dimension of this view, which he regards as ultimately an effort to barbarize the Greeks to meet the political needs of the present (pp. 161–2). Tragedy, he argues, is fundamentally an aesthetic affair. We needn't resort to rituals, however, to support our thesis that the *content* of tragedy exemplifies political realities and values of the society in which it is composed. Aesthetic affairs are, after all, often rich with political and ethical content. As Eva Figes has shown us in our discussion of Hansberry's *Les Blancs*, the tragic protagonist's actions usually pollute a community the response to which is the restoration of peace and order through the tragic hero's suffering.[12] It is easy to find support for Figes's view in actual tragedies, as our epigraph from *Antigone* attests. During the years of *de jure* and *de facto* colonialism, the "players" in the drama also were easily marked. I have argued elsewhere, for instance, that both Frantz Fanon's and C.L.R. James's writings exemplify powers of *pathos* primarily because of their status as tragic texts on violent, colonial realities.[13] In the present age, however, the violence and abject poverty persist, but the texts that are being produced by our avowed spokespersons on their theorization are of a different kind. We are therefore led to ask, What are the roles of contemporary theorists on the neocolonial scene? Unfortunately, like the mythological Hermes, who serves also as the etymological source of their practice, they have taken on a hermeneutical role of bringing flawed messages, messages of tricksters. This needn't have been so. But perhaps the chief reason lies in their postmodern (un)commitments and the postmodern antipathy to materiality that underscore their message. The former God of the age, if both Richard Wright and Jean-Paul Sartre were correct, is the Enlightenment Project of Progress and a better world—a project at least once thought best exemplified in the ethical dimensions of Marxism.[14] As John O'Neill sardonically puts it in *The Poverty of Postmodernism*:

> It is not the masses who have sickened of the injustice and exploitation that grinds their lives, weakens their families, starves their children, murders and terrorizes them each hour of the day and night in every corner of the world. No, it is not these people who have abandoned idealism, universalism, truth and justice. It is those of the oth-

ers. The two sides, of course, never meet. Each remains on the other side of the great wall of class upon which there flickers the imagery of mass culture, on one side, and the imagery of élite, professional culture, on the other. No one appears to own the wall. This is why those on each side of the wall see only themselves in their own cultures. Worse still, since the masses have no reason to believe they own anything—let alone the wall—those on the élite side have persuaded themselves that the wall is culture rather than property. This idea appeals to the cultural élite since what they own—as well as what they disown—is largely symbolic capital, especially language and its professional practice (p. 1–2).

O'Neill is not alone. In the midst of this situation is Africa as project. The African Divine was, and perhaps among some theorists and laypersons still is, *Pan*-Africa (as our discussion of Appiah attests). And while Africa's cultural élite, comfortably situated in the élite expatriate's First World conditions, deconstruct away language with which to articulate very modern demands on U.S.-European hegemony, African conditions—whether on the continent itself or through the micro-African experiences that dot urban centers—continue to choke under the weight of material reconfigurations of the global economy. When such intellectuals "speak out," what is the scene that is being laid by such a gesture? To whom are they speaking?

It appears that some spokespersons within this faction have laid claim to absolution by denying their obligation in the first place. For them, the question of audience conceals insidious demands for cultural, and often racial, authenticity—that the questioner fails to acknowledge an African identity by naming the Africana people as the most morally relevant audience in this situation. "How can we speak to the African audience," they seem to say, "when we are also members of the European community?" This question serves as a response, admittedly, to the disdainful *ad hominem* of the "Europeanized African." The problem is not, however, a matter of the authenticity of the "Westernized African." That problematic only reflects naive and ultimately absurd forms of cultural anthropology. After all, cultural purity, if it ever existed, no longer functions as a lived reality. Global capitalism has seen to it that no stone has gone unturned, and in that regard, the only accurate concern becomes one of *which* dimension of Western society is manifested by the Africana intellectual in Eurocenters. In those centers, the "distances," if you will, are not necessarily geographical; the boundaries are of the kinds described by Antonio Gramsci as *strata*—his euphemism for class, but also a convenient term for any socially separated segment of society. Tragic dimensions begin to emerge when we cut through the muck of obfuscating language, the morass of self-aggrandizing, narcissistic platitudes, and get to the point with vulgar language and the logic of the concrete: "When all is said and done, my friends, whose side are you on?"

Since the scene is primarily a circumstance of speaking to power from within its corridors, we may do well to return to *Antigone*, where, after all, there is a lesson to be learned from a tragic heroine speaking to the king from within the palace in the tragic situation of having "to choose sides." The lesson to be learned from Sophocles' *Antigone* is about flaws in the midst of obligation. Creon is, after all, a *flawed* king. Antigone is without fault save her origin. She is progeny of the unholy marriage of a righteously flawed king to his mother, a righteously flawed queen. All of these characters are oddly designed for suffering, for it is in fulfilling who they are, in fulfilling their publicly recognized roles of power and communal responsibility, in a word, their *characters*, that they encounter what they must do— or, more pointedly, *who* they are. For the community's demands to be met, the kind of rightful action that must emerge is the reconstitution of justice. In other words, the world must be placed back into a certain order. The tragedy in tragedies is that the "innocence" of the characters who occupy a wrongful place in the drama will not save them from suffering. Thus, the tragic protagonist finds herself or himself suffering, ironically, for the sake of justice.

Marilyn Nissim-Sabat has read this struggle of suffering for the sake of justice in Sophocles' *Antigone* as a conflict between narcissistic rage and love-motivated devotion to justice.[15] Narcissistic rage is the expression of hatred toward limitations on one's desire to be without limit.[16] The enraged narcissist wants to be the most beautiful, the most intelligent, the most talented, the most powerful. An enraged narcissistic artist wants to eliminate genius because the genius represents the narcissist's limit. Think of what Mozart meant to his rivals. Narcissistic rage calls for seduction. Baudrillard has argued that narcissism and seduction are companions because the narcissist calls for a lie to the self. The theme of narcissism is to be another's mirror. But instead of what the other "is," the image returned is an image of desire, an image of what the other would like to be. Beneath "I will be your mirror" is the truth: "I will be your lie." Think of the story of Snow White. There, the stepmother looks into the mirror and wants it to lie, but lie as a truth. Snow White is, however, the objective limitation of that lie. The mirror's answer to the query on the most beautiful was simple: Snow White. The stepmother needed to destroy Snow White to preserve her lie, to preserve her mirror. In *Antigone*, the goal is power: "For Creon, it is a narcissistic injury that the gods are all powerful," writes Nissim-Sabat, "and he, a mere mortal, so powerless" (p. 240). In advancing divine justice, Antigone becomes the brunt of this rage. According to Nissim-Sabat, "In a preliminary way, we can say that the unity of autonomy and empathy projected by Antigone terrifies Creon and the Chorus, and it does so because it is a manifestation of transcendence, and is, as such, an unequivocal moral demand" (p. 230).

In 1992, Jacques Derrida, whom we have already identified as a veritable guru of textual-poststructural cultural studies and, consequently, textual-poststructural postcolonial studies, declared that "the 'sufferance' of deconstruction, what makes it suffer and what makes those it torments suffer, is perhaps the absence of rules, of norms, and definitive criteria that would allow one to distinguish unequivocally between *droit* and justice."[17] Derrida advanced textual poststructuralism as a tragic hero.[18] I think Derrida is right, to the extent that deconstruction—through deconstructionists—constantly articulates the failure of narcissistic desire, including the narcissism of univocality and unequivocality in our moral and political systems. The irony here is that, if Marilyn Nissim-Sabat is right, this aspect of deconstruction makes it an "unequivocal moral demand." The generosity and genius of Derrida the man suggests that this conclusion may be what he means by deconstruction's tragic status as well. The stage was set by association, then, for the question of whether or not our Africana élite in first-world castles faced their flawed king as heirs to their revolutionary forebears' ghosts—as suggested by 1990s instances of elite postcolonial thinkers' textual and institutional identifications with past radical intellectuals.[19]

In Derrida's claim that "what makes [deconstruction] suffer and what makes those it torments suffer, is perhaps the absence of rules, of norms, and definitive criteria that would allow one to distinguish unequivocally between *droit* and justice," a great number of problems of audience ironically become clear. We already have seen O'Neill's remarks about delusions of criterial and normative "absence"—delusions that are apparently welcomed by Derrida, who has a penchant for undecidability in spite of the inclusion of Third World people among those whom deconstruction may torment by the advocation of blurring ethical distinctions. Now we may also add a dimension that separates tragedy itself from the sort of hero or antihero advanced by many North American Derridians.[20] For although the conflict of "right" may emerge Hegelian-style in most tragedies, the question of *audience* addresses a definite right: Atonement, after all, had to be made for Oedipus and Jocasta's polluting Thebes. Although Chinua

Achebe's Okonkwo was a strong man with flaws of tragic proportion, it is the Ibo people themselves who ultimately stand as the tragic heroes, like the Trojan Women, in the face of calamitous unjust justice. Whether it's *Oedipus the King, Things Fall Apart,* or, for that matter, *Les damnés de la terre, The Black Jacobins,* or Hansberry's *Les Blancs,* a hallmark of actual tragedies and, consequently, actual tragic heroes, is the demand for recompense.[21] Something must be set right.

Although North American deconstructionists suggest that they may not be able to distinguish unequivocally between right and justice, that may be a consequence of realities (or for that matter, unrealities) in which they live. The problem is in the bad-faith presentation of ideological commitment to begin with—signaled by a rightful, and often righteous, avowal against deciding rightness and justice itself. The tragedy of the situation can be realized, however, through the question of ethical ramifications in the face of current, global possibility. Nothing can be said, that is, to a Third and growing Fourth World people's violent response to First World opulence and the ongoing violence unleashed for the sake of its profit and, at times, preservation. The linguistic play of the African intelligentsia on American terrain becomes, then, a question of whose ideology they are protecting. Their attack on liberation that often accompanies the indecidability of *droit* and justice is all too obvious here.

Perhaps, then, the Westernized African should also take seriously a voice from the Western past:

Our happiness depends
on wisdom all the way.
The gods must have their due.
Great words by men of pride
bring greater blows upon them.
So wisdom comes to the old.
(*Antigone* 1349–1350)

It is a voice that is hardly alien to anything African.

Notes

1. For discussion, see Tsenay Serequehberhan, *The Hermeneutics of African Philosophy* (New York and London: Routledge, 1994), John O'Neill, *The Poverty of Postmodernism* (New York and London: Routledge, 1995), and *Marxism in the Postmodern Age: Confronting the New World Order,* ed by Antonio Callari, Stephen Cullenberg, and Carole Biewener (New York and London: Guilford Press, 1995).

2. See John Rawls, *A Theory of Justice* (Cambridge, MA: Harvard University Press, 1971).

3. *Fanon and the Crisis of European Man*, chap. 4.

4. For discussion, see P.F. Shelley, "Africa, Frantz Fanon and the Postcolonial World," *News & Letters* (June 1995), 8, and Olufemi Taiwo, "On the Misadventures of National Consciousness: A Retrospect on Frantz Fanon's Gift of Prophecy" in *Frantz Fanon: A Critical Reader*.

5. For an updated adaptation that suits our discussion perfectly, see Athol Fugard's *The Island*, in which black South African inmates stage a production of *Antigone* as an act of both protest and description of their situation. See also Cynthia Willett's "Hegel, Antigone, and the Possibility of Ecstatic Dialectics," *Philosophy and Literature* 14 (1990): 268–83.

6. This is my revision of Ingram Bywater's translation of the *Poetics* in *The Basic Works of Aristotle*, ed. by Richard McKeon (New York: Harcourt Brace Jovanovich, 1969). The Greek text from which my revised translations were determined is *Aristotle: "The Poetics"; Longinus "On the Sublime"; Demetrius "On Style,"* with an accompanying English trans. by W. Hamilton Fyfe (London: William Heinemann LTD, 1932).

7. See Søren Kierkegaard's complex discussion of tragedy in Problemata II of *Fear and Trembling*, trans. and ed. by Howard V. Hong and Edna H. Hong (Princeton: Princeton University Press, 1983) and Sartre's *Search for a Method*, trans. by Hazel Barnes (New York: Vintage Books, 1968), chap. 2; in the French, "Question de méthode," preface to *Critique de la raison dialectique*, tome 1 (Paris: Gallimard, 1960).

8. Oliver Taplin, *Greek Tragedy in Action* (London: Routledge, 1993), chap. 10.

9. For Hegel's discussion of tragedy, see his *Aesthetics*, trans. by T.M. Knox (Oxford: Clarendon Press, 1975), vol. 2; *Vorlesungen über die Aesthetic* (Frankfurt: Suhrkamp, 1978).

10. *The World as Will and Idea*, Vol. III, Seventh Edition, trans. by R.B. Haldane and J. Kemp (London: Kegan Paul, Trench, Trubner & Co., 1883), p. 213.

11. Again, for François Lyotard's ironically "classic" statement on postmodernism, see his *Postmodern Condition*, and for Gates's most influential assault on liberation theorizing, again see his "Critical Fanonism." Appiah is placed in this equation primarily because of the assault in *In My Father's House* on African philosophy of the liberatory kind (discussion of which is available in our chap. 6, above).

12. See Figes's *Tragedy and Social Evolution* (p. 12).

13. *Fanon and the Crisis of European Man*, chap. 4.

14. For some of Richard Wright's views, see "I Tried to be a Communist" in *The God That Failed*, ed. by Richard Crossman (New York: Harper & Row, 1965) and "How 'Bigger' Was Born," his introduction to the 1940 and all subsequent editions of *Native Son* (New York: Harper & Row, 1966); and for discussion of Wright's complex transition from Communism to Existentialism and then Black Nationalism, see Cedric Robinson, *Black Marxism: The Making of the Black Radical Tradition* (London: Zedd Press, 1983), chap. 11. Similar ethical and historical concerns launched Sartre's investigations into what became his *Critique of Dialectical Reason*. For discussion, see Ronald Aronson, "Sartre on Progress" in *The Cambridge Companion to Sartre*, ed. by Christina Howells (Cambridge: Cambridge University Press, 1992). It can easily be shown, by the way, that in both the cases of Wright and Sartre, their later stages are more concrete forms of their existential stages. Wright's black nationalism and Sartre's existential Marxism are ultimately premised on the demand for concrete foci of liberation struggles. For a discussion of philosophy of existence in the Africana context, see my "Black Existential Philosophy" and Paget Henry's insightful discussion, "African and Afro-Caribbean Existential Philosophies," both of which appear in *Existence in Black*, and for a discussion of existence and historical specificity, see *Fanon and the Crisis of European Man*, chap. 2.

15. Marilyn Nissim-Sabat, "Autonomy, Empathy, and Transcendence in Sophocles' *Antigone*: A Phenomenological Perspective," *Listening: A Journal of Religion and Culture* 25, no. 3 (1990): 225–50.

16. See Heinz Kohut, "Thoughts on Narcissism and Narcissistic Rage" in *Self-Psychology and the Humanities: Reflections on a New Psychoanalytic Approach*, ed. by C.B. Strozier (New York: W.W. Norton, 1985), pp. 124–60.

17. Jacques Derrida, "Force of Law: The 'Mystical Foundation of Authority' " (p. 4). Derrida's guru status is well-known, but his association with the textual-poststructuralist postcolonial studies set is based primarily on his influence on the individuals who emerge in the very influential *"Race," Writing and Difference*, ed. by Henry Louis Gates, Jr. (Chicago: University of Chicago Press, 1986).

18. If deconstruction as a tragic hero seems far-fetched, I urge the reader to examine Derrida's advancement of deconstruction as a contemporary Hamlet and, hence, "heir" to specters of Marx, in his book with the same title, subtitled *The State of the Debt, the Work of Mourning, and the New International*. See also Aijaz Ahmad's critical discussion of *Specters of Marx*, "Response to Derrida," in *New Left Review*, no. 208 (1994).

19. For example, Homi Bhabha wrote the foreword, "Remembering Fanon: Self, Psyche, and the Colonial Condition," to the 1986 Pluto Press edition of *Black Skin White Masks*. For a critical discussion of Bhabha's foreword, see P.F. Shelley, "Fanon, Africa, and the Postcolonial World," *News & Letters* (June 1995). That Gates oversees the W.E.B. Du Bois institute is an institutional instance.

20. "Many North American Derridians" refers not only to the individuals of *"Race," Writing, and Difference*, but also Gates's very influential "Critical Fanonism," where the people of color contingent of Derridanism are unwarrantedly advanced as chief spokespersons not only of "Fanonism" but also of postcolonial criticism. For criticism and critique, see chap. 5 of *Fanon and the Crisis of European Man*. See also Cleuis Headley's "Postmodernism, Deconstruction, and the Black Subject."

21. Sophocles references are from *Sophocles I: "Oeidpus the King," "Oedipus at Colonus," and "Antigone,"* trans. (respectively) by David Grene, Robert Fitzgerald, and Elizabeth Wykoff, ed. by David Grene and Richmond Lattimore (Chicago and London: University of Chicago Press, 1954). Full citation for Chinua Achebe's work is *Things Fall Apart* (New York: Fawcett Cress/Ballentine, 1959).

CHAPTER TEN

EXILIC "AMATEUR" SPEAKING TRUTH TO POWER: EDWARD SAID

The intellectual always has a choice either to side with the weaker, the less well-represented, the forgotten or ignored, or to side with the more powerful.
—*Edward W. Said*, Representations of the Intellectuals

Edward Said has always struck me as an intellectual with whom Jean-Paul Sartre, Simone de Beauvoir, Frantz Fanon, Almicar Cabral, and C.L.R. James would have enjoyed a cup of coffee. He is a man of great integrity and conviction, a man whose respect for his vocation and his avocation is of the highest order, a man whose respect for his fellow human being is matched perhaps only by those who now inhabit the world of the dead.

I stand guilty, like many young intellectuals today, of knowing Said's face before knowing his work. His relentless struggle against the anti-Arab *Geist* war, rooted in a profoundly existential struggle against dehumanization, fostered an environment in which he stared the rest of us in the face, by way of television and other popular media, as he appealed to our conscience and reason. A beautiful man. A man who understands morality, not as an abstract play of words or ideas, but as a passionate effort to reach the Other. Wherever that Other was being dehumanized, typified in Manichæan symbols of evil, Said was there, with a discursive arsenal at his command and a willingness, clearly, to be responsible for his actions. He is, in a word, a *mature* intellectual and, given the idiosyncrasies of violence and professional exclusion in our age, a *courageous* intellectual. His efforts have been such that they command even his critics' respect, in the least.

I heard about his life-threatening illness in an ironically appropriate setting: The 1996 State University of New York at Binghamton's conference on public intellectuals. I was at the post-conference party, drinking beer and engaging in idle chatter. I remarked that Fanon and Said would have been a good meeting both of minds and politics. The host agreed, and he added that Said's book on intellectuals supported that observation. Then he mentioned that Said was terminally ill. The room full of people immediately fell silent. It was as if we all realized at that moment what a treasure Said is, and like most people with such treasures, we also realized that many of us took him for granted. We forget that people like Said, in spite of the near immortality of their work, will not always be with us in the flesh.

Said has written quite a bit on intellectuals. His 1993 Reith Lectures, *Representations of the Intellectual*, stands, however, as his most developed articulation of that subject. Beautifully written, with clear sight (what Abdul R. JanMohamed calls *specularity*), Said has accomplished no less than a frank existential challenge to contemporary intellectuals: Speak truth to power.[1]

Said's counsel may seem simple, and perhaps even naïve, but that is far from the case. For one thing, speaking truth to power may in many instances entail torture or death. Implicit in the edict of speaking truth to power, then, is the virtue of courage. Although Said doesn't make it explicit, courage is a virtue that, added to the intellectual's talents and border-crossing capabilities, tips scales and expands the intellectual's spheres of influence. As I read *Representations of the Intellectual*, I was reminded of a story related to me by an African American scholar of an encounter between him and some faculty hosts at another university dinner party in Ontario, Canada. At that party were a Moroccan scholar of French studies, two scholars from Iran (one a professor of business, the other a professor of political science), a Jewish American sociologist, a Jewish American social worker, a Jamaican Canadian law student (who was also an antiracism activist), a Jamaican Canadian business student, an East Indian-Canadian graduate student of literature, and a French Canadian friend of the philosopher. Here is how it was related to me. The philosopher had presented a lecture on Frantz Fanon. The Moroccan scholar and the philosopher conversed a bit on North Africa, on the varieties of Islam there, on its racial diversity, on the fact that not all North Africans nor are all Arabs Moslem. The business scholar then joined the conversation, voicing his opinion that Fanon romanticized the Third World, that he placed too much blame on Europe for Third World problems.

The African American scholar was perplexed. "How could you say that," he asked, "when over two-thirds of *Les damnés de la terre* are devoted to the mishaps, greed, stupidity, blundering, and other misguided efforts of so-called 'postcolonial' régimes in the Third World?"

"But you don't understand," responded the business scholar. "He misrepresents Third World and non-Western revolutionary governments. He makes them seem better than they are. Situations like those in Iran are such that there is no room even for critical engagement. They are horrible, backward régimes. One has to be careful at all times. The student in your classroom might be an informant. What you say in public could lead to your disappearance."

This type of exchange went on for a while until the political scientist interjected, scoffing, "You people don't know what it means to live under a dictatorship, to live under a totalitarian state. No due process. None of the modern rights and entitlement enjoyed in North America."

"Really?" asked the business student. "Doesn't that type of thing happen all over the globe? Hell, my family's house was fire-bombed in Jamaica because of our oppositional political views. When we tried to run out, there were men with guns aimed at us. What do you mean by our not being able to understand?"

"That's still not the same," retorted the political scientist.

The African American scholar became sardonic. "Gee, I guess the peculiar relation blacks have with police forces globally doesn't count."

The political scientist became irritated. "They're not the same!"

"Of course they're not," replied the philosopher, "but for blacks in North America and, in fact, all of the Americas, there is a totalitarian reality, a reality difficult to explain to nonblacks primarily because a feature of being above the totalitarian line is its invisibility. Most nonblacks literally don't 'see' the claustrophobic reality under which black people live."

The law student then broke in. "Isn't all this a pointless case of who is more oppressed than who?"

"I know," said the literature student.

"Not really," answered the philosopher. "This is a case of placing a priority, in the United States and Canada, and at this dinner table, on the situation in Iran. Now I have no problem with acknowledging our colleagues' testimony about the situation in Iran. I'm just concerned about the refusal to acknowledge the reality of black suffering in North America."

"But that's not the point," interrupted the political scientist. "The levels of death and torture there can boggle the mind. It's not like the privileges we have here."

"And what is *your* point?" asked the African American. "I can name countless places of black deaths that have hardly resulted in any interventions. Do you think if the mortality and poverty rates of North American whites were to match those of ours there wouldn't be a call for full-scale reform, if not revolution? Think of Rwanda, Liberia, the Sudan; or think of Sri Lanka, of Indonesia. There are many."

The law student then encouraged the sociologist and the social worker to say something on the matter.

"Tonight, I'm just the cook," said the sociologist.

"And you?" asked the literature student, looking directly at the social worker.

"Me? I'm the hostess," answered the social worker.

"One is *never* just the cook and," looking at the social worker, "the host," said the law student.

"I know," replied the sociologist. "But you see, we've been this way many times before."

"Well," said the African American, "it's clear that we're not going anywhere with this. After all, what *are* we supposed to be doing by talking these issues through at a dinner table? Look, what we are all dealing with is the fact that all of us are either immigrants or intellectuals in exile. We're guilt-ridden about being here when part of our souls are elsewhere. Now it seems to me that conversations like these tend to conceal some basic facts about our existential situation. If one is living under a violent, totalitarian régime, there are few options available. You can stand up to that régime with the near-certain outcome of death or mutilation. Or you can be as quiet and as *incognito* as possible, which may increase your life chances a bit. Or you can become an informant for the state; you can turn your friends in, your relatives, perhaps even your own mother, for the sake of your continued survival or perhaps your career advancement. Or you can, if you have the economic resources and connections, leave. But the situation doesn't end there, does it? For although you may leave, your very identity is rooted in a place that forces certain obligations on you. In exile, or as an immigrant, you face some additional set of choices. You can play your role in supporting rebels against the régime by using whatever skills or connections you may have in North America to their interest. Or you can seal yourself in a world of indifference; adopt a new country and rise from the ashes of your past like a phoenix. Or you can simply criticize the régime without participating in any act to overthrow it. I can see why some intellectuals in exile choose the last alternative. Criticizing a government is one thing; participating in a struggle that fails is another. Criticism without praxis is a sure way to be held unaccountable. In my case, I do what I can by participating in organizations and by contributing what I can toward struggles that are clearly also mine. But again, the resolve is existential. Those struggles mattered to the point of their success or failure becoming irrelevant: Whether they win or lose wasn't the point. Such struggles have to be waged."

The conversation continued, with everyone but the students ignoring the African American scholar's questions. The African American wondered to himself afterward whether he had encountered a political conflict or a psychoanalytical one (which in some circles amounts to the same thing). Resentment and guilt take many forms. So does bad faith. Although intellectuals live, often, by the world of words, the gnawing presence of there being more *to do* hardly frees them from certain realities: One doesn't quite know how one would react in the face of state power and hegemonic structures that militate against one's existence.

The immigrant intellectual and the intellectual in exile experience problems of foreign policy from global perspectives. But the exile differs from the immigrant in some important respects. In Abdul JanMohamed's words:

> While both the exile and the immigrant cross the border between one social or national group and another, the exile's stance toward the new host culture is negative, the immigrant's positive. That is, the notion of exile always emphasizes the absence of "home," of the cultural matrix that formed the individual subject; hence, it implies an involuntary or enforced rupture between the collective subject of the origin culture and the individual subject. The nostalgia associated with exile (a nostalgia that is structural rather than idiosyncratic) often makes the individual indifferent to the values and characteristics of the host culture; the exile chooses, if indeed s/he has any choice, to live in a context that is the least inhospitable, most like "home." The immigrant, on the other hand, is not troubled by structural nostalgia because his or her status implies a purposive directedness toward the host culture, which has been deliberately chosen as the new home. Most importantly, his or her status implies a voluntary desire to become a full-fledged subject of the new society ("Worldliness-without-World," p. 101).

For the exile, to be "here" means, always, to be thinking about "there." Yet, JanMohamed's description calls for more evidence of difference when applied to both the exilic intellectual and immigrant intellectuals of color. I recall growing up in New York City in the 1970s, amid the many diverse immigrant communities there. What struck me as unusual in my youth was the extent to which the communities of color literally *rewrote* the Bronx,

Queens, and Brooklyn landscapes. This rewriting took the form of an intense struggle beneath the depths of calm waters. In my adult years, which brought opportunity to travel to Caribbean and Eastern European countries, it became clear to me that immigrant communities of color were communities literally frozen in time. For in trying to preserve their sense of being "there," which is often called "home," those immigrant communities developed a version of their "home countries" that depended on eternal presence; it is as if the country from which they emigrated was transformed into a Platonic eternal form. This fantasy of a home abroad that is eternally present is also nurtured by the racial and class realities of the First World nations these immigrants occupy. The situation is different for their children, who face the same existential-political dynamics as people of color who are born citizens, but for the first-generation immigrants themselves, the situation is more like limbo: They need to be welcomed in both places but are no longer members of either.

Although Said is formally an immigrant, his situation, as a man of color and a member of a dispossessed people, puts him in solidarity with the exile. What is remarkable about Said, however, is the extent to which he has avoided that living death of being frozen in what was or what could or should have been. For Said, the struggle for Palestinian liberation and the liberation of humankind is very much a *live* struggle. In that regard, he is an immigrant/exilic intellectual in the tradition of Frantz Fanon (in Algeria), C.L.R. James (in England and the United States), Chè Guevera (in Cuba), and even Ida B. Wells-Barnett (in the American South), and Karl Marx (in England).

Said, a Christian Palestinian, was born in Jerusalem in 1935 and spent his early years in Cairo. As an adolescent, he immigrated to the United States, where he studied English and history at Princeton University and comparative literature at Harvard University. A first-rate literary theorist and critic, he has made an indelible mark on literature, politics, and Middle-Eastern studies with his classic *Orientalism*.[2] Drawing on the work of Fanon and Foucault, he demonstrated the binary discourse of asymmetrical power as it manifests itself in Western conceptions of the Orient as Other, simultaneously subordinate and exotic. In works like *The Question of Palestine* and *The Politics of Dispossession* and in his service on the Palestine National Council, it is clear that Said is an immigrant intellectual who actively engages in humanist struggles in both the land to which he has immigrated and the land from which he has emigrated. He has chosen not to live "there," but he does what he can "here," with visits "there" as needed.

Said, in both his life and work, addresses nearly all the questions raised by our discussion of activism in the academy. Although he is clearly a charismatic figure, he is sufficiently aware of both his love for his profession, what he calls his area of "expertise," and the opportunity it has given him to engage in the *Geist* war. Among his contributions to that struggle is his discussion of representations of the intellectual.

For Said, the intellectual is primarily a critical voice in his or her society. Although he wouldn't characterize his position in that way, it is evident from his distinction between intellectuals who are merely professional experts and those who are what he calls "amateurs." He contends that the former are either parochial or too heavily influenced by the forces of power that govern their field. But the amateur, freed from such dictates, is able to forge a struggle, critically, toward truth and integrity. In many ways, Said's conception mirrors Immanuel Kant's positions on both enlightenment and duty. Kant demands the modern, secular intellectual to be a critical independent presence, and duty, he argues, is best exemplified by those who are not already inclined, by way of influence or nature, to obey.[3] But shared paths on a highway do not entail shared exits. There are as many differences between Said and Kant as there are similarities. Said will have nothing to do with Kant's ahistorical dictates. His intellectual must be attuned to history, with sensitivity and insight. He writes:

> An intellectual is fundamentally about knowledge and freedom. Yet these acquire meaning not as abstractions—as in the rather banal statement "You must get a good education so that you can enjoy a good life"—but as experiences actually lived through (*Representations*, p. 39).

Said's distinction between the professional and the amateur, with revolutionary potential being located in the amateur, rests upon the work of Antonio Gramsci. In his *Prison Notebooks*, Gramsci offers a distinction between what he calls traditional intellectuals and organic intellectuals.[4] Traditional intellectuals are professional experts who, by virtue of what the market offers their skills, tend automatically to represent the interests of the ruling class or bourgeoisie. They are usually physicians, lawyers, engineers, etc., whose skills can yield great profit and provide them with access to capital or the means of production. The organic intellectuals, on the other hand, need not possess expertise. And their lack of expertise often leaves them with nothing to sell but their labor. We can see immediately that skills create a structural relation to class: The traditional intellectual is structurally related to the bourgeoisie, and the nonexpert is often structurally related to the proletariat. (Think, today, of the difference between having a high school diploma and a doctoral degree in medicine.) Now, the organic link occurs through the particular intellectual's manifesting the values of the group to which he or she belongs. Because value-neutrality is ironically a value of the bourgeoisie, the modern intellectual is also an organic intellectual, organically linked to the bourgeoisie or upper classes. The worker, on the other hand, is organically linked to his or her class by virtue of *not* being able to afford value-neutrality. What is striking about Gramsci's analysis is that it demonstrates how avowed indifference can serve the interest of a ruling class. The scholar or natural scientist who believes him or herself simply to be engaged in a life of the mind and pursuit of knowledge is guilty of a form of self-deception. A specific class interest is being served, and its concealment can only be maintained through a determined evasion of historical reality. Gramsci doesn't, however, stop there. He points out that anti-traditional intellectualism works dialectically against itself as well. He defends the importance of the humanities and sciences against growing tendencies, in modern industrial societies, to reduce all education to vocational training. The humanities and sciences have their role in the development of the critical resources of each organic link:

> The tendency today is to abolish every type of schooling that is "disinterested" (not serving immediate interests) or "formative"—keeping at most only a small-scale version to serve a tiny élite of ladies and gentlemen who do not have to worry about assuring themselves of a future career. Instead, there is a steady growth of specialised vocational schools, in which the pupil's destiny and future activity are determined in advance. A rational solution to the crisis ought to adopt the following lines. First, a common basic education, imparting a general, humanistic, formative culture; this would strike the right balance between development of the capacity for working manually (technically, industrially) and development of the capacities required for intellectual work (*Selections*, p. 27).

What emerges in Gramsci's schema, then, is a case for the development of the critical resources of dominated and oppressed groups. Gramsci regards this transition as one from common sense understanding (in the sense of that which is mundane) to philosophical understanding (that which, for him, is critical and historical). Put differently, Gramsci regards a good education to be one that provides its citizens with the intellectual tools of a critical political consciousness. Unlike Plato, who saw philosophical potential and leadership in the few, Gramsci sees philosophical and leadership potential in the many.

Said takes up Gramsci's distinction between traditional and organic intellectuals and creates another distinction within the traditional stratum. A problem with the experts, he argues, is that they are often insular and discourage critical communication across fields. An expert in one field may simply be an amateur in another field. But as a professional intellectual, the resources at the expert's disposal are such that he or she can add a competent, perhaps even *creative* dimension to another field. The outsider's perspective may be more attuned to political realities that affect the insular world of the expert or political realities affected by the expert. The Manhattan Project, for example, was never simply an experiment. The Tuskeegee syphilis project was never simply an experiment. And in the human sciences, the same holds. The recent crop of studies in eugenics isn't simply scientific research; it is meant to achieve public policy agendas. The experts on terrorism who link Arabs with terrorism generally ignore the United States' oldest terrorist group, the Ku Klux Klan, which is well-known for countless deaths and maiming African American, Jewish American, Latin American, and Asian American citizens.[5] Such problematic linkages and significant evasions call for intervention from a critically informed outsider. Said's amateur intellectual is, therefore, far more complex than the word *amateur* suggests. Said's amateur is an intellectual whose task it is

> to try to deal with the impingements of modern professionalization
> . . . not by pretending that they are not there, or denying their influence, but by representing a different set of values and prerogatives. These I shall collect under the name of *amateurism*, literally, an activity that is fueled by care and affection rather than by profit and selfish, narrow specialization (*Representations*, p. 82).

Although we have been focusing on traditional intellectuals in the broad sense, it should be clear at this point that Said's main quarry are those intellectuals who specialize in politics. The problem dates back to Socrates' dialectical exchanges with Protagoras. Why should such an important part of human life—social reality and the science of the state—be left in the hands of a few experts? Could expertise in politics and ethics be taught? Like Gramsci, Said rejects the locating of a nation's critical political voice in its experts. Such a circumstance is not only anti-democratic, it also rests ultimately on a form of social investment that elevates such experts to the status of gods: Individuals whose knowledge claims on political matters become so incontestable that they might as well be divine authority. Yet, Said also parts with Gramsci here, for Gramsci was, after all, the leading organizer of the Italian Communist Party and its representative in the Italian parliament before his incarceration. Said is not a communist, but he is also not an anti-communist. He laments, in *Representations*, the political and moral bankruptcy of American and exilic intellectuals who have made "whole careers . . . upon proving the evils of communism" (p. 112), a ritual of which he will have no part. Said's concern, not only about totalitarian forms of communism, but also about fundamentalisms (of all sorts) and nationalisms, is the ideological reductionism they encumber: They are anathematic, in his view, to the critical intellectual's credo of knowledge and freedom. He states his position thus:

> I am against conversion to and belief in a political god of any sort. I consider both as unfitting behavior for the intellectual. . . . The hardest aspect of being an intellectual is to represent what you profess throughout your work and interventions, without hardening into an institution or a kind of automaton acting at the behest of a system or method. Anyone who has felt the exhilaration of being successful at that *and* successful at keeping alert and solid will appreciate how rare the convergence is. But the only way of ever achieving it is to keep reminding yourself that as an intellectual you are the one who can choose between actively representing the truth to the best of your ability and passively allowing a patron or an authority to direct you. For the secular intellectual, *those* gods always fail (pp. 109 and 121).

The irony of a figure like Gramsci—incarcerated, physically deformed, and an outsider—was his ability, *within a committed context of organized politics*, to speak the truth to power, which involved, also, speaking the truth *about* power. Like Kierkegaard, who suffered similar physical deformities and isolation in the midst of a struggle with Christendom, Gramsci managed to maintain an organic relation not only to the community for which he struggled, but also the dimension of the *Geist* war in which he was engaged. Unlike Gramsci (whose faith was in the Party) and Kierkegaard (whose faith was in Christ), however, Said faces a godless freedom. His situation is more like Sartre's, to whom he devotes more than a few pages of *Representations*. As an amateur intellectual, he faces the godless freedom of choosing how to meet the forces of dehumanization in the Present Age. His intellectual is in existential anguish.[6] Such an intellectual faces many opportunities to evade, to cop out. But what enables that intellectual to keep going, to stick to the struggle, is the extent to which he or she utilizes effective measures. Says Said, "Speaking the truth to power is no Panglossian idealism: it is carefully weighing the alternatives, picking the right one, and then intelligently representing it where it can do the most good and cause the right change" (p. 102).

At this point, a critic may declare, "Ah-ha! So when all's said and done, Said is a utilitarian, heh?"

To do what leads to the most good wreaks of classic utilitarianism, and a critic might also add that Said should be forgiven because he is, after all, a product of British and North American schools.[7] Yet such a charge would be ill-applied to Said. Throughout his work, Said regards dehumanization of all kinds to be immoral. Demonstration of the greatest good for the greatest number in the case of the Persian Gulf War would not have soothed his soul. An argument for permanent sacrifice of the Palestinian people for the sake of stability in the Middle East is one that he would find obscene. To understand Said's ethics requires taking seriously the existential, poststructural, and postcolonial dimensions of his thought. He regards the intellectual as living in a situation in which, echoing Sartre, de Beauvoir, and Fanon, he or she *must* choose. That is his existential side. He analyzes, however, the paradoxes of the relationships among institutions as they historically manifest themselves as discourses and formations of the self; he examines, that is, how institutions play a role in making us who we are. That is his Foucaultian influence. And finally, he sees the need to create new values against those constructed by an oppressive civil and political society. Those are the Gramscian and Fanonian elements of his work. When all these elements are put together, we encounter the problem of the hermeneutical or interpretative formation of the most good that constitutes the right thing and, simultaneously, the right thing that constitutes the most good. To some extent, then, the transformative dimensions of Said's *American* influences come to the fore here. There is a pragmatic dimension to his sober view of praxis. Affinities with Charles Peirce, William James, John Dewey, and Cornel West emerge. Compare the following passage from West's *American Evasion of Philosophy*:

> Prophetic pragmatism purports to be not only an oppositional cultural criticism but also a material force for individuality and democracy. By "material force" I simply mean a practice that has some potency and effect or makes a difference in the world. . . . The distinctive hallmarks of a prophetic pragmatist are a universal consciousness that promotes an all-embracing democratic and libertarian moral vision, a historical consciousness that acknowledges human finitude and conditionedness, and a critical consciousness which encourages relentless critique and self-criticism for the aims of social change and personal humility (p. 232).

In Said, then, we find an existential commitment to social change predicated on Fanonian and Foucaultian social analyses of oppressive structures and American pragmatic values toward social change.

Yet, it is not clear whether the intellectual can effect these aims without getting dirty hands. He is stained on the one hand by the system of which he is a part, and he is stained by the turns he may take against that system: Putting the good into place sometimes involves sacrificing the innocent; refusing to sacrifice the innocent in an evil world may constitute a good that preserves evil. What constitutes "carefully weighing the alternatives" in cases where there may not be any way of effecting change without, perhaps, declaring everyone guilty and thereby rendering some one or many dispensable? Would the powerful ever accept any demand for them to give up the power they hold? Wouldn't such a demand be interpreted by them as a sacrificial ethic?

We find, then, another criticism. Speaking truth to power ultimately *centers* the powerful. It presumes a moral willingness on the part of the powerful that is, given the context, absent. Shouldn't the amateur be one who speaks the truth *about* power to those who are without power (as the Marxist tradition attests) and thereby empowers them? Aren't the powerful those who by the luxury of their circumstances find the truth about themselves more a nuisance than a call to moral responsibility?

So we return to that dinner party in Ontario on a cold winter night. The African American scholar issued a question to an amateur in political theory (the business scholar) and an expert in exile (the political scientist), but an amateur and an expert in this case who, whether at "home" or in exile, were situated in their home country on a different point of the race-class divide than even the philosopher and the graduate students. In Iran, the business scholar and the political scientist were upperclass and white. In North America, they were always upperclass, sometimes colored, and never black. What was the African American to do in the face of their resistance to *those* types of question? Should he have persisted? Should he have been a nuisance?

Said's answer, I think, is that the intellectual in such cases should not only become a nuisance to the powerful, but also a comrade to the powerless in their struggle for freedom. He encourages the amateur exilic intellectual

> . . . to be unusually responsive to the traveler rather than to the potentate, to the provisional and risky rather than to the habitual, to innovation and experiment rather than the authoritatively given *status*

quo. The *exilic* intellectual does not respond to the logic of the conventional but to the audacity of daring, and to representing change, to moving on, not standing still (pp. 63–4).

Said has spoken to the powerful. The heartfelt sorrow that I and my colleagues experienced in Binghamton, a response that I've seen occur in almost everyone on the left intellectual scene, shows the extent to which he has managed to speak beyond the powerful as well.

Notes

1. Speaking truth to power is the concern of chap. V of *Representations of the Intellectual*. JanMohamed's essay is entitled "Worldliness-without-World, Homelessness-as-Home: Toward a Definition of the Specular Border Intellectual" in *Edward Said: A Critical Reader*, ed. with an intro. by Michael Spinker (Oxford: Blackwell, 1992).

2. Edward Said, *Orientalism* (London: Routledge, 1978).

3. See Immanuel Kant's *Foundations of the Metaphysics of Morals*, trans. by Lewis White Beck (Indianapolis: Bobbs-Merrill, 1995), which also includes his essay, "What Is Enlightenment?" as a postscript.

4. See Antonio Gramsci's *Selections from the Prison Notebooks*, trans. and ed. by Quintin Hoare and Geoffrey Nowell Smith (New York: International Publishers, 1971).

5. For discussion of the Ku Klux Klan's role in terrorizing blacks without being brought to justice, see, for instance, R. M. Brown, *Strain of Violence: Historical Studies of American Violence and Vigilantism* (New York: Oxford University Press, 1975); *A Common Destiny: Blacks and American Society*, ed. by Gerald Jaynes and Robin Williams (Washington, DC: National Academy Press, 1989), pp. 64–6; Homi and Winant's *Racial Formation in the United States*, pp. 118–19. See also Joy Ann James's *Resisting State Violence in U.S. Culture*.

6. For discussion of existential anguish, see *Bad Faith and Antiblack Racism*, chap. 3.

7. For two classic contemporary statements on utilitarianism, see Rawls's *A Theory of Justice*, and J.J.C. Smart and Bernard Williams, *Utilitarianism: For & Against* (New York and Cambridge, UK: University of Cambridge Press, 1973). Mill's most well-known formulation of his position is his essay, "Utilitarianism," which is available in *John Stuart Mill: A Selection of His Works*, ed. by John M. Robson (Indianapolis: The Odyssey Press/Bobbs-Merrill, 1980).

CHAPTER ELEVEN

BLACK INTELLECTUALS AND ACADEMIC ACTIVISM: CORNEL WEST'S ''DILEMMAS OF THE BLACK INTELLECTUAL''

Cornel West has issued several criticisms of the black intellectual in *Baking Bread*, *Race Matters*, and *Keeping Faith*. His criticisms are in stream with Russell Jacoby's influential work, *The Last Intellectuals*, in that he focuses on the black intellectual in the academy.[1] West's discussions also have gained considerable influence. They stand as classic criticisms of the black academic intellectual. It is fitting, then, that we examine them here.

Let us first clarify a few key concepts. It is evident that this discussion is premised on a context of political significance, which means it demands, then, a statement of the conception of the political assumed here. By *politics* I mean two types of activity whose objective is to affect a chosen community or the institutions by which conventional resources of power (conventional in the sense of flowing from or being influenced by facets of the state or a chosen administrative organ) are administered. The first type is what we shall call *consensus-building* activity. We also can call that type the democratic model, a model premised on speech and agreement. The second we shall call *instrumental* activity. We also can call that type the functional model. It should be clear that both types are related, in that instrumental activity, activity geared toward building up institutions or simply responding to immediate problems, can foster an environment that is conducive to consensus formations. Moreover, consensus *building* has instrumental or functional dimensions. In the American context, perhaps because of our tendency to treat democracy as our political *telôs*, we tend to treat consensus-building as a major objective of political action. Yet, when it comes to the ongoing praxis of maintaining and building political institutions, as well as combating the violence produced by right-wing and reactionary efforts to reassert hegemony, the mundane, often boring features of instrumental activity are essential for the success of any political objective.

Second, because the question is, after all, one of intellectuals, let me make clear what I mean by at least a specific type of intellectual—namely, the public intellectual. A public intellectual should be differentiated from a *popular* or *celebrity* intellectual. In the past two decades, there has been a trend—primarily through the ascendence of cultural studies, which centers popular culture as its "subject matter"—in which the celebrity intellectual has ascended as the model of the public intellectual. Although it is true that a celebrity intellectual is public, because one cannot be a celebrity without being in the public eye, it is not true that one will be a celebrity or popular by virtue of being public. There are many public intellectuals who have not seen, and may never see, themselves brought to the center stage of celebrity or popularity. But for these intellectuals, what marks them public are (1) that their work addresses issues that have an impact on the communities in which they live and (2) that such praxis often carries questions of responsibility regarding their roles in their communities. We can see how the distinction between celebrity and public intellectuals emerges in the difference between the Weberian charismatic leader/intellectual and the leader/intellectual who is guided by a sense of vocation, as both evince themselves in the Africana struggle against racism. Although W.E.B. Du Bois and Paul Robeson may have been charismatic consensus-builders, Ella Baker's and Claudia Jones's many hours of instrumental organizing and institution-building (for example, Baker's role in the development of the NAACP and the Student Nonviolent Coordinating Committee and Jones's in the development of the Communist Party USA) have been rendered nearly invisible. A similar observation can be made regarding the work of Charlene Mitchell, who is a founding member, a national co-chair, and coordinator of the Committee of Correspondence, the breakoff group of the Communist Party, founded in 1992. In black churches, we tend to locate political activity and leadership in the ministers, when in fact the day-to-day administering and development of those institutions are often carried out by the rarely seen but ever dependable boards and officers and key congregation members, who are often women.[2]

This brings us to the third concern. The context of an inquiry into the political role of the black intellectual is, on its face, one of classist, sexist, racist oppression. These forms of oppression function according to binaries of superior and inferior, white over black, masculine over feminine. What this means is that conditions of assessment tend to be skewed by ideologically distorted conceptions of progress and failure. For instance, the hire of a few blacks may be marked as progress, but the reality is that because blacks in our contemporary antiblack context function exponentially—which is to say that one counts for all—antiracist obligation is often misperceived as being accomplished when it has only been initiated.

Now to Cornel West.

Cornel West's work has received great praise as well as great criticism.[3] Given West's prestige and influence, however, it is safe to say that he can hold up well under the force of the latter. As for the former, praise both for his work and character are well deserved. He is by far one of the most outstanding and generous intellectuals of his stature. By virtue of his two classic works *Prophesy, Deliverance!* and *The American Evasion of Philosophy*, in addition to his many important articles and over eight other books, he has achieved a solid place in American intellectual history. His effort to conjoin pragmatism, Christianity, and Marxism into what he calls *prophetic pragmatism* continues to be an original, though at times strained, union. By the end of the decade in which those texts were composed, however, Marxism seems to have slowly dropped from the scene as West's thought becomes more pragmatic. The power of West's writings (especially his later writings), however, emerge from his use of *existential* concerns of dread, despair, and nihilism. In an ironic turn of events, the question emerges whether West's works reveal a pragmatic existentialist or an existential pragmatist? I recall raising this question at a 1996 discussion on black existentialism.[4] Sparks flew after I raised the question of whether pragmatism can articulate oppression. I argued that, at least in the case of West, pragmatism is supposed to function as his methodological point of departure. Yet every time West discusses *oppression*, he abandons the language of pragmatism for the language of existentialism.[5] Observe:

> For prophetic Christianity, the two notions of freedom are existential freedom and social freedom. Existential freedom is an effect of the divine gift of grace which promises to sustain persons through and finally deliver them from the bondage of death, disease, and despair. Social freedom is the aim of Christian political practice, a praxis that flows from the divine gift of grace; social freedom results from the promotion and actualization of the norms of individuality and democracy. Is this a pragmatic abandonment or a point of existential limitation? Existential freedom empowers people to fight for social freedom, to realize its political dimension. Existential freedom anticipates history and is ultimately transhistorical, whereas social freedom is thoroughly a matter of this-worldly human liberation.[6]

That was 1982. Although West has maintained his identity as a prophetic pragmatist, his trinity of Christ, Marx, and Dewey is more de jure than de facto. The fact of the matter is that West is a complex thinker who draws upon (perhaps pragmatically?) many intellectual resources. By 1993, West was writing on "nihilism" in black communities, and in a 1995 interview, he admits:

> For me, the issues on which religious discourse has traditionally fo-cused, such as death and dread and despair and disappointment and disease—the existential issues, the existential dimension of the human condition—have always been fundamental. So, for me, the role of religion, and not just religion, but also music—religion and music—is fundamental. It's a reflection of being a New World African and hav-ing to deal with the absurd: both the absurd in America and America as the absurd.[7]

Existential concerns are striking and directly emphasized in West's mid-90s works. The existential situation of the black intellectual, with which we are concerned here, emerges in at times poignant and self-defacing ways.

Of interest, as stated at the outset, are his discussions in *Race Matters* and *Keeping Faith*. Key to both discussions is West's focus on the black academic intellectual. Whether one thinks in terms of Gramsci's organic intellectual or the early Du Bois's Talented Tenth or most other models, it should be evident that an intellectual need not be an academic.[8] The common assumption that he or she must is a recent phenomenon.[9] It is a conse-quence of the growing influence of universities on every aspect of social life. As communities increasingly depend on universities for skilled labor and resources that emerge from their research—resources ranging from childcare centers to computer facilities—the influence of academics has led to the emergence of a new social class: knowledge producers. No academics in history have had the influence of contemporary academics. Unlike the past, where academics were on the margins of intellectuals who produced both the history they studied and the ideas they cherished, today academics are at the center. Their influence is so pervasive that we are in danger of forgetting what Audre Lorde had tried so hard to remind us: ". . . *survival is not an academic skill.*"[10] Because it is at least undisputable that the academic intellectual is an intellectual, there is no point hassling the reader with this issue. So, let us concede West's focus.

In *Race Matters*, the black academic is situated in the midst of West's diagnosis of the times as nihilistic, at least for black people. This nihilism stems from a persistent failure of viable responses to the social ills that spew forth from U.S. capitalism, a capitalism premised, in its roots, on racist ideology. A key problem of the leadership that emerges in this sorry state of affairs is their ideological and political-economic rootedness in the middle class, a class that West describes as "cynical and ironic" (p. 40). Since black academics tend to be middle class, the indictment of the leadership applies to them as well. Moreover, they tend to be divided, West argues, along taxonomical lines of "race-distancing elitists, race-embracing rebels, and race-transcending prophets" (p. 42). Since West is a well-known advocate of the third category, the reader will not be burdened with his criticisms of the first two.[11]

West offers James Baldwin as an example of a race-transcending prophet. This assessment is out of line with his earlier depiction—in *Prophesy, Deliverance!* (pp. 83–5)—of Baldwin as a "marginalist," and it is pretty clear that the model of race-transcending prophet is how West may see prophetic pragmatic thought. I will not burden the reader with the obvious problems in constructing Baldwin as "race-transcending," especially because whereas West is an academic, which is the group under focus here, Baldwin was not.

In the section of *Race Matters* entitled "What Is to be Done?," echoing V.I. Lenin's famous tract, West issues the American rallying cry for consensus-building politics:

> The crisis in black leadership can be remedied only if we candidly confront its existence. We need national forums to reflect on, discuss, and plan how best to respond. It is neither a matter of a new Messiah figure emerging, nor of another organization appearing on the scene. Rather, it is a matter of grasping the structural and institutional processes that have disfigured, deformed, and devastated black America such that the resources for nurturing collective and critical consciousness, moral commitment, and courageous engagement are vastly underdeveloped (p. 56).

In *Keeping Faith*, the black academic intellectual is discussed with more specificity. There the contemporary black academic intellectual finds her or himself, on one hand, isolated in a world without black institutional support and with too much hostility from black communities, and on the other, denied full entry into the academic white world. In both cases, there is a form of legitimation crisis—because the black academic's credentials for "belonging," so to speak, are held hostage, by both communities, to suspicion and incredulity. A traditional response by black academic intellectuals has been embodied in what West calls the Marxist model and the bourgeois humanist model. The former attempts to respond to the activist demands of black communities, the latter attempts to respond to the uni-

versal, "humanistic" demands of white academe. He rejects both, ultimately, on postmodern grounds (if postmodern "grounds" are possible):
They fail to respond to times in which liberatory and humanistic projects
are supposedly deemed passé and ultimately terrorizing.[12] He argues that
Marxism stifles black specificity, and bourgeois humanism is existentially
debilitating because of its skewed values of meritocracy and hierarchies that
are ultimately racist. He also considers the Foucaultian model of "postmodern skeptic":

> By conceiving intellectual work as oppositional political praxis, it sat-
> isfies the leftist self-image of black intellectuals, and, by making a
> fetish of critical consciousness, it encapsulates black intellectual activ-
> ity within the comfortable bourgeois academy of postmodern
> America (pp. 81–2).

Here West concedes the bourgeois dimensions of the Foucaultian, then
concludes that this model does not fully address the uniqueness of the black
intellectual predicament. In its place, West offers what he calls the "insurgency model," where, "The major priority of black intellectuals should be
the creation or reactivation of institutional networks that promote high-
quality critical habits primarily for the purpose of black insurgency" (pp.
82–3). He makes this declaration because, echoing Immanuel Kant's admonition in his *Critique of Pure Reason*, "An intelligentsia without institutional-
ized critical consciousness is blind, and critical consciousness severed from
collective insurgency is empty" (p. 83). Moreover: "Black intellectuals
must realize that the creation of 'new' and alternative practices results from
the heroic efforts of collective intellectual work and communal resistance
which shape and are shaped by present structural constraints, workings of
power and modes of cultural fusion" (p. 84). So, now echoing Fanon, he
concludes that "The future of the black intellectual lies neither in a defer-
ential disposition toward the Western parent nor a nostalgic search for the
African one. Rather it resides in a critical negation, wise reservation and
insurgent transformation of this black lineage which protects the earth and
projects a better world" (p. 85). One wonders what is meant by the expression "the future" here. Does it mean what the black intellectual should do
for the welfare of humankind? Or does it mean what black intellectuals
should do to avoid obsolete? Why is the black *intellectuals'* welfare so
important? If this path is so clear, why are the other paths *dilemmas*? And
finally, are the two stated paths the only options available? According to
Joy James:

Liberation praxis is arguably a third indigenous African American intellectual tradition that produces significant intellectuals. West's emphasis on conventional structures (and the Protestant work ethic rather than the political protest tradition) does not demonstrate how radical resistance for a democratic society is a site for knowledge.[13]

West's analyses, both in *Race Matters* and *Keeping Faith*, are guided by two major assumptions. The first is consensus-building politics as *the* focal point of political activism. This facet forces him to situate resistance and struggle in terms of *discourse* and *discursive* practices. The second assumption is that black communities are like the caricatures that he constructs in both volumes. It is not only a monolithical claim that the black middle class is "cynical and ironic," but also a claim that is based, ultimately, on black yuppies as representative of the black middle class. (We will set aside the vagueness of the term "middle class" in the American context, where even blue collar workers may find themselves among the "middle class.") We can count among the black middle class such professionals as university and college teachers, as well as primary and secondary school teachers, nurses and physicians, clergy persons, and community-resource administrators. An interesting feature of each of these groups is the array of black resources they support.[14] Many of them constitute those "background figures" mentioned earlier in our discussion of instrumental politics. They pay their dues and keep many black aesthetic, knowledge, and other market productions afloat, albeit often barely so. And in their places of employment, they have access to sites of power that are rarely discussed in contexts where *activism* is the focus.[15]

It is the consideration of instrumental politics in sites of power to which this discussion will now turn. The ideas in this chapter were first presented at the American Education Research Association's meeting in San Francisco, CA. When I mentioned to friends that I was going to talk on academic activism, they smirked. After all, "academic activism" is treated as an oxymoron. The obvious reason for this is our tendency to articulate the world of theory and practice as worlds separated not only by foci, but also by genus—as worlds, that is, of different *kinds*. Since the academic world is associated with the realm of theory and the activist world with the realm of practice, the caricature emerged of inactive thinkers in opposition to people of action. Yet if the model of instrumental politics were considered, where political activity focuses on and is borne out of the political situation, it would be clear that the academy is but one political situation in the midst of many others. Universities are not simply collections of individuals engaged in an exchange of ideas. They also are workplaces in which income is generated to support families and communities. These communities also are consumers, to which businesses sell their products, which in turn generates income that, again, supports families and communities. Members of academic communities also are political advocates, which means they have an impact on the communities in which they are located. And universities also are intellectual training grounds, from which a cadre of next-generation professionals/intellectuals can develop resources with which to challenge and contribute to their own communities. What these features of university communities suggest is that we should rethink the way we look at academic communities. We should ask ourselves what kinds of resource are they.

A key feature of instrumental politics is the requirement of a track record. West's discussion of the distrust that black communities have for black academics raises the question, Why should they not be distrustful? Why should a black academic have a presumed place in black communities? It may be vital for black communities to "test" their intellectuals by awaiting demonstrated performance before accepting or even articulating the professional intellectuals' roles in various facets of their praxes.

For example, a black professor in a small, economically depleted New England town once took it upon himself to go out into the "streets" and play his role in the community's ongoing struggles against poverty and violence. He joined a local black male, predominately working-class group whose aim it was to have an impact on gang activity in the area. He attended a few meetings, but contributed nothing beyond his name and phone number. By the third meeting, it was clear that he could be depended upon at least to come to more than one meeting. As time went on, others in the group asked where he worked, and he told them. He was also asked to participate in the planning of certain activities. He agreed, and he played his role in the planning of some events. Eventually, a circumstance emerged that necessitated a response for which he had a specific skill. There was a great deal of attack on that organization because of its male identity. Although women participated in the organization, it was constantly misrepresented as sexist and "racialist." It was vital for that organization to be in solidarity with female groups and a number of predominately white left groups. The organization decided to create a brochure, in addition to organizing public forums.

At this point, it was clear that the professor had something to offer not only by virtue of his writing skills, but also by virtue of his work site. In the university, there were computers and copying machines and departmental offices, which he had access to throughout the days and evenings. The professor simply took advantage of the wonders of computer graphics, a pair of scissors, and the copying machine to generate two hundred brochures. The brochures quickly worked their way into the local community, where the organization was now accessible to groups that had previously believed it to be a stereotypical black male organization. This example is a clear case in which instrumental politics led, through a succession of dependable efforts, to consensus-building politics.

It is worth noting, also, that it was the organization that gained the recognition of the community, not the professor. Thus, one can easily see how black middle-class participation would be rendered invisible, and therefore absent, in such a process. And although the group would have found a way to get brochures done, perhaps by a professional printer, the fact remains that the alternative solution was not only cheaper but it enabled the group to devote its limited funds to other activity. Moreover, with the cost of more brochures being simply a matter of money for copies, their costs were significantly low.

Now let us go to the professor on campus. On the campus, the academic activist's task becomes one of forging specific sites of praxis. We illustrate again by way of example. Another college professor realized that race relations could not be addressed on her campus unless predominant sites of people of color were engaged. In her institution, it was the custodial workers. So, she asked them if she could participate in a meeting of custodial workers of color. They permitted her to participate, and she did just that— *participate*, not lead. In that meeting and subsequent meetings, the members discussed problems of verbal abuse, unequal pay, and slim chances of promotion. The professor spent her time with similar meetings in the community—the churches, the public union meetings, the peace groups, etc. In all cases, she simply sat in, and went to at least three meetings. In each case, she signed in and gained the address and phone numbers of various organizers. Eventually, through her, the custodial workers at her university were speaking with all the organizations whose meetings she visited. When the custodial workers' concerns reached the form of a strike, communication was so strong among the various groups in the community that the city literally shut down. The workers received their best contract in more than a decade.[16]

Moreover, because of various class and race presumptions (for instance, that black custodial workers are those who are "seen" but do not "see"), the custodial workers, as it turned out, had access to more information about the university than some of the university's key administrators. The information enabled various members of the community to confront the university—the town's largest employer—about its systemic failure to employ members of the local community. The pressure of the strike made it clear that the university had to make concessions.

When it is remembered that universities and other research centers are sources of employment, other dimensions of academic activism come to the fore. After my first semester as an academic, it became clear to me that a good portion of a black academic activist's time is spent on a single local praxis: forging employment for people of color. Black academic activists do not only attempt to get other black academics hired, but they also play a role in the employment of staff personnel. In fact, the black-based institutions they develop usually translate into black employment. It was through the creation of black studies and black cultural centers, for instance, that a vital source of income for black academics, administrators, and staff emerged after the sixties. In that process, because of black studies' interdisciplinary structure and usually interdisciplinary appointments, black academics gained access to more than one site of struggle for employment of applicants of color.

Black academic activism includes another stage: the production of more black intellectuals. Here, the black academic treats the vocation of teacher as a fundamental dimension of her or his praxis. The roles of mentoring and advocacy stand out here, but added is a clear articulation of the role and tactics to be implemented after the formal educational process. The protege is expected, that is, to be added to the number of black intellectuals who engage not only in knowledge production, but also in the production of jobs and other resources.

Among the many resources available to, and in many ways developed by, black intellectuals are informational and advocacy resources. The work of black academics can contribute significanly to the dissemination of knowledge that is vital to the advancement of the communities in which they live. Black academics usually have, through their access to various informational resources, ways and means of challenging the criminal justice system and, on national and international levels, contributing to the fight against institutional violence at the state and other levels. Among black academics who have functioned well in this regard are W.E.B. Du Bois, Alain Locke, William Fontaine, Broadus Butler, Eugene Holmes, Angela Y. Davis, Manning Marable, Eleanor Norton, Derrick Bell, Anita Allen, Rosemary Brewer, Tommy Lott, Barbara Ransby, Joy Ann James, William R. Jones, Toni Morrison, Leith Mullins, and, of course, Cornel West.

All of this brings us, finally, to the ideological work of black academics. In that capacity, the black academic's activism is, so to speak, the *Geist* or spirit war. In that war, there is a struggle for no less than self-identity from the local level straight up to the global level. In that task, the black academic activist's task is to help forge an identity of her or his institution that facilitates all of the other levels of activism highlighted above.

It should be clear by now that academic activism in the sense discussed here lacks the charismatic appeal of most popular conceptions of activism. Yet it is clear that the more charismatic model, while galvanizing populations with consciousness-raising rhetoric and appeals, suffers from a serious limitation: It cannot be sustained. Not to say that it is not needed, but we must instead consider the dimension of exigency and relevance that is needed for any political praxis to work. In effect, then, the instrumental turn of letting consensus emerge from praxis, albeit boring to some and taxing to others—with its obvious demands for committee meetings, job searches, curriculum designs, contract negotiating, monitoring state and international procedural and substantive violations, and the accumulation of local information—is the model that is needed. Ironically it also is the model most often practiced by black academics who are less known than such academics as Cornel West and the intellectuals he cites as examples of the failures of black leadership in *Race Matters*. And in fact, the behavior of these individuals can hardly be characterized by cynicism and irony, ultimately, because many of them are too *busy*, at least, for cynicism. As for irony, a lack of that hardly stands as a sign of human advancement.

In closing, although black academics are not above criticism, the importance of their role demands a more complex and creative understanding of political activism than the popular consensus-building model allows. Toward the end of his life, the dean of black academics, W.E.B. Du Bois, came to this realization when he reflected upon his existential situation:

> Very early in my work in Atlanta, I began to feel, on the one hand, pressure being put upon me to modify my work; and on the other hand, an inner emotional reaction at the things taking place about me. To note the latter first: as a scientist, I sought the traditional detachment and calm of the seeker for truth. I had deliberately chosen to work in the South, although I knew that there I must face discrimination and insult. But on the other hand I was a normal human being with strong feelings and pronounced likes and dislikes, and a flair for expression; these I could not wholly suppress nor did I try. I was on the other hand willing to endure and as my dear friend, Henry Hunt, said to me in after years, "I could keep still in seven different languages."[17]

Today, with the gift of multiple sight and many souls, black academic intellectuals face the task of seeing before them the world in which they have chosen to work. A vital dimension of that task is to see, through a coherent understanding of what it means to be political, both why and how they need not stand still.

Notes

1. See Russell Jacoby, *The Last Intellectuals: American Culture in the Age of Academe* (New York: Basic Books, 1987) and for criticisms, see Said's *Representations of the Intellectual*, chap. IV. See also Robert S. Boynton, "The New Intellectuals," *The Atlantic Monthly* (March 1995).

2. For discussion of these women's important work, see Joy Ann James's *Resisting State Violence in U.S. Culture* and her *Transcending the Talented Tenth*. See also James's article, "Ella Baker, 'Black Women's Work,' and Activist Intellectuals," *The Black Scholar*, 24, no. 4 (Fall 1994): 8–15. See also Marcia Riggs's *Awake, Arise, and Act: A Womanist Call for Black Liberation* (Cleveland: The Pilgrim Press, 1994).

3. For critical assessments, brutal and gentle in kind, see *The American Philosophical Association Newsletter on Philosphy and the Black Experience* 90, no. 3 (Fall 1991), which featured Robert Gooding-Williams, "Evading Narrative Myth, Evading Prophetic Pragmatism"; Konstantin Kolenda, "The (Cornel) West-Ward Vision for American Philosophy"; Elizabeth V. Spelman, "Theodicy, Tragedy and Prophesy: Comments on Cornel West's *The American Evasion of Philosophy*"; Robert S. Corrington, "The Emancipation of American Philosophy"; Cornel West, "Response"; and Lorenzo Simpson, "On the Historicist Turn in American Philosophy: A Reply to West"; Mabogo P. More, "Review of *The Ethical Dimensions of Marxist Thought*," *The South African Journal of Philosophy* 11, no. 4 (1992); Lewis R. Gordon, "Review of Cornel West's *Race Matters*," *Political Affairs* 73, no. 2 (February 1994); David Theo Goldberg, "Whither West?: The Making of a Public Intellectual," *The Review of Education/Pedagogy/Cultural Studies* 16, no. 1 (1994), reprinted in David Goldberg's *Racial Subjects*, chap. 6; Leon Wieseltier, "The Unreal World of Cornel West: All and Nothing at All," *The New Republic* (March 6, 1995); Adolph Reed, "What Are the Drums Saying, Booker?: The Current Crisis of the Black Intellectual," *The Village Voice* (April 11, 1995) and the exchange it prompted, "Discussion on Black Intellectuals," which featured Danny Postel, "In Defense of Adolph Reed," Norman Kelley, "Notes on the Niggerati," Peniel E. Joseph, "In the Post Civil Rights Era," Reed, "Protect the Legacy of Debate," and Manning Marable, "Manning Marable Responds," in *New Politics* 5, no. 4 (Winter 1996); Joy James's *Transcending the Talented Tenth*, pp. 157–169; George Yancy, "Cornel West's Postmodern Historicist Philosophy of Religion: Problems and Implications," *The Journal of Religious Thought* 25, no. 1 (1997). Clarence Sholé Johnson, "Cornel West as Existentialist and Pragmatist" in *Existence in Black*; and Clarence Sholé Johnson, "The Humanistic Scholarship of Cornel West" in *Key Figures in African American Thought*.

4. The panel included Robert Birt, Clarence Johnson, and Robert Westley. It was a meeting of the Radical Philosophy Association at the American Philosophical Association Easter Division Meeting in Atlanta, Georgia, December 1996.

5. The best evidence for this concern of West's language is achieved by reading his books. For an examination of West in an existential context, see Clarence Sholé Johnson, "Cornel West as Pragmatist and Existentialist."

6. Cornel West, *Prophesy, Deliverance!: An Afro-American Revolutionary Christianity* (Philadelphia: Westminster Press, 1982), p. 18.

7. Cornel West, "American Radicalism" in *A Critical Sense: Interviews with Intellectuals*, ed. by Peter Osborne (London and New York: Routledge, 1996), p. 127.

8. See, for example, George Yancy's "Where One Finds Black Intellectual Exchange of Ideas," *The Philadelphia Tribune* (Tuesday, May 7, 1996).

9. I have already stated my view of its relation to the ascent of cultural studies (and, to that matter, postmodernism), but an interesting discussion of its black-Jewish connection has been advanced by Robert S. Boynton in his article, "The New Intellectuals," *The Atlantic Monthly* (March 1995), pp. 53–70.

10. *Sister Outsider*, p. 112. See also *Transcending the Talented Tenth*, p. 158, where Joy James takes West to task for failing ". . . to cite political activism as an 'organic' black intellectual tradition."

11. But for those who "must," see *Race Matters*, pp. 42–3.

12. For a critique of these postmodernist conclusions, see chap. 4 (above) of this volume and *Fanon and the Crisis of European Man*, chap. 5.

13. *Transcending the Talented Tenth*, p. 160. For additional discussion of the New World radical black tradition, see Cedric J. Robinson, *Black Movements in America* (New York and London: Routledge, 1997) and Brian Meeks's *Radical Caribbean*.

14. For discussion, see Bobby Dixon's "Toting Technology: Taking It to the Streets" in *Existence in Black*.

15. Discussions of convergences and class are numerous, but the classic statement on why there is no bourgeoisie proper among blacks, see E. Franklin Frazier's *The Black Bourgeoisie* (New York, London, Toronto, Sydney, and Singapore: Free Press/Simon and Schuster, 1997 [1957]) which originally appeared in French as *Bourgeoisie noire* (Paris: Librairie Plon, 1955).

16. None of this is to say that the custodial workers couldn't have organized this communicative environment without the professor. It is only to say that this was one contribution she was able to make, and so she did.

17. W.E.B. Du Bois, *The Autobiography of W.E.B. Du Bois: A Soliloquy on Viewing My Life from the Last Decade of Its First Century*, p. 232.

Chapter Twelve

Right-Wing Celebration, Left-Wing Nightmare: Thoughts on the Centennial of *Plessey v. Ferguson*

The Spanish-American philosopher George Santayana once declared that those who do not learn the lessons of history are destined to repeat historical mistakes. Santayana was rather charitable in his presumption that some people may want to move forward on matters of grave historical importance. But for those whose main objective is to thwart the course of history, to steal away its progressive possibilities and offer regressive alternatives, repeating history may be exactly what they hope to achieve.

There are many ways to read the present in terms of the past. On birthdays, we try not only to recount from where we have come, but also to reminisce and bring to life the significance of where we have been. In U.S. politics, right-wing elements decided to celebrate 1996 by reinvigorating 1896, a year of irony. That year was the culmination of every effort to turn back the clock on what both the thirteenth amendment (which outlawed slavery in the United States) and the fourteenth amendment (which guaranteed equal legal protection to members of this society) represented. Court cases in the 1870s, 1880s, and early 1890s outlawed "preferential treatment" of blacks and Native Americans. Legislation implemented under the banner of "civil rights" actually curtailed efforts to further the course of African American equality. The crowning achievement was *Plessey v. Ferguson*. That 1896 ruling effectively sealed the course of regression with a "separate but equal" administration of the law of the land. Segregation was affirmed, and a mock equality, where procedure rules over substance, became the mark of U.S. civilization well into the present century.

For many progressives, the 1950s represented the second U.S. Civil War. It is remembered today as the civil rights struggle, but we should not delude ourselves. It was a war. It continues to be one. It was a war with revolutionary aims, such as William Patterson and Paul Robeson's bold effort to make the United States come to terms with its genocidal activities.[1] The civil rights struggle stands in relation to the 1990s pretty much as the Civil War stood in relation to the 1890s. What tales do the 1990s tell?

We find, first, the scores of cases and legislation against the efforts of the 1950s and 1960s. The attack on affirmative action has taken a course from court rulings on such absurd notions as "reverse discrimination" and "meritocracy" to contemporary legislation against progressive programs for blacks and other people of color.

This course of action has organized resources from the left and used them to effect a conservative, right-wing agenda. Thus, just as the concept of discrimination has been perverted to meet the needs of the haves instead of the have-nots, so, too, has the very meaning of the terms "civil rights" and "revolution." We find, as in the so-called "civil rights" initiatives of California, Oregon, and Illinois, the use of the *notion* of civil rights against any material example of civil rights. In Marxist revolutionary theory, this technique is a form of reactionary idealism.

Reactionary idealism emerges when we separate concepts from their material conditions and instantiation. When the notion of civil rights is separated from the people who most embody questions of exclusion, one can float freely over constituencies who lay claim to representation. One can level out political and economic realities and conceal how both power and representatives of power go about acquiring capital and alienating the general citizenry's access to concrete political participation. Rights become a rallying cry for the protection of the most-advantaged's disenfranchising the least-advantaged.

We find a similar metamorphosis of the concept of revolution. When revolution is divorced from its historical meaning of radical systemic and systematic change, then used to describe any *coup d'etat* in which one group of rulers is replaced by another, we find ourselves facing the obscenity of a right-wing government that refers to itself as "revolutionary."

In the 1890s, reactionary groups were able to implement a well-orchestrated contract on most of America: the separation of the poor and the downtrodden into divided, easily accessible fodder for a capitalist machine that was ready to shift gears into an industrial–military complex with which to make manifest the "destiny" of a profiting elite. In 1996, that cause found its *Plessey v. Ferguson*. It was called the Republican Contract with America, aptly derided by progressives as the Contract *on* America.

The 1996 return of *Plessey* was accompanied by a strangely familiar set of players. In *Plessey*'s day, Booker T. Washington ideologically prepared a black conservative faction that E. Franklin Frazier later referred to as a *lumpen-bourgeoisie.* A lumpen-bourgeoisie is a group whose primary "capital" is political. They have no material means of production. They are puppets who profit from illusions of power.[2] In Washington's time, the black lumpen-bourgeoisie served as a liaison between communities of color and the Wall Street–District of Columbia center. It made sense that their intervention destabilized issues of racial justice and shifted the focus of theoretical and practical debate to notions of black pathology (laziness, licentiousness, greed, etc.) and black exoticism (the flourishing culture of entertainment in the midst of social misery).

We found, in 1995–1996, a similar preparation in place. It is no accident that a powerful, neoliberal cadre of black scholars formulated its interests under the banner of *The Future of the Race.*[3] W.E.B. Du Bois has become an empty signifier, in this regard, for Booker T. Washington's contemporary Tuskegee Machine up north.[4] This academic textual response stands as no surprise, especially since the "historical textual event" was written but a few months earlier in the fall of 1995. When an unprecedented number of black men (and an untold number of black women) gathered together and stated their case of social and moral pathology in Washington, D.C., it was no surprise that the current heirs of *Plessey* responded with sound agreement:[5] "But isn't that what we've been saying all along?"[6] Translated: "Perhaps the right wing is more in touch with black values than the liberals and progressives."

What happens to any notion of class struggle when the interests of management and the interest of workers are blurred? What happens to the struggle against racism when blacks begin to organize in such a way that we can even imagine the Klan declaring, "But isn't that what we've been saying all along?"[7]

We should be on the alert.

Look at the record. In education: During the Reagan administration, too many workers were available in an economy that wasn't absorbing their labor in the form of jobs. The response, through a number of ideological resources like the infamous *A Nation at Risk*, was to declare the American worker incompetent and ill-equipped.[8] As resources were generated away from school systems that functioned as community centers, as sites of progressive political education, and then rechanneled into the military with leftovers devoted to research facilities that study school systems, many of the fictional problems of 1983 became material realities by the end of the 1980s.[9] The assault on social welfare programs took a similar course. As resources were rechanneled away from programs that were working, their devastated remains were left to be studied as the standards that existed all along. What right-wing forces learned very well in the 1980s was that, with the proper capital, they could make a social pathology exist simply by virtue of declaring it (which enabled a redistribution of resources), then confirming it (after having made it become so). With such a pattern, we need to be asking what is to be made from what has been declared in 1995 and put fully into place by 1996.

In 1995, there was a resurgence in eugenics research that declared black people to be constitutionally stupid, criminal, and nymphomaniacal. There was then a march on Washington, D.C., that provided the moralistic dimension to that turn: Black men suffer from a failure to take responsibility for the travails they have supposedly brought upon their communities. Is it not clear that, in the conservative blame-the-victims rhetoric that underlay the Million Man March, hope was voiced for a transformed black population that could meet the growing right-wing, retrograde agenda? A black population, in other words, that was to be too stupid and morally deviant to fight instead of *atone*?[10]

While the anniversary candles burn in celebration of *Plessey*'s coming full circle, we on whom the current contract has been issued, as we face the battles that will mark our entry into the next millennium and the insanity of their right-wing *bicentennial* celebration, would do well to take heed of a prescient voice of a century ago:

> Let me give you a word on the philosophy of reform. The whole history of the progress of human liberty shows that all concessions yet made to her august claims have been born of earnest struggle.
>
> This struggle may be a moral one, or it may be a physical one, and it may be both moral and physical, but it must be a struggle. Power concedes nothing without demand. It never did and it never will.

Echoing Frederick Douglass, we now must join hands and develop creative techniques, instrumentally and otherwise, in struggle against the possibility of another élite anniversary celebration that promises to be no less than our common nightmare.

Notes

1. See Patterson's and Robeson's accounts in their autobiographies: William Patterson, *The Man Who Cried Genocide: An Autobiography* (New York: International Publishers, 1971) and Paul Robeson, *Here I Stand* (Boston: Beacon Press, 1958).

2. The classic formulation of this class is E. Franklin Frazier's *Black Bourgeoisie*.

For a similar analysis, see Frantz Fanon's "Mésaventures de la conscience natio-nale" in *Les damnés de la terre.*

3. Henry Louis Gates, Jr., and Cornel West, *The Future of the Race* (New York: Vintage, 1996). West's association with the contemporary version of the Tuskegee Machine has perplexed members of the black radical community. His association could be regarded as his continued belief in dialogue with power in addition to dialogue with the disadvantaged. It could also be regarded as consistent with his background from his college days: West's educational and professional life (at Har-vard, Princeton, Union Theological Seminary/Columbia University, Yale Divin-ity School, and Oberlin College), like Gates's (Yale, Cambridge, Cornell, Duke, and Harvard), has always been among first-tier institutions. Such institutions repre-sent only a small portion of interests of any group in the nation, however, so the future of blacks in the United States calls for representation beyond Harvard iconography. Finally, the future of the black "race" should be articulated beyond the borders of the United States.

4. This assessment is well-covered terrain and needn't be labored further. In-terested readers should consult the references to Henry Louis Gates, Jr. in chap. 4 above. The hegemony that Gates exercises over black scholars in literature may invoke a stream of confessionals in future autobiographies of "the race." Gates is no atypical example of this type of hegemony. Houston Baker held this prestigeous role. And I'm sure that there will be others ready to assume the mantle when Gates steps down. There are many scholars who would like to embody the spirit of W.E.B. Du Bois today, but in truth, the radical Du Bois would easily recognize many of our contemporaries who sit in chairs that bear his name to be possessed in the end by the spirit of Booker T. Washington's infamous Tuskegee Machine. Cornel West does not hold a Du Bois chair, but his strong association with radical politics makes him at home in an institute that bears the great scholar's name.

5. For discussion, see the collection of articles that comprise volume 25, issue number 4 of *The Black Scholar* (Fall 1995).

6. This response came from Newt Gingrich in a CNN interview after the march. It was echoed by other conservatives as well, including William Bennett on *The Charlie Rose Show.*

7. The rhetoric in the Million Man March ironically matched an infamous letter from a Klansman that circulated in Chicago churches and found its way to New Haven in 1992. Here is a sample: "The Ku Klux Klan would like to take this time to salute and congratulate all *Gang Bangers, all Alcohol Drinking Abusers,* and *all Drug Users* for the slaughter of over 4,000 black people since 1975. You are doing a marvelous job. Keep killing each other for nothing, the streets are still not yours. . . ." The complete letter is reprinted in *Bad Faith and Antiblack Racism,* p. 109.

8. *A Nation at Risk* (Washington, DC: National Commission on Excellence in Education, 1983).

9. For discussion, see Ira Shor's introduction to *Freire for the Classroom: A Sourcebook for Liberatory Teaching*, ed. by Ira Shor, afterword by Paulo Freire (Portsmouth, NH: Boynton/Cook Publishers, 1987).

10. On the absurdity of atonement in this context, see Ernest Allen, Jr.'s nuanced analysis, "Toward a 'More Perfect Union': A Commingling of Constitutional Ideals and Christian Precepts," *The Black Scholar* 25, no. 4 (Fall 1995): 27–34.

PART III

AISTHESIS DEMOKRATÊ

CHAPTER THIRTEEN

SKETCHES OF JAZZ

"*Jazz* is a misnomer. Our music," said the instructor, "is African American classical music. Remember that. Remember that colonization of our works of art must stop. And if there is anywhere it stops, it is right here—at Jazz Mobile."

The Saturday afternoon was cold, and the intermediate school in which hundreds of young musicians had met for the Jazz Mobile Workshop at 127th Street and Park Avenue in Harlem, NY, was well-known for its lack of heating fuel and important equipment.

Yet the place was hopping, and the teachers, some of the best practitioners of African American classical music, faithfully assembled there every weekend at 8 a.m., after performing in clubs at times until 4 a.m., with a sense of mission that transformed the place into no less than a place of worship.

I love African American classical music. I realized this when, on one freezing Saturday morning, as my trombonist friend and I walked through ice-covered streets on our way to the subway station, our faces covered with petroleum jelly to protect us from the sub-zero cold, our scarves wrapped tightly around most of our faces, with only a space to see in front of us, our bodies puffier than usual as we negotiated our way through many layers of clothing, we looked at each other and asked:

"What are we *doing*?"

The IRT subway station at Gun Hill Road was cold. So was the train. And by the time we walked into that freezing intermediate school on 127th and Park, we were so numb that it seemed unlikely that my friend would be able to blow a note and that I would be able to generate a buzz role on a snare drum or a decent "ride" on my cymbals.

But by the time we walked up those cold stairs and began to hear the snippets of instruments warming up here and there—a Charley Parker riff shooting out of one room, some Modern Jazz Quartet's coolness from a vibraphone nearby, a sprinkle of Thelonius Monk's "Trinkle Tinkle" tickling a piano, a syncopated "boom!" reminiscent of Max Roach from another room, a bit of Clifford Brown fluttering through the air down the hall—heat radiated from within our chests as we took in the glow and excitement of the moment, of the scene, of the special way of talking about and looking at the world that mattered so much to us.

"Wednesday Night Prayer Meeting" beckoned my soul. A Charles Mingus tune. I first heard it broadcasted from a public radio station out of Columbia University. The year was 1977. At that time, I also was able to catch a barely audible public station coming out of Newark, NJ. WBGO. Commercial jazz stations no longer existed in the tristate area, so the torch was being carried on by public radio. WBGO also played Mingus. Mingus wasn't the first jazz icon to color the world with thoughts and images that touched our souls. And he won't be the last. But Mingus had a style that was so political, so nasty in a provocatively and paradoxically reverential way, that I found myself listening to his music with an explosion of apperception, with an awareness of what I was feeling while listening to his work. The stomping. The dissonant notes. The humming. The polyrhythmic surges into various stages of African American and Latin American history. Even alone on the piano, he explored the thresholds of aesthetic possibility with ironic reflection, as he announced in "Myself When I am Real." Ourselves when *we* are real? Yes, Mingus played African American classical music.

A great deal happens at once when one plays and listens to such music. Have you ever watched the audience? They synchronize themselves with the song, they participate, they give and take from the musicians, they contribute to the music, which seems to transcend the temporal moment as the West African 6/8 pattern dances over whatever time that is counted and frees their soul into what John Coltrane called "another place."

That other place was cool. It was truthful. It was free of dichotomies between subject(ivity) and object(ivity), passion and rationality, illusion and reality. In that place, the world was truthfully aesthetic. Truth, in that world, had set itself free as what it was, as value.

Miles Davis once forgot his trumpet, so he had to use a cornet at the gig. Horace Silver was there on piano. Paul Chambers, funky with the rhythm and always plucking just the right note on bass, while Kenny Clarke on drums set the rhythms free. Some classic tenor sax was thrown in by Coleman Hawkins, joined by some classic trombone by J.J. Johnson, and the coolest version of "Walkin' " was born.

On hot summer days, my trombone friend and I used to sit out on the porch of his back yard, open some beers, and tap our feet and bob our heads while the sun slowly went down and Miles and company ushered in the night.

That cool, hip rhythm, accompanied by offbeat statements from well-chosen chords on the piano, brought to new levels by melodies that jazz musicians call "heads," took the Hucklebuck into a different dimension when Charley Parker declared, in his typical atypical fashion: "Now's the Time."

At Jazz Mobile, Parker's famous riff that opens his solo—"*bi-bop-dapa-dooliadapa-dapa-dapa-doodliadapa-dap-dadaaa*"—is heard over and over again, in warm-up snippets perhaps to this day.

African American classical music. Once called "nigger music." Called many names over the ages.[1] I remember a horrid movie, *The Birth of the Blues*, in which Bing Crosby and a few other white actors played some hip New Orleans musicians who transformed black spirituals and European popular music into "the blues," and then jazz.[2]

Yeah. *Right.*

The all-white Original Dixieland Jazz Band.

Original?

George Gershwin, it has become legend, "Made a Lady out of Jazz."

So, was she a whore?

Benny Goodman, "king of swing."

King of swing? So, while black musicians were being stereotyped for their rhythm, white musicians could still claim the highest accomplishments over it.

Harold Cruse chronicles the rejection of Duke Ellington for the Pulitzer Prize for "long-term achievement" in American music.[3] Some white critics wondered whether Ellington was any Mozart or Gershwin. I say this: Neither Mozart nor Gershwin was any Duke Ellington.[4]

Imagine how it felt, however, when in 1980, while taking a break from an afternoon jam session in a club, I walked outside and had the following exchange with three African American boys, each about ten years of age:

"Would you like to come in and check out the session?"

"What y'all playing?" asked one of the boys.

"Jazz," I said.

"Jazz? Naaa, that's white people's music!" he shrugged, and he and his friends went on their way.

Yeah, "white people's music." White people seen for many years even on public television presentations of jazz. Yeah, Benny Goodman, Gene Krupa, Tommy Dorsey, Dave Brubek, Gerry Mulligan, Stan Getz, Chuck Mangione as a crossover symbol in the '70s, and many, many more. Excellent though those white musicians were—geniuses, in some cases—the problem wasn't that white "cats" were playing African American classical music. It was that they were serving as its most popular, media-constructed representatives. Think of the difference more recently between the Marsalis brothers, popular though they may be, and the saccharine and well-marketed phenomenon Kenny G.

Being a black jazz musician was and continues to be almost synonymous with being out of work. But fortunately, when I was a teenager, those who were working were also spending a great deal of time away from their paid gigs on a mission to bring the music to another generation.

"I need young drummers who can read music," declared Eddie Locke, former drummer for Coleman Hawkins and Roy Eldridge.

"What for?" asked Charley Persip, the Jazz Mobile multipercussions instructor.

"For the Newport Jazz Festival."

Being young and a drummer was one thing. Being able to read music was another. I was fifteen and was able to sight-read music at 450 metronome speed. The other drummers pointed their sticks at me.

So began weekend rehearsals for a drum octet on Saturdays at Riverside Church in Morning Side—that is, Columbia University's Harlem—and a wonderful moment with a teacher *par excellence*. Locke was an incredible drummer. But most of all, he was, and continues to be, an incredible human being.

He offered to give me free drum lessons on Wednesday afternoons. So after school, I hopped the train and found my way down to West End Avenue, where I took drum lessons from the famous Eddie Locke.

"You play melodically," he used to say. I was less concerned with keeping time then. I was with what the drums had to *say*. But time also had to be kept, and what a drummer has to say must also be remembered as something to be shared rather than left alone.

"Would you like to come down to Jimmy Ryan's Night Club?" asked Locke one afternoon after showing me how to "stew" the brushes.[5]

So began more train-hopping. And there, in that little club, was "Little Jazz," Roy Eldridge, blazing through the night with unbelievable riffs.

Then, there was the famous "Caravan," in which Locke performed an incredible fifteen-minute drum solo. His hands glided through the air like a butterfly flapping its wings, while he kept a beautiful, continuous buzz-role. He thumped and banged out low and lower tones on the tom toms of his tiny, four-piece multipercussive instrument, and he massaged them with his hands to bring out their cries from ages past. Modestly, thinking only of the music, he made those drums tell a story, a story that I and my occasional company of high-school friends had the good fortune at that moment to experience.

I returned to that club at least one Thursday night each month for about a year and a half.

"You don't have to become a professional musician," Eddie used to say. "But you must always play the music as best you can."

African American classical music is a dialectical music. It recognizes a world of order, but it simultaneously embraces a world of unpredictability. It cherishes the "standards," but each musician's task is to be original.

African American classical music has a politics all its own. Total strangers can meet, choose a tune, and strike up a performance that seems almost like magic. A form of virtue-based democracy emerges in which first the melody is played, then choruses are taken in which each accompanying musician's task is to "drive" the soloist toward the best possible solo he or she can accomplish. Like the gospel chorus who cheers on the speaker or simply hums along, as we hear in Charles Mingus's "Wednesday Night Prayer Meeting," the other musicians speak out now and then—the bass drum booms an "Amen," or a "go on, go on!" and the pianist or, in big band, the trombones, hit the chords, "left-hand," to punctuate each bar—all in the name of the music. The community, the musical moment, the people assembled, all understand that the music is to be played, and played well. A good jazz performance is a moment of and for communal celebration.

In African American Classical Music, one's duty, always, is to play the music in one's own way. A melody, then, is a suggestion, not an edict. I have played "Take the A Train" in 4/4, 6/8, 3/4, 5/4, and many other meters. To accomplish this, one must take many liberties with the melody. Yet, the audience always knows the tune. The music presents many phenomenological insights and a view of the world that is anathema to the philosophy of language and mathematics that undergirds European classical music. In the world of African American classical music, one plays a tune or sings a song in a particular way but once. Modern European philosophy, which reflects back upon its aesthetic bases, regards European classical music, on the other hand, as lending itself to the gods Chronos (Time), Phanes (Appearance), and Apollo (Order); it burdens the music with, in its essence, European science and its market's quest for predictability and control. It generates laws. It generates repetition. It generates order. These features are far removed from the creative experience of many European composers and musicians. Bach, in spite of the complexity of his fugues, wrote many of them spontaneously and grooved. Mozart and Beethoven did the same. But European classical music eventually collapsed, in European society's quest for order, into a leader-led relation. The musicians are guided by a leader, a conductor. Even popular appropriations of African American music—for example, white rock 'n' roll, "the baby," as Little Richard says, from Rhythm and Blues getting together—center on a highly marketable individual, in spite of claims to rebellion. White rock 'n' roll bands exude a form of centered libertarianism that celebrates the market through the *one* who sings or the *one* who performs *the guitar solo*. It is as if the whole art form has been reduced to a single instrument. With the rise of rock 'n' roll, a world of gadgets and technology burgeoned in the midst of market-centered music; at the edges of the radio dials, the darker, non-profit peripheries vied for smaller and smaller places and time slots.

Any instrument, even the drums, can carry a melody, as Max Roach's "Oom Boom!" demonstrates. African American classical music, when performed and written well, presents its own language, which one learns in ways that are not part of the stock of European tonality and pedagogy.

Think of the voice. European male classical singers opted for castration to sail in the higher registers.

African American classical musicians opted for singing in the higher registers through using their falsetto.

European music sheets: *Allegro, adagio, pianissimo, forte.*

African American classical music sheets: *Pick up the tempo, soften the groove, get funky, slam it, swing!*

The tones: dissonant, quarter-toned, beckon pentatonic instead of hectatonic scales. Think, here, of what Thelonius Monk and Cecil Taylor do on the piano.

When African American classical musicians communicate their music to each other, many European terms are also used, true, since most African-American musicians learned the musical language from the instruments and the historical experience of the European context. But more emerges as well, when that context no longer governs as the only direction in which to groove. It is a testament to the aesthetic and political prescience of jazz that no one who plays it well is someone who looks "out of place." Given that there are many ways to play a jazz melody, we find also that there are many ways to "be" a jazz musician. Membership in that world is not a function of the extent to which one is able to leave oneself behind. It is, instead, a call for us to suspend seriousness in the everyday world for the sake of creative and aesthetic experience.

Coltrane spoke of "A Love Supreme." He looked back, back to Africa and found himself looking ahead, like a Sankofa bird, to its future. He also spoke of "Om." The spiritual dimension of the music permeates the world of what Arthur Schopenhauer called *Will*. As the swing-time stretches the contours of physical time, opening up durational dimensions of experience, the world's seriousness is suspended, paradoxically, in a serious way. Coltrane used to make his saxophone snort and growl and cry and tear at consciousness itself as it let loose possibilities that, to this day, stand as spiritual. The music stands between the rational and the irrational, in the world of a form of passionate rationality, the world in which one is angry because the truth is an angry truth, happy because the truth is a happy truth. It is a world in which moods function not as a subjective condition of an agent's perspective, but as an important feature, among other features, just as a particular interpretation of a melody stands as one among others, of the world.

I did not only see housing projects when Coltrane played "Afro Blue" and twilight walks through Central Park when he played "My Favorite Things"—I *felt* them. Coltrane had a way of making one's soul tremble. Fear and trembling. Fanon was suspicious of the blues and by extension much of African-American classical music, primarily because he equated their existence with black misery. But like tragedy, whose pathos can purge an audience into a condition of joy, so, too, are there "happy" blues. Nearly all of Count Basie's blues are "happy."

In African American classical music, one catches a glimpse of how vast the world might really be if one were to open the floodgates of aesthetic perception. That is why there have been so many geniuses in African American classical music. On genius, Immanuel Kant wrote:

> *Genius* is the talent (natural endowment) that gives the rule to art. Since talent is an innate productive ability of the artist and as such belongs itself to nature, we could also put it this way: *Genius* is the innate mental predisposition (*ingenium*) *through which* nature gives the rule to art. . . . (1) Genius is a *talent* for producing something for which no determinate rule can be given, not a predisposition consisting of a skill for something that can be learned by following some rule or other; hence the foremost property of genius must be *originality*. (2) Since nonsense too can be original, the products of genius must also be models, i.e., they must be *exemplary*; hence, though they do not themselves arise through imitation, still they must serve others for this, i.e. as a standard or rule by which to judge. (3) Genius itself

cannot describe or indicate scientifically how it brings about its products, and it is rather as *nature* that it gives the rule.[6]

Kant regards the genius as the expression of others' limitations; like the
sublime, in which our encounter with nature's vastness reminds us of our
limitations while eliciting an overwhelming feeling of wonder, so, too,
does the genius. The genius appears as nature expressing itself, but the
genius, being a human being, transcends nature in any reductive sense. The
response to the genius, then, is usually one of both wonder and anxiety;
there is not much for pure creativity in our world of measurement, dicta-
tion, and scripts, except as *ex post facto* determinations of what *has been
created*. Many musicians, from many heritages, can be found devoting hours
of practice toward doing what Louis Armstrong, Fats Waller, Duke Ellington, Art Tatum, Charlie Parker, Dizzy Gillespie, Bud Powell, Thelonius
Monk, Billy Strayhorn, Miles Davis, John Coltrane, Clifford Brown, Max
Roach, Elvin Jones, Tony Williams, Mary Lou Williams, and many more
did and continue to do spontaneously. If we suspend the nature talk for the
moment and substitute the language of culture, then the genius is one
who can make creative use of the cultural resources available. One African
American cultural resource, due primarily to material scarcity, is spontane-
ity. As an existential music, African American classical music gains sustenance from the African American situation in a unique way: Writing occurs
through performing. Its existence, if you will, precedes its essence.

Jazz is existential. Jazz is spiritual. Jazz is dialectical. One must first lay down
the "head" by performing one's interpretation of the melody. That is the
thesis. But then many possibilities emerge as many *other* theses are played,
all of which allude, at times only minutely, to the original thesis, the original melody. That is called taking choruses. One can imagine a jazz tragedy,
wherein the harbinger comes out and declares the scene, then the chorus
helps us interpret the action here and there while it pushes the agent who
is now presented as leading that which is also leading him or her through
to the next stages of the performance. Then there is the moment of epiph-
any, where the music "wails," where catharsis is achieved, and after which
the early theme, the thesis, returns and makes its effort to reconstitute itself.
    African American classical music comes out of a tragic tale. It comes out
of a world that was ripped apart at the seams, vivisected, and set to wander,
as did the *tragos*, the proverbial goat who bore the community's burdens,
amid a loud cry of suffering. But through this suffering, through this wan-
dering and wondering, there was no time for self-lamentation. One had to,

and has to, go forward. But as one does so, one constantly affirms bits of the past. That past keeps repeating itself under the jazz soloist, and every time it does so, like Sisyphus's journey to his rock, it strikes out possibilities of freedom in a world plagued by a threat of despair. It is cognizant of an absurd world while it celebrates the beauty of every element it can choose through the possibilities it creates.

Jean-Paul Sartre wrote that play is one of the primary antidotes to a spiritually serious world. In play, one constructs a world in which one brings to the fore one's role in that construction. One finds oneself aware of a world for which one is responsible. That world is multi-interpretative. It is a world that simultaneously recognizes the possibilities of its transcendence and the fact of its facticity. In a jazz performance, the musical composition stands not as a constraint upon freedom but as an opportunity for it.

Mercer Ellington once wrote, "It don't mean a thing if it ain't got that swing." To swing is to bring to our practices and our praxis that special element that can also be called *doing it right*.

Wouldn't it be wonderful if we could live the folkways and mores of our society in the form of a jazz performance? Imagine what would happen if the laws and economic structures were opportunities for freedom instead of constraints upon it. Each generation of our society could recognize and interpret what had been handed down—without slipping into epistemological conundra—and simultaneously recognize its active role in the constitution of its meaning and where it was going. And the task of every generation? To live in a way that brought out the best possibilities of their society's ongoing composition of itself.

Our current society is like an orchestra with a music sheet, but no groove. It fails to recognize that to play the music the people need their instruments. It is not that it is our turn to take a chorus, but instead that we've missed our beat. It is that this society, from its inception, has failed even to begin to groove. The downbeat that has been taken is not one committed to swinging.

There are individuals who are trying to stultify any creative philosophy of life in the hope of repeating a performance that was believed to have been the repeat of some other mythical performance of a long, long time ago. Communication is breaking down. There are no chords accenting decisions like choruses in a Greek drama, an Asante festival, or a call-and-response black church. Whereas in jazz, there is a conception of community in which, although synchronized, each member or performer exemplifies his or her uniqueness. Contemporary, mostly neofascist claims to democracy have no clue of this conception of community. They lack *asthesis demokratê*—democratic perception. They offer "opinions."

There are no opinions in African American classical music. The music interprets the world in many ways, but those interpretations are always intersubjectively established, either among the group, or between the performer and the audience. One cannot articulate in advance the conditions of a particular jazz performance's meeting the conditions of being jazz primarily because the performance itself doesn't exist prior to the *performing*. Existential reality is socially embodied.

Jazz musicians don't refrain from judgment. If the performance stinks, they'll tell you so. And if you're committed to the music, there is no time for egotistical self-delusion and bad faith. You will admit it was so and move on. You will admit to yourself what you are doing.

Our political society, on the other hand, suffers from polite self-delusion. The conditions of communicative speech are set aside for intrasubjective, solipsistic, self-indulgent, opinionated reality. A truly democratic society needs speech, not as reverberations over physical reality that amount to no more than "sounds," but instead as those moments in which sounds and electromagnetic radiation and gases are transformed into symbols, into meanings, into thoughts, into worlds. Yes, the music aims not simply to speak, but also first to communicate.

I have spent many hours listening to the world as expressed through the sight and voices of Billie Holiday, Ella Fitzgerald, Dinah Washington, Johnny Hartman, Sarah Vaughn, Joe Williams, and Abbey Lincoln. I have seen my children and my brothers' children move their legs to the rhythms that accompany these singers and their faces brighten with delight as their voices permeate the air and light their soul. I say to my colleagues, whenever I buy a compact disk collection by one of these singers and hurry home to play them to my children, "I gotta start them off right."

Yeah, I've gotta start them off right. They need to know about "Strange Fruit," "God Bless the Child," and *The Freedom Now Suite*. They need to know "Haitian Fight Song" and "Meditations on Integration (Parts I & II)."

So I think back about my friend and me walking down those cold Bronx streets, and I wonder about a saying that C.S. Lewis gained from the father of one of his students. That wise man said the reason we read is to know that we are not alone. Every bit of the music for which we endured so much stood as an effort to move the veil, if but for a moment, to see the many ways in which even our aloneness could be heard.

Notes

1. For a lively, concise history of African American classical music, see John Fordham's *Jazz: History, Instruments, Musicians, Recordings*, foreword by Sonny Rollins (London, New York, and Stuttgart: Dorling Kindersley, 1993).

2. The group on whose achievements the film was most likely based was The Original Dixieland Jazz Band. The group is attributed with performing the first jazz recording, "Livery Stable Blues" and "Original Dixieland One-Step," in 1917. The record sold a million copies. For a brief history of The Original Dixieland Jazz Band, see Fordham's *Jazz*, espcially p. 10.

3. Harold Cruse, *The Crisis of the Negro Intellectual: A Historical Analysis of the Failure of Black Leadership* (New York: Quill, 1984), pp. 107–9.

4. Black artists and intellectuals contend with this dimension of Eurocentric arrogance all too often. In philosophy, a familiar insult is, "Why aren't there any African or African-American Platos, Aristotles, Descartes, and Kants?" Perhaps it will one day occur to such critics that if they were Platos, Aristotles, Descartes, and Kants, they wouldn't be their own intellectual giants on their own terms. The legacy from Plato to Kant contributed to *Europe*'s identity. How could thinkers who contribute to *Africa*'s identity even be respected if the European worldview has been centered? We know of Lao Tze and Confucius in China, but it is important to note that they are their own terms. Similarly, in Africa there is a legacy from St. Augustine through to Zar'a Ya'aqob, Walda Heywat, and many others, and in the twentieth-century, the importance of Frantz Fanon and C.L.R. James is being understood in terms that are very different from those of their European counterparts. I have cited texts in Africana philosophy in Part I, but again, readers are encouraged to look at D.A. Masolo's *African Philosophy in Search of Identity*, Kwame Gyekye's *An Essay on African Philosophical Thought*, and Tsenay Serequeberhan's *The Hermeneutics of African Philosophy*. For extant work by the sixteenth-century Abyssinian philosophers Zar'a Ya'aqob and Walda Heywat, see *Ethiopian Philosophy*, vol. 2, ed. by Claude Sumner (Addis Abeba: Addis Abeba University Commercial Printing Press, 1976).

5. For the uninitiated, stewing is the circular twirling of the brushes, as if gently twirling a spoon in Gumbo, for a steady, delicate stream during ballads.

6. Immanuel Kant, *Critique of Judgment*, trans. by Werner S. Pluhar (Indianapolis and Cambridge, UK: Hackett, 1987), §46, pp. 175; Prussian Academy: 307–8.

CHAPTER FOURTEEN

AESTHETICO-POLITICAL REFLECTIONS ON THE AMTRAK: RAP, HIP-HOP, AND ISAAC JULIEN'S *FANON* ALONG THE NORTHEAST LINE

In the latter half of the 20th century . . . all the thaumaturgy of mythology has been realized or, at least, approximated to the point of being . . . ready to become enfixed in the matrix of daily intercourse. We are entering into a period during which we will see the death of mythology through the nonritualistic tangible enactment. Technology, predominantly in long distance travel and communication and medicine and surgery, has subsumed mythological accomplishments; we can go anywhere, see everything, change sexes, transplant organs, and in some cases nearly raise the dead. It is as if the Aboriginal dreamtime has all returned to Earth and operated in real time.
—*Gary Schwartz, "Toni Morrison at the Movies:*
Theorizing Race Though Imitation of Life*"*

Here the new horizons opened by the film text's visual medium and its narrationally foregrounded signifying practices directly impact on the new question posed implicitly by Fanon as to how the human subject is itself instituted as specific modes of the sociogenic subject by the signifying practices of each culture's order of discourse.
—*Sylvia Wynter, "Rethinking 'Aesthetics':*
Notes Towards a Deciphering Practice"

I need some black-on-black love, baby. . . .
—*Me'Shell NdegéOcello, "I'm Diggin' You (Like an Old Soul Record)"*
Plantation Lullabies

A wonderful feature of living in the northeastern United States is the array of intellectual and political activities going on throughout the year. One can, with small funds, hop from neighboring state to neighboring state to attend anything from a conference on phenomenology and existential philosophy to a conference on Frantz Fanon or a conference on Léopold Senghor. Movement. The world of learning shifts. The model of the meditating scholar, alone in his or her office or study, quietly reading perennial texts, quietly thinking through what needs to be thought, such a model falls to the wayside. Instead, there is a sense of hustle and bustle. Something is always happening where one lives, true, but there is *always* something equally and at times more interesting happening elsewhere, nearby. The environment is conducive to a form of traveling scholarship. One hops on the AMTRAK or the Metroliner and reads to the shake and chug of trains along the rails; an ever-present sense of motion permeates one's consciousness; Boston, Providence, New Haven, New York, Newark, Philadelphia, Washington, Richmond, cities flicker by eyes raised from many texts; a nap here and there, passengers here and there, conversations with strangers as passionate as lovers; morning coffee in styrofoam and toasted bagels with cream cheese release their spell at morning's light; all to a rhythm of the train and its bland prism of gray, brown, and occasional blue; moments of surprise—a past friend coming on board. When I lived in the Midwest, professional travel invariably meant the cramped, sterile environment of the airplane. The trauma of recent flight disasters and the foreboding sense of vulnerability and caprice—one's life is, after all, totally in the hands of two or three others for the flight's duration—compel one to suspend the gravity of the moment with the mental facility of a yogi; for a time, not much must really matter. Flights are terrible for me when I reflect on my loved ones. So I read, and when times are good, I speak to my neighbor, who at times is interesting enough, but most often I sleep. The train, on the other hand, invites sleep *only* for the sake of passing time. The café cars, however, are places to sit down for a while and converse. They're unavoidable. Passengers returning with coffee, donuts, or the smell of food that has permeated their clothing, work better than television snack commercials. I have ridden on trains in the past, and having been a seasoned New Yorker, the subway grind had its own drama. Traveling from state to state along the eastern coast is a different matter. I often discover how little I have been socialized into certain class dynamics of travel. For instance, on one occasion I found myself traveling to a talk in New Haven. The university at which I was to speak had bought my ticket. After boarding the train, I found a window seat and took out my books for the trip. When the conductor came along and looked at my ticket, he declared:

"Well, you're on the right train at the right time on the right day, but you're in the wrong car. You belong in custom class. You need to go to the back of the train, past the café car."

Now, as a scholar on human sciences and studies of race and ethnicity, thoughts of Freud's nightmare about trains, about being Jewish with the wrong ticket, or Fanon's reflections on being "caught" in the train, or the multitude of reflections back to Jim Crow, emerged with full force. Worse, I didn't know what "custom class" meant. I presumed it was for my fellow Plebeians and me. So, I caught myself. If I have a ticket to be among my fellow working-class passengers, then so be it. How is *my* right instead of my *class'* right being violated here? Being among my class origins shouldn't be beneath me. "You don't want to be bourgeois, do you?" I reminded myself. So, I proudly got up and walked back to join my "class." When I arrived in the "custom car," it was immediately apparent, however, that custom class was a euphemism. The car was furnished with large, blue seats. Electronic conveniences were everywhere. About eight people were in the entire car. The passengers? The price of their manicured nails probably exceeded my mother's daily income. Then I realized: the price of my blazer exceeded my mother's *weekly* income. And then the image of what would have happened if I had fought passionately to stay in the car I was in, and on the ground that I belonged, say, in a higher class' seat, when I was in fact in a working-class one. Paradoxically, my ignorance of how the upper classes ride the train made my working-class identity, although not necessarily my working-class identification, all the more apparent: I thought that coach seats were high-quality seats.

"*Duh. . . ?*"

I found myself on another occasion hopping by train from one conference to another, from one state to another. Art was on my mind. I was sick of expending my political energy on projects that were increasingly political automata. Political and academic meetings were increasingly resembling my childhood experiences of going to church: It was sometimes fun but most often stifled under the crushing weight of obligation; whether I *wanted* to go was irrelevant. So I decided to seek out and at times organize dialogues on politics and aesthetics. The conjunction of the two may seem odd to some readers, for the political dimensions of aesthetics have a rich history in the world of ideas. The aesthetics of politics, on the other hand, receive little attention. It's as if aesthetic reality has been reduced to mere conduits, like the trains I take on my intellectual sojourns across the northeast. Art for art's sake, a bourgeois ideal, no?

Must that be so?

I am not enamored with a world without art. Such a world strikes me as the epitome of an ascetic ideal. Why should we choose to live in undecorated houses? Aren't such houses spaces that have not been transformed into *homes*? Do I hang a picture on my wall simply because walls need pictures, or do I hang a picture on a wall because it transforms the wall into a wall I "like"? Perhaps I simply "like" the picture?

I decided to get off the train in New York City. The stop afforded a multitude of possibilities: a conference at New York University, a chance to see some friends, an opportunity to visit my mother and my grandmother, perhaps an opportunity to leaf through some books, and, of course, a chance to pick up some gifts for my family on my way back to Providence. The conference at NYU was entitled *Finding Fanon*. It was a conference that this Fanon scholar wasn't invited to, but I decided to "crash" the scene, because of my curiosity about the types of Fanon that might be "found." So, on I went. On my way, the question of art continued. The conference was occasioned by the completion of Isaac Julien's *Frantz Fanon: "Black Skin, White Masks."*[1] Art, politics, technology, philosophy came to mind. A film, a docudrama, history, art, and politics merged. To see political art and the art of politics merge in a setting like NYU, a place in the heart of New York's equivalent of Paris' Latin Quarter. And all this in the hope of "finding" Fanon as in Julien's past search for Langston Hughes. Near the end of this book, this moment's journey, on Her Majesty's other children, we have come full circle to Fanon and in ways beyond him. We face here the world of aesthetics, a world whose shaky travel cars are ones in which Fanon was suspicious about riding but nevertheless rode so well; his prose is, after all, a work of art. He held the strange view that black aesthetic productions would disappear in an age without racism. In spite of his suspicion that beyond modern racism there was only whiteness, he struggled to break down the systemic semiotic dimension of racism and colonialism in addition to their political economy of inequality.

The "struggle" takes many dimensions. Economic and institutional dimensions provide us with what we need to stay alive. Theoretical dimensions focus on how we make sense of things and the possibilities we can imagine. But the aesthetic struggle is a paradoxical struggle: It is a need that does not seem like a need. The aesthetic emerges from a suspension of exigency. Yet, on its own terms, the aesthetic is an urgent play.[2] It is a need that emerges from the suspension of our material needs. It is a need that emerges when we seem no longer in need. Without the aesthetic realm, we slip into concrete boredom, a gray world of excess. The aesthetic emerges when we see that we are no longer *too* serious about the material world. A South African artist paints a picture of Township life, a moment typical of many moments—zinc roofs, morning coal burning outdoors under makeshift pots, dirt paths calling for asphalt, baskets atop wrapped heads as the women who carry them sway with the morning rhythms, an alert dog barking, the hills in the distance, and in the midst of it all a youth with his back to our gaze, his blazer is bright yellow with tiger stripes as he bops home. Dignity emerges beyond the abstraction of a Kantian kingdom of ends; a bright yellow blazer, an object though it may be, signals a reference to the self: "I matter."[3]

The importance of an independent black aesthetic is a subject of great debate.[4] The terrain is familiar: Should black aesthetics serve the cause of black advancement or is such an appeal an irrelevant demand and perhaps unfair onus to place on black artists? Isn't a consequence of such a functional turn the strangulation of artistic creativity?

Such questions carry a load of assumptions. Their tone is that of a dilemma. But dilemmas in the human realm are often false. They are moments of crises that mark points of indecision: "Oh, which shall I choose? What shall I do?" Such questions fail to identify an important dimension of black advancement: that such advancement may also be an aesthetic one. The subordination of art to politics that is implicit in the question of art's function or "role" fails to account for art as a worldview. Revolutions in art may or may not accompany revolutions in nations. The former is sometimes ahead of the latter. What kind of "being ahead" can art be? Art is no less than the identity of hope and despair without the intrusion of what to do with either. Whatever *we* do with what art makes us see, hear, feel, taste, and wonder, the art remains "there," in its world, waiting, reminding us that, although we have our moment with it, there will be others. Think of references to "lost" creations, how we seek them out, how we wonder about them. Dead? Their presence lacks horizons; Henry Ossawa Tanner's *The Banjo Lesson's* frame is but an artificial surrounding for the eye to see, for its borders have not been reached; art passes through all of us, even in its immitations—compact disks; "copies" for decorating our homes; television viewings—never complete though always distinct. Black aesthetics have many revolutions: spirituals, blues, jazz, rhythm and blues, reggae, calypso, salsa, rap, etc; jitterbug, jazz dance, twists, the hustle, freestyle, etc.

The "color question" is at the heart of the arts dilemma here. It is not that Europeans don't ask these questions about art. Tolstoy was concerned about art's relation to morality. Marx was concerned about art's relation to revolution, though he, unlike many of his successors, wasn't fond of the idea of becoming boring and predictable. Heidegger was concerned about where art "dwells." Sartre liked art's tendency to suspend seriousness but later demanded its service for a cause. Color, as we've seen throughout these sketches, problematizes a reality, obscures vision and sense, and translates the ordinary into the strange. Unusual causes must be found; language of investigation changes to language of pathology. Black artists become like the Fanonian black child; such artists are abnormal artists. Their work flows from naturalistic forces; like the black athlete, whose effort, determination, and skill have been ideologically transformed into biologically determined forces (black basketball players were once thought unlikely but now inevitable). Black artists become, then, manifestations of an overflow of biologically determined eros. "Black art" is a flicker, like those stations whose signals have been scrambled on the television screen behind which are those themes for "mature audiences." There, in their blackness, flows disruption of the normal scheme of things, a Foucaultian *episteme* that is a disruption of *epistemic* conditions, an *abnormal episteme*: When the black walks in the door, Reason walks out; when the black artist walks in the door, "normal art," whatever that is, walks out. Contradictions reign.

I will speak of two contemporary works of art. The first is less a work as a body of works. Since a black work often collapses exponentially into all black works, the interplay of work and works is the inevitable consequence of pathological "play." That work(s), then, will be "rap" and hip-hop. The second work will be a filmic essay, a docudrama, Julien's *Frantz Fanon*.

The rap on rap, as it were, has taken on absurd dimensions. MTV, for instance, which once had a "no black videos allowed" policy, now predominates rap for its middle-class white suburban teenage audience. I recall a special, early '90s report on that station: "Racism in Rock 'n' Roll." There was much talk about racist *artists*. That Michael Jackson had to sue MTV to get on the air, and thus broke the MTV color line, was absent from that report. The reality of power—who bankrolls racist, sexist, and homophobic white artists and limits opportunities for black artists who don't, as Dizzy Gillespie reminded Charlie Parker, "fuck up"[5]—remains "behind the scenes." Rap artists have taken their cue in the ongoing drama of black pathology; they have become the voice of the black "inner city," or the " 'hood," and, consequently, the presentation of black Americans.

"Rap is the voice of the black community," declares the white progressive.

"Really?" objects a black activist.

"It's what black people listen to. Isn't it?"

"Consider this," urges the black: "There are supposedly thirty-three million black people in America. I'd say more, much more, but all that

depends on how one defines 'black people.' There are many black teenagers in the world, true, but there are many more black mothers, fathers,
aunts, and uncles, many more small children. Although there are teenage
consumers, there are many more adult consumers, and in the black middle
class, there are many consumers who purchase reflections of *their* communities. So, if you're a musician planning to make a quick buck, whom
should you focus on? The easiest route is gospel. There, you speak not only
to the heart of black communities across class, but also to a forum in which
your music will be needed; black churches are many and their audiences
listen to gospel in great numbers. The gospel charts rarely make the popular
stations with their secular and often postmodern rallying cries, but those
stations target, we often forget, only so*me of* the nation's music listeners.
Although gospel speaks across the classes, the black middle class likes R &
B. Anita Baker and Luther Vandross are examples of artists who focus on
that constituency. Black teenagers are similarly broken down into class and
regional constituencies. Now, think of the audiences whose experience rap
and hip hop represent. They are poor urban black teenagers. But even
black teenagers under those designations differ. There are large gangs, but
there is an even larger group of black urban teenagers who are not in gangs
and for whom and about whom the rap artist does not speak."

Some time ago, at the beginning of my tenure teaching African American studies and philosophy at a large Midwestern university, I experienced
an encounter that has now become mundane in my academic career. A
familiar feature of the African American studies dimension of such a post is
the ritual visit from the student who is "down with what's happenin' in
the black community." Such a student invariably "examines" the professor
by testing his or her insight on the latest developments in black popular
culture. These days, like the question of women in feminist theory, a faculty member's position on black music has become the litmus test for student acceptance. One can say in this regard that Michael Eric Dyson, Tricia
Rose, and Houston Baker know their constituencies well. In my case, the
student wanted to see if I were in agreement with the view that rap is a
revolutionary art form with revolutionary political potential.

"That depends on what you mean by *revolution*," I started. "If by revolution you mean radical political and economic change, then no, I don't
think rap is revolutionary. Now, if you mean something radical on every
dimension of social life, I will again have to say no. Revolutionary talk isn't
your usual type of talk. Simply producing something 'new' isn't the same
as producing something revolutionary. Rap and hip-hop are additions to

popular culture in the last third of the twentieth-century. But revolutionary?"

"But don't you think that there is revolutionary potential in rap? After
all, it is coming from the streets, from the excluded," retorted the student.

"Revolutionary potential isn't the same thing," I responded. "And besides, not all rap is from the streets. The boys from Long Island [Public
Enemy] don't come from the streets, and they may not have to. Grand
Master Flash and company did speak of alienated urban experience for a
time, and so do many gangsta rappers. But so, too, do Will Smith and Kid
'n' Play. Arrested Development speaks in a quasi-spiritual Afrocentric
voice. The Jungle Brothers have their story. Queen Latifa has hers. I particularly like De La Soul and Me'Shell NdegéOcello's powers of critique. The
list goes on. In the end, the groups are too diverse to be a single voice not
only for black communities but also for revolution. Look, we need to put
rap into perspective. It's a popular music, and it is one that comes out of
black America."

Revolutionary talk demands revolutionary "assessment." If we assess our
productions without revolutionary insight, we may be blind about the extent to which they are more of the same. Blacks, as we've seen in our
discussions of Fanon, live in a negrophobic world. That negrophobic world
often reinscribes a Manichæan chain of values onto loci of black embodiment. What this means is that the discourse of pathology, of ossified hate
or beguiled exotica, usually emerges. *"Salé Nègre!"* ("Dirty nigger!") takes
many forms: criminal demographics; rape; teenage pregnancies; sexually
transmitted diseases; deviant sexuality (from the right-wing's perspective);
underclass; gangbangers; low IQs; laziness; disloyalty; vice; savagery. In antiblack environments, there are also "affectionate" forms; the noble savage
is, after all, still a savage. Think of: the exoticization of Rastafarians; the
black athlete; the negress; the hipster; the buck; the black homosexual,
lesbian, and bisexual (from the left's perspective). White and black anti-
blacks can drool at a popular overflow of "noble" black pathology; black
pathology that titillates through its accessibility to desire in the midst of
underlying themes of danger. The popularity of gangsta rap among white
suburban youth signals the imaginary leap articulated by Fanon in 1951:
"God knows what those people really do in bed. . . ." Rap's location in
the ongoing inscription and reinscription of black pathology signals a far
from revolutionary appeal.

On the economic level, there is a bit of the ridiculous in the discussion
of rap as politically revolutionary. Capitalism is the dominant economic
system of the modern age. Because of this, it has often had to conceal its

agenda under prescriptive claims. Only capitalism feels compelled to defend what is selling. That is because the naked fact is often too crass to tolerate: In the end, it is only profit that counts. Capitalism, then, is the relativism of egoistic self-interest. It is about getting one's own, as the saying goes. The claim of rap artists to be doing "more," then, is tragicomic. Although rap and hip-hop are art forms born out of inner-city black youth culture— summer dance parties ("jams") in the Bronx, Brooklyn, and Manhattan parks; house parties; home "mixes" given and sold here and there—their path into *white* and, therefore, mainstream popular culture is a classic tale of the subordination of values for the sake of profit.

The story is as follows:[6] Consider the radio dials. To the extreme left, there is usually college radio, with short-range signals. There, "art" and less commercial music is played. To the far right of the dial, one usually finds popular music that is not considered "pop." In many U.S. states, that is where one usually finds black stations. The tones are conspicuously low in that region. Then there are the stations round the middle. That is where "pop" and "rock 'n' roll" are usually played—in other words, the "white" section of the dial. Now, logically, if one moves from the middle of the dial to both ends and then back to where one began, one is likely to cross the middle twice and hear the middle three times. Thus, whatever one prefers, the middle is a better place at which to reach listeners. That is important for advertisers to know. (One can push it to the extreme and point out, also, the associations with the "left" in Western semiosis: *Sinister* is, after all, Latin for left; the negated is on the left; the cold is on the left; the feminine is on the left; the dark is on the left. That black *popular* music is often found on the far right is an interesting challenge to this rule.) Thus, when *new* music emerges, it is most likely to find a place on the far left of the dial, where there aren't advertisements and other incentives to play that music nor its artists often.

When rap first emerged in the 1970s—with MC's (master of ceremonies) rappin' over the drum sections of a popular polyrhythmic funk song with congas called "Apache"—radio play (if any) was limited to the college end of the dial. For the most part, however, the art form was heard "live," at parties and other celebrations. (I recall being amazed at how *West African* these large dance sessions were in both rhythm and style.) Tapes were often sold; independent production groups were formed; challenges and competition between groups were emerging; the art form was being made. Then there was the hit "Rappers Delight" by the Sugar Hill Gang over the Chic song "Good Times." I recall how excited we were at my high school, Evander Childs: The drummer on that recording, Pumpkin', was in his senior year at Evander then; he became the epitome of *cool*. Before we knew it, small production companies and local labels were popping up. Salt 'n' Peppa were independently produced and managed to make gold. These groups knew their audiences and, as such, offered a form of black economic independence from the major record labels that dominate mid-Manhattan and the world of popular music. Their economic independence encouraged independence of views and creative risks: Something new was seemingly appearing everywhere as if, literally, "out of thin air."

Eyes in high places were not entirely closed during the growth of these developments, and eventually large labels not only began to sign these artists but also to absorb their independent labels into the satellites of larger labels—all, of course, in the name of profit. As these absorptions became more frequent and intense, and as these earlier "East Coast" artists became more familiar in their local venues (rap on television in NYC, for instance, was only available by way of a public television program, *Video Music Box*), the "danger" element of the music lost its force. Think of the maturity announced by the emergence of Whodini's rap ballad "One Love" in the mid-'80s. In addition, the usual phenomenon of asserting white hegemony surfaced: the Beastie Boys and Vanilla Ice were specific embodiments, but also, among black artists, Hollywood iconography—Steppin' Fetchit, Buckwheat, Amos and Andy—reached out for its players.

It was at this point that the West Coast brought its contributions to the fore: anger; gangs; the 'hood; violence; no, absolutely no, political correctness; bigger, bigger, Bigger Thomases. Here, at last, is the negative moment within rap and hip-hop's own dialectic. Capitalism needs the outlaw; outlaws do not only save the system with the underground economy they provide, they also embody a nihilism of values beyond the system. One becomes an outlaw because there is no other way to make it *within* the legal system; outlaws, in other words, don't fight against the capitalist system, for what *is* an outlaw who is not out for getting, at all cost, his own piece of whatever pie is available? In the end, as labels and artists literally sold out, the promisory note of rap, in political terms, was an affirmation of U.S. capitalism. The disgruntlement of gangsta rappers in particular is not over the fact of exploitation but *who* is exploited.

With developments of controversial art and cultural forms like rap and hip-hop, the inevitable slew of social commentators and academic critics climbed down from their towers to diagnose the terrain. I have avoided commenting in print on rap in particular because of a confessed disdain for the opportunism represented by those individuals. Congressional hearings on misogynist groups, in which noted academics testified with explanations of those groups' "signifyin'," is but an instance. But in the end, I was wrong. One should try one's best to contribute to the understanding of any human production that has a controversial impact on public debate, especially if one cares about the art form and the people who practice it. I admit a love for nearly all black music forms. So, commentary now emerges for me, as we see, here.

The discussion on rap is, however, dominated by postmodern cultural studies' approaches. This in itself is not a bad thing because the practitioners of these approaches often focus on, and at times even appreciate, black popular cultures.[7] Moreover, that rap and hip-hop are undeniably recent *cultural* productions makes them suitable subjects for *cultural* studies. As the musical epiphenomenon of hip-hop culture, a culture marked by other artistic productions like graffiti and "break" dancing, special varieties of black and brown urban youth dialects, and a host of other cultural features, rap's cultural revolutionary potential can be appreciated there. Unfortunately, some of the drawbacks of that approach emerge as well. Cases in point are the various presentations of some rap artists as radical public intellectuals with radical messages to tell. Listening to what these artists had to say reflected some form of social progress, true, but after all was said and done, *what* these artists often had to say amounted to clichéd opinions on our social situation. In other words, *that they were being listened to* is what really mattered. They got their say, even if they weren't saying much.[8] Eventually, an effort to *legitimate* these artists emerged. The odd thing is that in white popular culture, one cannot find a single instance of white academic intellectuals apologizing for, or trying to legitimate, the public intellectual potential of heavy metal artists, artists who spoke in far more misogynist, homophobic, and racist terms than most rap artists. And why should they? After all, these "intellectuals" are mostly teenagers. The nature of the business is such that, by the time any of them is beginning to develop an informed opinion, his or her career is on the wane, if not already over. In white popular music, perhaps the closest instance is John Lennon, but he manages to achieve an *adult* (albeit youthful) sensitivity. In black popular culture, rap and hip-hop, unlike jazz and the blues—where an artist improves with age—are such that an artist degenerates with age: Even if the artist's work is better, the sight of a mature artist performing the work is a liability to the work. A middle-aged rap artist?

In the cultural studies arena, another drawback that emerges is the bad memory that marks popular scholarship. I recall attending a talk by Tricia Rose, for instance, in which she claimed that black female rap artists are the first to present strong, assertive musical images of black women.[9] I wondered if Rose had heard of Bessie Smith, Dinah Washington, and Aretha Franklin. Where would she place Billie Holiday's "Strange Fruit"? Or Dinah Washington's "Evil Woman"? What about the many black women blues and jazz artists who *managed* their own productions, led orchestras (for example, Ella Fitzgerald, and Shirley Bassie), and asserted themselves— always—during times when it was not only black men who risked dangling from trees after standing up for themselves?

In the art form itself, the representation of black revolutionary history was similarly saturated by amnesia. KRS One, an artist who often showed great political insight, used a famous photograph of Malcolm X holding a shotgun while looking out an apartment window, with the caption, "By Any Means Necessary." Not only was the "necessary" element lost in translation to popular imagination, but so, too, was the fact that he was watching out for *black* enemies at the time—namely, the Fruits of Islam, the trained militia of the Nation of Islam. That portrait truly became a free-floating-signifier, though it was never able to shake off residues of black pathology.

A similar devolution occurred in the political consciousness of music from the Caribbean, particularly reggae. There, we witness a path from a spiritually charged liberation theology (Rastafarianism) of protest as we find in the work of Bob Marley and Peter Tosh—with such songs as "Natural Mystic," "Slave Driver," "War," and "Redemption Song"—and Mutah Baruka's poetry to the dominating dance-hall, "ragga muffin'," Caribbean version of the gangsta scene. Reduced to a whisper are the cries of liberation and turned up full blast are monotonous grunts and unimaginative lyrics to the gyrating, marketable combinations of sex and tacky aesthetics: gold jewelry, hair extensions and contemporary "konks," undersized clothing, and the exoticism of the market's current heirs to the thrown of the noble savage. The Caribbean sage has fallen to the Caribbean jester. A familiar and tired motif in popular cultural presentations of blackness. The decline is not without historical significance: Marley, Tosh, and Baruka are from Michael Manley progressive politics of the 1970s; the current strata are consequences of the International Monetary Fund (IMF) and the World Bank's strangulation of the Caribbean economies and protest thought; "Don't Worry, Be Happy" served (against Bobby McFerrin's protest) Reagan politics of evasion; the jester now serves a New World order in which sexual *simulation* (since free sexual practice is now perilous) offers symbolic displays of resistance: pelvic thrusts and grinds signify a concrete moment of power, which affords, albeit misguidedly so, some sense of dignity from being beyond it all; in the end, there is no systemic critique nor threat to systems there.[10]

The story of reggae is an important tale for the *politics* of black aesthetic productions: When black politics and aesthetics sway from their spiritual bases, they suffer the fate of going nowhere. Think of what happened to the popular group Earth, Wind, & Fire when they swayed (at least in their musical production) from their spiritual messages. Think of African American classical music, which by comparison has maintained its spiritual presence throughout: Ellington's "Come Sunday"; Holiday's "God Bless the Child"; Mingus's "Wednesday Night Prayer Meeting"; Roach and Lincoln's "Take Me Back Where I Belong"; Coltrane's "A Love Supreme" and "Om"; Sun Ra's cosmic excursions; and Oscar Peterson's recent live explorations of spirituality through musical performance. In soul, the obvious examples are Aretha Franklin and Marvin Gaye, whose *What's Going On* album is a benchmark not only in black aesthetics and political thought, but also black spirituality. An important difference between these musical forms and rap and hip-hop is the space the former offered for *mature* contributions. Bob Marley explored spirituality in his youth, but his most persuasive statements emerged in his thirties. Marvin Gaye's situation was similar. Franklin's remained throughout because she is also a gospel singer and soul is a spiritual music. There have been moments of spiritual striving in rap—moments that were quite effective, if groups such as Arrested Development and A Tribe Called Quest are representative, but for the most part, the theologies that emerge in rap and hip-hop, when they emerge, pale next to the protest theological music of the '60s and '70s.

My suspicion is that these limitations emerge from a lack of textual exegesis and constraints upon historical memory: Ellington, Holiday, Coltrane, Marley, Gaye, et al., were informed by the liberation motif of the book of Exodus and, with the exception of Marley (who used Marxist themes of alienation in his theory of oppression—as in "Crazy Baldheads"), the gospels' sermons to the meek—the poor, the indigent, the oppressed. Although there have been efforts to articulate a *postmodern* black theology (Cornel West, bell hooks, Michael Eric Dyson, Victor Anderson) that is sensitive to the spiritual demands of black music, it is not often clear whether these theologies are prescribing postmodernism or simply accepting it as a condition in which to theorize.[11] If the latter, then the project of a *liberation* project is not lost. But if the former, then the arsenal of antiliberatory assessments from Foucault to Lyotard needs to be taken into consideration: Is there really room for the spiritual in a postmodern age? Only if part of postmodern resistance is against modern secularism. In truth, when

I read avowed postmodern theological texts, I am often struck by the absence of the spiritual as a legitimating voice. Philosophy and cultural criticism are more the rules than the exceptions. Thus, if we return to the second possibility, where the social context of postmodernity is conceded, we arrive at my next and final concern in this regard: The holistic postmodern assessment of rap and hip-hop musical productions in postmodernist cultural studies.

Although there is a sense in which rap and hip-hop are postmodern, they are not often so in terms of what their artists actually talk about. Black postmodernity has always been a problematic ascription because many of the *aims* of black communities are toward forms of *modernity*. Modernist notions of selfhood and universality dominate many rap songs. In its early stages, rap music focused, for instance, on an elevated egological self. The early songs of the Sugar Hill Gang and Grand Master Flash had MCs who declared how great they were. In the popular rap movie *House Party* (1990), there is a crucial face-off scene in which the dozens were acted out in the form of each artist's rappin' skills. The *content* of the exchange was praise for each artist's self through a negation of the other's. Moreover, who claims to represent black communities, and often with claims to being more "authentically black," than rap artists? Far from postmodern anti-essentialists, in these artists one often finds even biological notions of blackness. Blackness emerges, often, as a Manichæan opposition to whiteness, and in the midst of these oppositions is usually a desire for the *material* benefits of modern industrial society: the mansion, the cars; the power.[12]

There are, however, exceptions. LL Cool J's career charts a course of temperance and growing maturity. With early "art" recordings and videos like "Going Back to Cali" and "Mamma Said Knock You Out," LL Cool J has managed to maintain a uniquely *aesthetic* vision of hip hop. In the *MTV Rockumentary* focus on his career, he points out that he has a family and is careful about spending and the "high life." He is also careful about the roles he plays in films. His self-image is, in other words, that of a responsible entertainer. In LL Cool J, there may very well be the mature rap artist. A similar conclusion can be made regarding KRS One, whose philosophical ruminations, rooted in Afrocentric cultural motifs and existential considerations of self-creation, mark a mature presence throughout the 1990s.[13] By further contrast, there is the work of the extraordinarily talented Me'Shell NdegéOcello, whose brilliant *Plantation Lullabies* evinces musical and literate black nationalism of a kind that defies most stereotypes of black nationalist productions. In its aesthetic scope and critical power, NdegéOcello's work has few (if any) equals in recent popular music: It is black in a way that is critical, liberatory, historical, and beautiful, and in those regards, it defies ascriptions of at least the politically pre- and post-modern.

I can go on, but instead I would like to turn to the aesthetic dimensions of rap and hip-hop, for by this point, the reader may mistakingly think I don't see anything positive in these art forms. It is my hope that the discussion thus far shows that I think the way in which these art forms have been discussed is problematic.

On the aesthetic level, rap is, without question, a *postmodern* art form. It is postmodern to the extent that it breaks every rule of modern aesthetics. Take, for instance, motifs of repetition, harmony, resemblance, and similitude.[14] We can think of how singing, poetry, and musical accompaniment play out in these terms.

Singing. Rap songs are called "songs" and are therefore registered with such music societies as BMI or ASCAP. The artists' copyrights are registered with the Library of Congress under categories of music with lyrics—in a word, songs. Yet, in rap we hear songs that are not quite songs, singing that is not quite singing. Most rap artists don't sing on key, because whether they do or not is *irrelevant.* Further, the sound of "rappin' " is often best achieved *without* being on key. Perhaps the most gruesome example of this assault on tonality is the rap artist Biz Markie's "You Got What I Need." Dressed in eighteenth-century attire—white powdered wig and all—Biz Markie simulates playing the piano, looking into the camera and, therefore, the audience's eyes, with a broken-heart puppy-dog face that is well-suited for ballads, then sings, wretchedly off-key, but wonderfully with passion, "You got what I need. . . ." I've seen the response of audiences to this song in many settings. After a visceral shiver, as if nails were scratched across a blackboard, there is an elation of realizing that *any one* can sing along to this tune and, with its heavy beat, dance to it as well. So they join in, to a chorus of off-key ecstasy. Rap, in this regard, takes a very postmodern attitude to harmony and dissonance: Neither really matters. Not to be pinned down, rap singing simply emerges as whatever the artist attempts. *Singing* talent is irrelevant. Audacity is all that counts. Again, it is a singing that is not singing as *institutionally* understood.

Rappin'. Moreover, a challenge to singing in rap is the activity of *rappin'.* To rap (a new verb) is to talk with a flare, with "hipness," about things that matter. It is a talking that is not ordinary talking. Think of the '60s' version, where "hip" young people would "rap" about what's goin' on. Singing in rap music is therefore much like a side dish; it is only part of the event.

Rappin' is a vernacular of its own. There is no pretense here of emulating the dominant idiom. Rap vernacular is constantly changing; rap and hip-hop artists experiment, they twist and turn and stretch the contours of the language; they take on a corporeality that points (with curved wrists and curlicued fingers) and props of the self—strong, embodied, fierce (even female rappers' shoulders are "broad")—in a visual aesthetics of the form, "Why don't you see. . . ?" The semiotics of rap syntax is polyvalent: ensemble rappin' isn't unusual, and even when there is a single rapper, the rhythm and grammar of the performance takes on a constant shifting of the body from left to right, from high to low, from perspective, that is, to other perspective. Although *tolerance* may not be high among some rap and hip-hop artists, one cannot help but think that a psychodrama of changing perception is at work in the bodily shifts that mark nearly all rap perform-ance. Dodging in and out, from side to side, there is the appearance of a boxing match, true, but it is not often that a jab or fist is thrown at an imaginary opponent instead of a pointing finger. Again, "You see. . . ?" A fighting that is not fighting; a talking that is not talking; a play that is not entirely play; a language that is not quite the dominant language. Look at rap in German, French, Italian, Hindi, Kiswahili. Its syntax remains the same.

Poetry. As in song, rap poetry is poetry that is not poetry. Again, the "not" here refers to conventions handed down from modernity. Rap artists *rhyme*, but they rhyme to beats and structures that are not dictated by mod-ern, and even antiquarian, conventions of pause and stanzas. Further, with-out the music, the rhymes often don't work. They are not like other poetic forms, which, when applied to music, become just that: poetry *applied* to music. In rap, there is no such application. The rhymes *are* part of the music.

Music. The not-quite theme continues here with many twists. The music *heard* is similar to most musics. It has time, pitch, rhythm, tonality, etc. What is different, and awfully postmodern, is its challenge to author-ship: Rap music has become music without musicians. Most rap music is "sampled." Sampling is the taping of an isolated section of a musical re-cording and "looping" or recording it in succession, over and over, for the purpose of background music for one's lyrics. Thus, the artist often plays no role in the *musical* production that accompanies his lyrics. It is taken from another artist's performance, an artist whose performance now con-tinues in part as mimesis of the original performance, but is now different because its context has changed. Imagine: An artist playing to James Brown leaves a string of musical signifiers that *now* signifies Kid 'n' Play. Or Kool and the Gang's and Brothers Johnson's music now signifying Coolio. Once removed enough, stored perhaps on a library of samples, the artists lose all reference: On the original recordings, the accompanying musicians would be listed in the credits. Although their performance remains, they have disappeared. The death of the author has taken concrete form as the death of the artists who *composed* and *performed* the accompaniment. Beyond the question of sampling, there is also musical equipment designed so that, with the aid of the proper studio equipment, one can compose music without being a musician. *How* music is produced is becoming a piece of knowledge like that associated with the inner core of the technologies we use: One knows how to push buttons, but not how they produce our desired effects. How things work is often lost to making them work for us. Modern instrumentation is, therefore, becoming lost as well: Horns are for classical and jazz musicians, not popular ones. A generation of people will evolve who think drums are the electronic boxes that now imitate them. Far-fetched? Modern Euro-music has honed itself down to a few key instruments; how many of us know or even care about the difference between the many types of brass, string, or percussive instruments that existed in the Middle Ages and antiquity? The musical innovation, then, is music without musicians and music without musical instruments. In their place are floating signifiers and digital technologies. In rap, one doesn't *perform* instrumental music. One *programs* it.

Now, this is not to say that rap cannot be done with musicians performing music. There have been instances, for example, *MTV Unplugged*, a program in which acoustical instruments are used. But even there, an important electronic device had to be added: the turntable was present for the sake of "scratching" records. Scratching is the use of the turntable's needle to scratch out a rhythm to syncopated turns of records on the turn table. But even here, there is a postmodern turn: The turntable was not designed to be a musical instrument but a conveyor of prior musical performances. Its potential as an instrument was realized by rap artists. The obvious limitation in an age of compact disks, however, is that even that innovation will eventually give way to its version of a drum machine: a scratch machine or synthesizer, perhaps.

We find in rap, then, an unquestionable site of postmodern aesthetics beyond the *ennui* that attracts a postmodernist like Jean-François Lyotard to the avant-garde; the postmodernism that undergirds rap and hip-hop aesthetics can be compared to birds in flight: warm-blooded creatures who are not mammals but find suddenly that their long arms, bereft of dexterity, also are wings; clumsy on land, in the air, they soar. It is no wonder that

rap and hip-hop emerge in even conservative cultural contexts; it has become the syntax of popular expression; even polished politicians and academics add a little polyrhythm to their four-four timed steps throughout
the '90s—think not only of Jesse Jackson but also of President Clinton's
embodiment and punctuation (in spite of his avowed preference for jazz).

Having ruminated on rap and hip-hop, let us now go on to a film. It is
indicative of the political climate at the close of the millennium that films
by such luminaries as Charles Burnett, Haile Gerima, Julie Dash, and Euz-
han Palcy are not greeted by Her Majesty and her other children as major
cultural events. In their stead, perhaps because of the heightened *academic*
attention Frantz Fanon has been receiving or because of the aura around its
filmmaker, Isaac Julien's *Frantz Fanon: "Black Skin, White Masks"* has taken
the moment by storm. Screenings pop up at nearly every "art" films event.
I saw a fifty-minute version of the film at York University in Canada.
Controversy loomed then, but the retort to all criticism lurked in the
wings: The film was not complete.

Then I found myself in an auditorium at New York University Law
School, where a seventy-minute film lay in waiting. Preceded by day one
of a star-studded conference, *Finding Fanon*, the film served as a star in its
own right, awaiting its "cue" to be unveiled, as it were, to all.[15] The conference and film became, then, a complete text: Stuart Hall, Françoise
Vergès, Maryse Condé, Mark Nash, and Julien, who appear in the film,
were present. In addition, major contributors to Fanon studies—Irene
Gendzier and Ato Sekyi-Otu—were there. James Forman attended, with
the announcement that he was still working on a book on Fanon in progress for over two decades. Some major contributors to postcolonial theory
also were there—namely, Ngugi wa Thiong'o and Gayatri Spivak. Then
there were the rest: Teresa de Lauretis (who spoke of Fanon's and everyone's "unconscious limitations"), Manthia Diawara, Robin D.G. Kelley,
Ella Habiba Shohat (who derided Fanon's supposed "nationalism" and lack
of diagnostic specificity), and Robert Stam (who extoiled Julien's film, especially its presentation of the powerful, sexualized homosexual gaze). Because of its relevance to Julien's film, Djamila Sahraoui's *La Moitié du ciel
d'Allah* (*The Other Half of Allah's Heaven*), a film that focuses on women of
the Algerian National Liberation Front and the situation of Algerian
women today, also was screened. Sahraoui was thus listed as a participant
of the meeting.[16]

Paget Henry and I had decided to make it our point to attend, especially
since Ato Sekyi-Otu and Ngugi wa Thiong'o were on the same panel. So

there we were. Perhaps misunderstanding about Fanon's supposed "nationalism" will be cleared up through their presentations? I hoped. I wasn't disappointed. The session was brilliant. Two memorable moments: Ngugi's articulation of *capitalist fundamentalism*. Hmmm. Sekyi-Otu, overjoyed and in respect to Ngugi, cited an Akanian proverb: "If I dropped dead today, I'd never regret it!" Then he pondered: "One wonders about the ancestor's reasoning about being able to regret at all after one has died. . . ."[17]

Later, as I sat next to Ngugi and Ato at the screening of the film, I began to appreciate the power of the ancestors' wisdom.

Before talking about the film, let us say some words on *film*.

Unlike music, film embodies the integration of many media. Long gone are the days of silent film, with at most a leitmotif by organ or orchestra. With the advent of sound technology, television, and videotape, the impact on interpretation raised by the range of mimetic interplay between screen and real world stepped onto new terrain. Crucial moments in a story can be "blacked out" while the soundtrack continues, creating an impact on interpretation, on imagination. Creative filmmakers drew upon a plethora of techniques with which to elicit moments of wonder, laughter, pain, sorrow, anger, horror, titillation, and, let us say it, *pathos* and *catharsis* to billions of people over the twentieth century. By the century's end, even music has become nearly unbearable without the inclusion of visual interpretation; a classic case of role reversal, in musical videos, we find *visual* leitmotifs, where sight accompanies sound. Within cinematic aesthetics, there are now so many genres, each of which mirrors various other aesthetic forms, that only a few can be mentioned here. There are the cinematic genres born from theater and burlesque: drama, comedy, musicals, tragedies, horror, and pornography. The cinematic and video genres drawn from historical, biographical, political, scientific, and journalistic essays: documentaries, news reports, and "talk" shows. There are "how to" films and videos, which are, in effect, manuals and learning aides. We already have mentioned music videos. As the technology gains sophistication, various *interactive* media—in cinemas, on televisions, and on portable computers—have evolved that may create new genres as well. Then there are the many variations that emerge among the avant garde. All this is to say that film is an evolving medium with seemingly endless possibilities. Key to these possibilities is imaginative power of interpretation.

Now, Isaac Julien is well-known in contemporary "art" and "cultural studies" film circles for approaching his subject matters with bold interpretive license, particularly with regard to subtextualizations of homoerotica. His *Looking for Langston* and *Darker Side of Black* are instances. In the first,

Langston Hughs's homosexuality is addressed through a thematic of his not being homophobic; in the second, Jamaican homophobia is addressed through a portrait of the regressive lyrics and attitudes of dance-hall reggae. Although Julien's context is aesthetic production, his expression is, in the end, the essay.

The advancement of the essay under the name of aesthetic creativity is not unusual. Yet there is an element of bad faith when an appeal to aesthetics is made in such cases. If appreciated, the text rings as "true." If challenged, the author denies truth and reminds us of the text's aesthetic status. "It's only a film" is a familiar retreat. A danger, where misinformation can be considered damaging, is that such productions are not always taken for aesthetic statements alone, and why should they be? After all, an essay, in the end, is not mere opinion or artistic vision. An essay can be contested not only for its validity but also its claims to and denials of truth. Consider, for instance, the work of Alice Walker. Walker has contributed to a number of understandings and misunderstandings of black *historical* reality through the essays that serve as subtexts of her fiction. Although she has coined the term *womanism*, as Aimé Césaire coined *negritude*, she also has provided context for an antiblack and antiradical feminist revisioning of one of the greatest radical activists in American history: Ida B. Wells-Barnett. Walker's short story, "Advancing Luna—and Ida B. Wells," presents an Ida B. Wells that is so blinded by race loyalties that she fails to admit gender injustices.[18] In a brilliant, genealogical archaeology of the motif of the "regressive race woman" Joy James traces the path from Walker's fictitious account of Wells-Barnett through to Valerie Smith's portrayal of her as "counterfeminist."[19] James's conclusion is worth a long quotation:

> Historical revisionism and historicism based in selective and skewed information concerning Wells-Barnett's sexual politics elide or distort the praxis of past radicals in order to shape perceptions and depictions of present-day race politics. Erasing the specificity of past radicalism promotes a doctrine of evolutionary leadership in which contemporary political or feminist leadership is uniformly taken to be more progressive than its predecessor. . . . Writers may construct contemporary womanist or black feminisms as more (gender) progressive than the views of women such as Ida B. Wells-Barnett, who led the antilynching campaigns. Walker's reading of Wells-Barnett as intimidated by racist violence into fearful denials and Smith's reading of Wells-Barnett as a counterfeminist place contemporary black feminist thought above the political thought of historical activists. This evolu-

tionary ascent toward the black feminist writer counters traditional notions of public intellectual as engagé; it allows the contemporary to transcend her predecessor in progressive agency, as the writer replaces the activist. In fictional dialogues between ancestry and progeny, the contemporary heroine, as moral and political agent, consistently triumphs over her militant race-woman predecessor. In our postmovement era the postmodern, professional writer and/or academic reigns as an intellectual. Validating progressive gender and race ideology in the symbolic analyst, one may supplant the activist with the commentator-essays as representative of ideal political leadership (*Transcending*, p. 80).

As I sat in the NYU Law School auditorium, I kept thinking of "Advancing Luna." The script of *Frantz Fanon* is, in a word, inscribed in its cast of "experts"—Homi Bhabha, Maryse Condé, Françoise Vergès, Stuart Hall—none of whom has written a major study on Fanon, although Vergès and Bhabha have written some essays.[20] Bhabha's essays are influential primarily among those who do not read Fanon at all.[21] Of interest is the caption "Cultural Critic" that demarcates these scholars in the film. One wonders why "cultural critic" is more appropriate than "Fanon scholar" for a film on Fanon. Although a popular designation in cultural studies these days, the notion of a cultural critic has always struck me as a problem. It betrays an arrogantly aesthetic and elitist attitude toward culture and politics: "Oh, we don't know what we are saying. Let us call in the *critic*." Or, "Oh, we have been blindly accepting our cultural allegiances. Let us call in the critic for some critical insight." Imagine perhaps a television show where two or three cultural critics hash it out on the *performance* of historical and recent popular events. Perhaps that's what's going on in the many so-called journalistic roundtables on news events: critics sitting in a circle hashing events out among themselves for the benefit of our enlightenment. With the exception of Bhabha—who hardly says anything about Fanon in the film, but instead walks stoically through the streets of London (or Chicago?) and stares with a solemn face at the camera in front of a portrait of Fanon and a copy of *Black Skin, White Masks*—most of the "critics" criticize Fanon in a portrayal reminiscent of the digression from Walker to Smith on Wells-Barnett. True, there are exceptions: M. Confiant, who reminds us of the racial conservatism of Martinique and the liberating impact of Fanon's writings on subsequent generations; J. Azonlay, with whom Fanon wrote some of his medical papers;[22] and an unforgettable moment of Fanon's brother and best friend, Jobi Fanon, attempting to read his brother's deathbed letter from Bethesda, MD.

The film begins with somber music (with all the evocative power of the cello) over which an Arab mental patient recites, in Arabic, a call for freedom. The Arabic is without English subtitles, although French interviews receive English subtitles for the audience and most interviews and dramatized segments are done in English. One rationale for not using subtitles for the Arabic is that Fanon's experience of first entering the corridors of the asylum is thereby better conveyed, since Fanon did not speak Arabic. An Arabic scholar, Nada Elia, has objected, in a conversation on the film, that what the Arabic patients were *saying* was important for the film and should be conveyed to the non-Arabic-speaking audiences who, after all, are not Fanon.[23] I find her argument persuasive. In any event, as the film moves on we find a weaving of docudrama with documentary footage and other dramatizations—often presented without explanation—the effect of which is to make unclear to all but experts what is going on *when,* and what is fact and what is fiction. I won't relate the film point by point because in the end the reader should see the film for her or himself and experience the effect of its various efforts, some of which are, as Angela Davis remarks in a blurb for the *Library of African Cinema Supplement,* "visually stunning."[24] Instead, I would like to focus on the politics that mattered most to the filmmaker by virtue of the absence of Fanon's revolutionary diagnoses of oppression and prescriptions for revolution in Africa and the rest of the Third World. Sexual politics, and consequently psychoanalysis, take center stage in this film. The portrait that emerges is a homophobic, misogynist Fanon obsessed with white women and a suprastructural white colonial father. At first, the sexual motifs may strike some viewers as innovative and perhaps even transgressive. For this viewer, however, they were in the end regressive. Let me explain.

First, the homoerotic subtext: The actor who plays Fanon walks around bare-chested and broods as Kobena Mercer and a male lover kiss each other passionately; and there is a portrait of a Martinican man in drag, referring to Faron's comment that although there were men who dressed up as women in Martinique, he was convinced that they led "normal sex lives." The homoerotic is an interesting dimension of the film, albeit without the lyrical and artistic sensitivity and intensity of, say, Marlon Riggs's *Tongues Untied.* That film's criticisms of homophobia in African American communities are inspired by profound love for those communities. Fanon spoke of homosexuality, and he did so in negative ways; however, the passages in which he spoke of homoeroticism in *Peau noire* require some discussion. Since they are all from "Le Nègre et la psychopathologie," where the black is discussed as a phobogenic object (in other words, a pathological object and a stimulus to anxiety), where could there be room for "normal" sexuality beyond that expressed by dominant European society? Not only do we need to consider how problematic it is to expect Faron to manifest contemporary sexual mores, we need also to consider homosexuality in clinical psychological terms: The shackles of "deviant sexuality" remain in clinical research. That is why there is controversy over whether one is born a homosexual or becomes one. Fanon's reading was, in fact, far more complex and advanced for the time in which *Peau noire* was composed (1951). He argued, for instance, that both a negrophobic white man and a negrophobic white woman regard the black man as a putative sex partner.[25] Since the white woman is not supposed to desire the black man, the sexual tension takes on the phobothematics of rape. For the white man, however, the tension is one of homosexual violence. We can see how these themes manifest themselves in the elaborated footnote from which Fanon's remark about "normal sex lives" emerged. I will use Markmann's translation, because it is quoted in the film:

> Let me observe at once that I had no opportunity to establish the *overt* presence of homosexuality in Martinique. This must be viewed as the result of the absence of the Oedipus complex in the Antilles. The schema of homosexuality is well enough known. We should not overlook, however, the existence there of what are called "men dressed like women" or "godmothers." Generally, they wear shirts and skirts. But I am convinced that they lead normal sex lives. They can take a punch like any "he-man" and *they are not impervious to the allures of women*—fish and vegetable merchants. In Europe, on the other hand, I have known several Martinicans who became homosexuals, always passive. But this was by no means a neurotic homosexuality: For them it was a means to a livelihood, as pimping is for others (*Peau noire*, p. 146, n. 44; *Black Skin*, p. 180, n. 44; my emphases).

Notice that Fanon implies here that Martinican heterosexual transvestites and Martinican bisexuals were not uncommon, and that black homosexual "passivity" was marketable in Paris perhaps because it fulfilled white male customers' fantasies of conquest.[26] Further, Fanon here has a category of "neurotic" homosexuality, which he suggests comprises masochistic and sadistic homosexuality. For Fanon, at least in this note, homosexuality that is neither masochistic nor sadistic is not neurotic. More problematic, however, is Fanon's later remark:

> I have never been able, without revulsion, to hear a man say of another man: "He is so sensual!" I do not know what the sensuality of a

man is. Imagine a woman saying of another woman: "She's so terribly desirable—she's darling. . ." (*Peau noire*, p. 163; in *Black Skin*, p. 201).

Fanon's confession of not knowing the sensuality of a man is his announcement of his heterosexuality. He aims these remarks against physician Michel Saloman, who referred to black men as "sensual." Fanon's point is not only that Saloman, a heterosexual, places himself in a homoerotic relation to every black man, but that even if Salomon were a homosexual, he fails to acknowledge that not every black man could be interested in being in a homoerotic relation with him. The racial codes displace homoerotic attraction through homoerotic "triggering": A homosexual who finds another man sensual is "normal." A heterosexual male who ascribes sensuality to males who are black suffers, in Fanon's view, from racist psychosexual displacement.

Given Fanon's reference to women in this passage, however, another question emerges. One wonders why Fanon does not point out rape and lesbian erotics with regard to the desires of white men and white women for black women. In a much quoted passage, he announces that he knows nothing about the woman of color, even though he has discussed quite a number of them starting with his chapter on the woman of color and the white man.[27] Fanon is here speaking about information from his clinical practice. The history of *clinical* studies or, for that matter, *any* studies of the mental health of women of color is recent, and, I would add, for reasons that are all too understandable. Most psychiatrists and mental health workers were white men. The client needs to visit the mental health professional at times of great vulnerability. Probabilities of sexual violence are high in those instances, and because most interracial sexual violence/exploitation was by white men on women of color, I don't see how the paucity of colored female patients could have been otherwise.[28] The problem is exacerbated by what white men signify in relation to black women to this day: When white men are involved, women of color, particularly black women, are considered unrapable. Given this logic, the rapist that emerges in the black woman's reality as a structural phobogenic object, then, may be the black man. A young African American woman reporter for CNN was recently interviewed by *USA Today*. In the interview, she announced that she was dating white men exclusively because "they are more feminist than black men."[29] She then added, after some critical responses from another black woman, that she is now strongly interested in one day dating a black man. I wondered how she could determine what black men think *romantically* if she had not in fact dated any. In a conservative environment, there are matrices of permissible interracial relations. Because the black penis signifies a violent moment, the conclusion is simple: permissible racial crossings emerge only upon or from women of color. One would not get much mileage from sounding an alarm on black female sexual violence upon white men and white women.

Why this detour?

The film's second sexual theme is Fanon's supposed policing of black women's bodies through his criticisms of Mayotte Capécia's autobiographical novel *Je suis martiniquaise*.[30] At a crucial moment, Françoise Vergès declares that if Fanon can argue that his being with his white wife was nobody's business, why not Capécia with her white man? Behind Vergès is a picture of an anonymous Martinican or Guadeloupian woman in traditional headdress. A powerful image, indeed. As a black woman in the audience responded at that moment, "Yes, why not!" What is missing, however, are some crucial facts. Fanon never claimed that black women should not be romantically involved with white men. He argued that it was pathological to be romantically involved with whites on the sole basis of their being white, a position many of us share today. Capécia had declared that "I should have liked to marry, but to a white man" (p. 202).[31] A white man with the worst character is better than a black man with the highest virtues save one—being white. Vergès claims that Capécia was destitute and avoiding an abusive father, but in the autobiography she is a high-French laundress who supports her white lover. Her obsession with whiteness is such that she wears mostly white, European clothing and her profession, Fanon argued, exemplifies her associations with whiteness—cleanliness, purity, goodness. Here we find a point of dishonesty in the film, because for nonexperts, the recurring portrait of an anonymous Martinican or Guadeloupian woman "is" Capécia, in spite of the fact that Capécia wouldn't be caught dead in such an outfit. Moreover, it is strange reasoning that destitution and an abusive father lead to universal condemnation of a particular *race* of men. Do abused white women who, given declarations of abuse these days, are multitude, run in search of colored male lovers? At the end of the autobiography, when Capécia's lover abandons her and their child, she returns immediately to her father. How does this event comport with Vergès's interpretation of her actions? Vergès should also have added that Fanon called Capécia's work cut-rate merchandise for good reason: The literary award the book received, the Prix des Antilles, was from a panel of six white men. Capécia's is a familiar tale of pathological fantasy. No wonder she followed up with a "coming out" text: *La Négresse blanche* ("The White Negress").[32] In that work, Capécia unleashes much venom against black men and particularly black women, whom she not only refers to as "dirty niggers," but also as sluts and as an array of other invectives. Unlike the anonymous Martinican woman in the portrait behind Vergès, Capécia was a classic example of the French *evolvée—blanche*, straightened hair, at home in white clothing and white apperception, and especially hateful of the abased *négresse*. Observe:

> [Lucia, the négresse] sought pleasure with such a frenzy, she was worse than a cat in heat. Isaure [the mullata] listened to her with a mysterious smile. Sometimes she was envious of the black woman who didn't have any more scruples than an animal (p. 37).[33]

I am here reminded of Audre Lorde, who asked, "What is the theory behind racist feminism?"[34]

After scenes castigating Fanon's chauvinism, other scenes emerge with Fanon entering a bedroom, where a white woman awaits on a bed. Still photos of his wife, Marie-Josèphe Dublé Fanon, flicker on the screen as subliminal statements. Eventually, the woman is naked. Fanon, nude, sits next to her. She is still, and the photography is such that, although there is daylight, the room seems sterile and cold. The woman's body looks as though she is about to receive an intrusive examination. She is inert. Divorced from herself. Disembodied in ways reminiscent of the woman in Sartre's *Being and Nothingness*, whose hand lay, as pure "thing," in the hands of her suitor. Fanon's right hand moves up to her shoulder and gropes her flesh in an effort at a caress.

Now, why not issue some reality here? Fanon, a handsome black man in the 1950s walking into a room to make love with a white woman (who may or may not be his wife), would no doubt find himself in a situation of mutual desire.[35] Why not her reaching for him as he reached for her? Why not conversation, kissing—all those things that *lovers* do? Carefully woven into the scene is the negation of the woman's desire for Fanon and, by implication, white female desire for black men. A truly racially transgressive, and perhaps progressive, portrayal would be their mutual lust. What complicates the scene further is that later in the film the actress in the bed is also the actress who plays Simone de Beauvoir, who wrote in her autobiography, *The Force of Circumstances,* of her and Sartre's meeting with Fanon in Rome. Who was the woman in the bed? By implication, she was Josèphe Dublé *or* Simone de Beauvoir or sufficiently both to signify that *any* white woman would have sufficed.

Why do I say that the scene is racially regressive? Return to the case of Capécia. Why wasn't there a dramatization of Capécia in bed with her white lover? Why weren't passages from her texts read? Capécia was spoken for; Capécia was referred to but never *seen*. An anonymous French West Indian woman's portrait stood in her place. The woman in the portrait is passive; her head tilted to the right, her eyes—awkward; her persona—controlled; her gait—oppressed; her agency—erased.[36] Capécia's relations with her white lover are kept hidden and are thus private and "pure." Fanon, on the other hand, is called upon to play the role of predatory black male of the hour.

The charge of racial regressivism pertains especially to what is supposedly the film's most controversial scene. Again: Fanon stares at the camera while Kobena Mercer kisses a lover (who, by the way, resembles Fanon more than the actor chosen for the role). Fanon turns and looks at the lovers. Mercer turns and stares at Fanon. Supposedly unable to take the homoerotic look, Fanon turns away and looks back at the camera. Fine. But what if one of the homosexual lovers were white? Why not continue the motif of interracial transgression and go with it, especially since Fanon's actual discussions of homosexuality and homoeroticism have to do, as we have seen, with *interracial* relations? Aren't we in a society that already presumes homosexuality exists in colored communities? And consider again Fanon's remark about mandatory black passivity in *public* interracial homosexual liaisons. What might have been the effect if (was against such films as *The Crying Game* and *Pulp Fiction*, in which interracial homosexuality is in fact interracial *heterosexuality*) Julien were to articulate a form of interracial *homosexuality*, where both the black and the white male lovers had agency?

In the end, we see in *Frantz Fanon* the same set of images with which popular audiences are familiar: black men who want to jump in bed with everybody, including each other, and who are thereby violent predators of white women. Black females have no agency, and white males are so normative that they are afforded a protected space of anonymity and privacy through assumed, suprastuctural, and abstract desire.[37] One "sees" only black predators, black homosexuals, and victimized women—a far cry from transgressive and progressive politics.[38]

There is much more that can be contested in the film. Mohammed Harbi, who is well-known for two books on the Algerian war, claims that Fanon was a member of the most conservative factions of the Algerian National Liberation Front. In addition, Harbi and the other critics assert that Fanon romanticized the liberatory role of Algerian women in the struggle, a romanticization produced by his utopic vision of postrevolutionary Algeria.[39] All this is said in spite of Fanon's having been a member

of the secularist faction, which can hardly be seen as conservative or fundamental. With regard to Algerian women, there is a telling contrast between
the experts' testimonies in Julien's film and the portrait that emerges in
Sahraoui's *La Moitié du ciel d'Allah*. Sahraoui's film shows that women in
fact did *more* than many of us imagined. Thus, while Fanon is accused of
exaggerating women's relationship with the revolution in Julien's film, he
is left with a possible charge of underrepresenting women's roles in the
second film, in which he is, by the way, not mentioned. To Fanon's credit,
he pointed out in *L'an V de la révolution algérienne* that for purposes of
security he could not state the full scope and nature of women's involvement in the Algerian liberation struggle. How effective could they have
been if *all* Algerian women were suspect? Moreover, what is of great importance but rarely mentioned is Fanon's continued discussion of the Algerian woman in the Algerian family. The Algerian family, he argued, was
thrown into a direct, internal conflict between its traditional identity and
its revolutionary one. This conflict, he claimed, would permeate the whole
society. Fanon's thesis was, therefore, that the liberation struggle was raising
an *internal* discourse on women's rights.

History has confirmed Fanon's theory. The current conservative back-
lash in Algeria is in response to a multitude of issues—for instance, as Irene
Gendzier pointed out in her discussion at the conference, the impact of the
Algerian economy's dependence on exporting oil in the midst of major
markets (e.g., the United States) focusing on Saudi Arabian oil instead of
North African oil, and the social and political instability of such impact
in the midst of an Algerian internal struggle on gender, secularism, and
modernity.

In the end, despite a melancholic theme, grand shots of deserts and col-
orful, robust flowers, it is clear that the filmic essay's goal is such that,
besides the Fanonian encomium for his body to inspire curiosity and wonder, sexual identity politics have subordinated radical revolutionary politics.
Fanon's revolutionary praxis having been occluded, the only criteria of
assessment remaining are his stands on gender and sexual orientation. It is
fitting that the film ends with Fanon in a desert. His politics, the film
intimates, are barren and lead nowhere.

So I went to a bar with some fellow searchers at the end of the evening.
Our guide was a graduate student who helped organize the conference.
We drank and talked politics a bit. Afterward, we went to 1st Avenue to
get a cab for Ato Sekyi-Otu. "Let us see if see if five black men can get a
cab in New York!" I said.

Fifteen minutes later, as cab after cab passed by or whose driver waved "no" or drove around us to whites who had only to tug an ear, our graduate student host was emboldened enough (perhaps through embarrassment and anger) to walk in front of a cab. As that cab stopped, Henry called us from the other corner. A cab had stopped for him without duress. So we took that one. Walking over, I said to Ato, "You know, the only time a yellow cab ever stopped for me, the driver turned out to be from Ghana." As we entered the cab, I smiled. The driver was a Sikh.

After saying farewell to Ato, I took the subway up to my grandmother's house in the Bronx. It was odd being on a New York subway again, especially at 1 am. I took out reading material to prepare for the next week's seminar at Brown: Foucault's *The Order of Things*. Later that day, I was on the AMTRAK again, riding home to Providence. Although I was on the right train at the right time and had the right ticket for the cars I explored, it took a while to find an empty seat—crowded as those cars were on that autumn Saturday morning. A spot between duffle bags and some sleeping students. I was relieved that I need never block that train in order to make my way home.

Notes

1. Isaac Julien, *Frantz Fanon: "Black Skin, White Masks,"* produced by Mark Nash (London: Normal Films, 1996).

2. For a portrait of this dimension of aesthetic resistance, see M. Nourbese Philip's pamphlet, *Caribana: African Roots and Continuities—Race, Space and the Poetics of Moving* (Toronto: Poui, 1996).

3. The work described here is Vusi Khumalo's untitled painting of a scene from a South African township. It appears at the end of this volume, courtesy of the painting's owner, Karen Baxter.

4. Sources are numerous. For discussion, see especially *The Black Aesthetic*, ed. by Adison Gayle, Jr. (Garden City, NY: Anchor Books/Doubleday, 1972); and Sandra Adell's *Double Consciousness/Double Bind*.

5. The story is well known and related in Clint Eastwood's biographical drama *Bird* (Warner Brother's). Gillespie told Parker that a white man will one day produce a film on him but not on Gillespie, because Parker lets whites see him "fuck up." As is well-known, the drugged-out jazz musician is now a cliché on the cinematic screen. For more on both Parker and Gillespie, see Bill Crow, *Jazz Anecdotes* (New York and Oxford: Oxford University Press, 1990), chapters 38 and 39. See also John Fordham's *Jazz*.

6. The following account is based on my experience of growing up in the Bronx in the 1970s. I was among the few who literally got to see rap evolve by attending the outdoor jams and Saturday-night house parties of the 1970s. Living in New York City in the 1980s was ideal for observing the commodification stage of rap and hip hop until the "West Coast" invasion near the decade's end. My goal here is philosophical, not historical, so there will be some artists and their music left out. Full-scale accounts are available in Tricia Rose's *Black Noise* (Middletown: Wesleyan University Press); Houston Baker's work; and Bakari Kitwana's *The Rap on Gangsta Rap* (Chicago: Third World Press, 1994). See also chapters 1 and 2 of Michael Eric Dyson's *Reflecting Black: African-American Cultural Criticism* (Minneapolis and London: University of Minnesota Press, 1993) and various sections of Gilroy's *Black Atlantic*, especially chap. 3. See also *Vibe* 4, no. 6 (August 1996) for interviews with some of the artists discussed in this essay; and George Yancy, " 'Gangsta Rap': Let It Speak for Itself," *The Philadelphia Tribune* (Friday, January 6, 1995), p. 9E.

7. An important text in this regard is *Black Popular Culture: A Project by Michele Wallace*, ed. by Gina Dent (Seattle: Bay Press, 1992).

8. Cases in point are Angela Y. Davis's 1993 interview with Ice Cube in *Transition*, the journal edited by the team of scholars in Harvard's Afro-American studies program and Du Bois Institute, and bell hooks' interview of Ice Cube in *Outlaw Culture*. Ice T went on a college speaking tour. I must confess, however, that both Ice Cube and Ice T weren't saying any *less* than some of the celebrity intellectuals who tour the college circuit, so in the end, their entry into the world of celebrity intellectuals represents a critique, if anything, of some of those scholars' intellectual bankruptcy.

9. This talk was a Purdue University Black Cultural Studies consortium held during the fall 1995 semester.

10. For a succinct discussion of the Jamaican economic situation, see Claremont Kirton, *Jamaica: Debt and Poverty*, with additional material by James Ferguson (Oxford: Oxfam, 1992). For an account of Michael Manley's political philosophy and the U.S., Canadian, and British response to it, see Michael Manley, *Jamaica: Struggle in the Periphery* (London: Third World Media Limited, 1982).

11. Their texts are many. I have already mentioned West's *Prophesy, Deliverance!* See also his *Prophetic Fragments* (Grand Rapids and Trenton: William B. Eerdman's and Africa World Press, 1988), where a number of essays focus on black music. Michael Eric Dyson's *Reflecting Black* and *Between God & Gangsta Rap* (New York and Oxford: Oxford University Press, 1996) are two instances. And finally, see Victor Anderson's *Beyond Ontological Blackness: An Essay on African American Religious and Cultural Criticism* (New York: Continuum, 1995). For a critique of these academics' discussions and role in the dessimination and presentation of rap and hip-hop to academic culture, see Kitwana's *The Rap on Gangsta Rap*.

12. For discussion of materialism in rap and hip-hop, see Bobby R. Dixon's "Toting Technology: Taking It to the Streets" in *Existence in Black.*

13. See, for example, a memorable session of the BET talk show, *Youth Summit* (February 23, 1997), in which KRS One is the special guest.

14. There are more, but these categories work well enough for the textualization of the "classical period," which for most of us is the modern era, developed by Foucault in *The Order of Things*, part I.

15. *Finding Fanon: Critical Geneaologies* (The Center for Media, Culture, and History and the Africana Studies Program and Institute of Afro-American Affairs, New York University, October 11–12, 1996).

16. Of equal interest were Fanon scholars peculiarly absent: Edouard Glissant, a countryman of Fanon and his living intellectual rival (if it is proper to use that term), who was in residence on Manhattan island, at the Graduate Center of the City University of New York; bell hooks, who appears in a volume precipitated by the film, *"The Fact of Blackness": Fanon and Visual Representation*, and who lives just a few blocks away from NYU; Hussein Abdilahi Bulhan, who we may recall is the author of *Fanon and the Psychology of Oppression* and who lives just down the way in Washington, D.C. Then there were the many other uninvited Fanon scholars in the U.S. at the time: Lou Turner, author of *Frantz Fanon, Soweto & American Black Thought* (Chicago), Olufemi Taiwo (Chicago), Dismas Masolo (Louisville), Sonia Kruks (Amherst and Oberlin), Nada Elia (Boston), Nigel Gibson (New York City), Sylvia Frederici (Long Island), Abdhul JanMohamad (Berkeley), Sylvia Wynter (Palo Alto), Tsenay Serequeberhan (Boston), Neil Lazarus (Providence), and Edward Said (New York City), to name a few. Perhaps they all couldn't have been there.

17. I recently heard my mother invoke this proverb. It is a proverb that has survived in the African diaspora, especially among Jamaicans.

18. Alice Walker, "Advancing Luna—And Ida B. Wells" in *You Can't Keep a Good Woman Down* (New York: Harcourt Brace Jovanovich, 1981).

19. Valerie Smith's "Split Affinities," in *Conflicts in Feminism*, ed. by Marianne Hirsh and Evelyn Fox Keller (New York: Routledge, 1990). Joy James's critical genealogical discussion appears in her *Transcending the Talented Tenth*, chap. 3: "Sexual Politics: An Antilynching Crusader in Revisionist Feminism."

20. I have already listed some of Bhabha's essays in my discussion of Fanon in part 1 of this volume. Vergès's only publication on Fanon at that time was a highly informative article she wrote for *Fanon: A Critical Reader*, entitled, "To Cure and To Free."

21. Bhabha is not my focus here, but one need only look at the recent texts in Fanon studies cited throughout this volume for instances of nearly universal rejec-

tion by Fanon scholars. Bhabha's hegemony is in postmodern cultural studies, where no full-length study of Fanon has emerged and where perhaps the most historically uninformed set of essays have come into print. This is not to say that cultural studies' interpretations of Fanon are necessarily problematic. What is at the heart of the matter is the problem of disingenuous scholarship: Reading Fanon is not the primary concern among scholars there; it is Fanon as occasion for alternative projects. Now, this practice of using Fanon as a context I do not entirely reject. What concerns me is the extent to which such scholars present their work as nonrevisionary. In many instances, as with Gwen Bergner, Henry Louis Gates, Jr., and Bhabha, to name a few, the instructive story is not what they include (which is too often easily shown to be false) but what they *exclude*. As we have already seen, it is important to read the works of the people Fanon has criticized before we take it upon ourselves to defend them. Similarly, when Bhabha presents a Lacanian Fanon—ahistorical and well-suited for contemporary postmodern cultural studies—he interestingly excludes discussion of Fanon's *rejection* of Lacanian psychoanalysis in his discussion of psychopathology in *Peau noire, masques blancs*.

22. For instance, Fanon and Azoulay, "La socialthérapie dans un service d'hommes musulmans: difficultés méthodologiques," *L'Information Psychiatrique* 4, no. 9 (1954). In the film, Azoulay announces that patients were not held in chains in Blida-Joinville Hospital. Fanon's arrival, he said, was galvanizing and liberating. The "chains" of legend were metaphorical.

23. For some of Nada Elia's views on Fanon, see her article, "Violent Women: Surging into Forbidden Quarters" in *Fanon: A Critical Reader*.

24. *Library of African Cinema Supplement 1997* (San Francisco)—*The Decolonized Eye: Six Films from Africa and the Caribbean*, p. 3. Note also how, with my criticisms of this film, we are again in Lugosi land, where bad press is still press.

25. See *Peau noire*, p. 127/*Black Skin*, p. 156.

26. I am reminded by contrast of Malcolm X's remarks in his *Autobiography* on his hipster days in New York City. He mentioned friends who were invited to affluent white men's homes to perform sexual fantasies. Among them was the white males' desire to be dominated by black men and women. Fanon's discussion of *observed* activities suggest that publicly, many white men express desire to dominate. Privately, however, stories differ. Some desire domination and some desire to be dominated.

27. The passage is in *Peau noire*, p. 145; in *Black Skin*, pp. 179–80.

28. The now-classic discussion and critique of interracial sexual demographics is Angela Davis's *Women, Race, and Class*. See also Joy James's discussion interracial rape in *Resisting State Violence in U.S. Culture*.

29. Ann Oldenburgh's interview with Farai Chideya under the title, "Serves Up Gen. X Politics for CNN," *USA Today* (October 1996), p. 4D.

30. Mayotte Capécia, *Je suis martiniquaise* (Paris: Corréa, 1948). Fanon's criticisms are in chap. 2 of *Peau noire*.

31. For discussion, see T. Denean Sharpley-Whiting's, "Anti-Black Femininity and Mixed-Race Identity: Engaging Fanon to Reread Capécia" in *Fanon: A Critical Reader*.

32. Mayotte Capécia, *La Négresse blanche* (Paris: Coréa, 1950).

33. This translation is T. Denean Sharpley-Whiting's from her article, "Anti-Black Femininity and Mixed-Race Identity," p. 160.

34. *Sister Outsider*, p. 112.

35. This is not to say that there wouldn't be desire if the woman were black, but Julien's scene dictates the matrix. Prior to marrying Jose Dublé, Fanon had relationships with black women as well. See Peter Geismar's *Frantz Fanon* (New York: Dial Press, 1973). I mention this because the film only identifies his relationship(s) with white women.

36. This tactic of portraying passive women of color in literature and popular culture, especially when black men are being portrayed as *victimizers*, is all to familiar. For some discussion, see Ama Ata Aidoo's "Literature, Feminism, and the African Woman Today," in *Reconstructing Womanhood, Reconstructing Feminism: Writings on Black Women*, ed. by Delia Jarrett-Macauley (London and New York: Routlede, 1994).

37. For discussion of anonymity in colonial and race contexts, see *Fanon and the Crisis of European Man*, chap. 3.

38. On the limitations of this form of seeing, see my essay "Existential Dynamics of Theorizing Black Invisibility" in *Existence in Black*.

39. Harbi's books are *La Guerre commence en Algérie* (Paris: Histoire Julliard, 1954) and *Le FLN: mirage et réalité*. Paris: Éditions Jeune Afrique, 1980).

Epilogue:

The Lion and the Spider
(An Anticolonial Tale)1

"Gee, Mama, why is the lion called the king of the jungle when on nature programs we only see lions on the plains?" asked Asani.

Asani's mom thought for a moment and seemed to disappear into another time, as her face broadened into a warm smile.

". . . Mama?"

"Yes, dear?"

"What are you thinking about?"

"Oh, I'm thinking about a story my great-grandfather told me when I was a little girl like you."

"A story? What kind of story?"

"A story about what might have happened long ago. A story about how the lion lost his title as king of the jungle. Would you like to hear it?"

Asani was excited with curiosity. "Of course, Mama!"

Asani's mom drew her closer and onto her lap. Comfortable in her mom's arms, Asani snuggled up and prepared to listen to the tale of long, long ago.

၃၅

The lion, king of all the jungle, often let out a loud roar to make sure that everyone knew who he was. He would sneak up behind other animals while they drank at the pond and roar a mighty roar, scaring them into the water. Sometimes he would sneak up on a monkey and frighten the poor monkey straight up the tree and on to another tree!

"I am the mightiest in the land!" Mr. Lion would declare, pounding his chest and kicking up a lot of dust and leaves.

One day, while sneaking around the forest with his usual stealth in search of a victim, he came upon a spider, a toad, and a lizard who were discussing the matter of where to settle down for a nice forest picnic.

"Well—*rebbit!*—I think we should settle down by the pond—*rebbit!*," said Ms. Toad.

"Oh, no," said Mr. Lizard, "we would be in great danger there. The birds like to gather there for thirsty little creatures."

"But it is oh so hot," added Ms. Toad. "We could have a delightful swim there after our meal."

Ms. Spider was about to state her opinion on the matter when she was suddenly interrupted by an unusually loud roar.

It was Mr. Lion.

Ms. Toad and Mr. Lizard were nearly frightened out of their skins! Ms. Toad hopped into a hollow log, and Mr. Lizard quickly scurried up a tree.

But Ms. Spider didn't budge. She looked at Mr. Lion and shook her head from side to side. "How rude," she said.

Mr. Lion was shocked.

Who did this little spider think she was? She wasn't afraid of the mighty Mr. Lion!

He roared again.

But Ms. Spider didn't move.

He roared again and again and again until he was nearly out of breath.

"Why aren't you afraid of me!" he cried. "Don't you know that I'm the king of the jungle?"

Ms. Spider shook her head from side to side again and said, "Tsk, tsk, tsk. Too bad."

Mr. Lion was puzzled. "What do you mean?" he asked.

"Well," she said. "How could you be the king of the jungle when everyone knows that the bravest, the toughest, and the smartest creature in the jungle is Ms. Spider?"

Mr. Lion couldn't believe his ears. He chuckled—

"You? *You*?"

And then he laughed,

"YOU? Ha, ha, ha!"

But Ms. Spider wasn't amused. "Oh, yes," she said. "Me."

"Why, I could crush you with my eyelash," said Mr. Lion, smugly.

"Oh, I see," answered Ms. Spider. "You laugh at me because I am small. But size has nothing to do with strength and courage. I tell you what, let's make a bet on who is the most brave and the most feared creature in the forest. Whoever wins will be the rightful king or queen of the jungle."

Mr. Lion thought Ms. Spider was joking. So to humor her, he said, "I would most certainly like to do so. And since I am a very good sport, I shall let you choose the terms of our bet."

"How very considerate of you!" exclaimed Ms. Spider. "Okay. We shall each attack the largest animal that passes through the forest today. Whoever of us can jump on that animal's back, bite her, and leave her frozen with fear so that she refuses to fight back, wins."

"Hmmm," thought Mr. Lion out loud. "You like to live dangerously, don't you, Ms. Spider?"

"Are you *scared*, Mr. Lion?"

"No, no, no. Nothing scares me. I am the king of the jungle!"

"We shall see," said Ms. Spider. Just then, a herd of elephants came upon the edge of the forest to munch on some delicious leaves. Ms. Spider's lips stretched into a plotting smile. "Mr. Lion," she said, "here are my terms. Each of us must jump on the back of one of those elephants and bite her. Whichever of us she fights back and throws off of her back will be the loser."

"Nooo problem," said Mr. Lion confidently. He rushed over to the elephants and paused. As he looked up at them, his head went back so far that it almost touched his spine. "Uhm, uhm," he began to stutter.

"Wait!" yelled Ms. Spider. "Since these are my terms, let *me* go first."

Mr. Lion didn't hesitate. "Okay, Ms. Spider. Being a gentleman, I shall let you go first."

"Thank you." Ms. Spider spat some webbing onto the top of a tree, swung through the air, and landed on the back of the largest elephant, Ms. Gigantuan. She sunk her choppers into Ms. Gigantuan's back and bit away!

But Ms. Gigantuan Elephant did nothing. She simply continued her business of picking off leaves and fruits from the trees with her trunk.

After a few moments of snarling and biting, Ms. Spider spat some web into the air, swung off the elephant, and landed right in front of Mr. Lion.

"Wow!" exclaimed Ms. Toad—while cautiously peeking out of her hollow log.

"Incredible!" declared Mr. Lizard from the top of the tree.

"Gee," said Mr. Lion. Then he remembered—*he* was supposed to be the king of the jungle. So, he declared, "Not bad, Ms. Spider. But *I* can do much better." He puffed up his chest, clenched his paws, pressed his lips, and marched—no, stomped!—his way over to the herd of elephants.

He roared and then leaped into the air onto the back of Ms. Gigantuan and began to bite and scratch and claw and . . . and. . . .

Ms. Gigantuan Elephant raised an angry eyebrow. "Enough!" she screamed, raising her trunk over her back and grabbing Mr. Lion. She threw him to the ground with a loud THUMP!

Mr. Lion screamed in pain.

Then Ms. Gigantuan ran up to him, grabbed him again, and pounded him over and over into the ground.

Ms. Toad and Mr. Lizard covered their eyes at the terrible sight.

Finally, Ms. Gigantuan Elephant let Mr. Lion limp away, with his tail curled up between his hind legs and his head hung low.

Mr. Lion now knew that he could no longer call himself the king of the jungle. He felt so ashamed that he continued on his way, limping and licking his wounds, until he was far out of sight from any of the animals in the forest and found himself on the open plains. To this day, that is where lions remain.

But spiders, as we all know, live everywhere. Thanks to Ms. Spider they all carry the knowledge that on that special day, long, long ago, one of them outwitted a lion and in so doing, reminded all of us that improbable odds are not always impossible ones.

Note

1. Dedicated to the following children: Mathieu Alexandr Gordon, Jennifer Seren Gordon, Anthony Christopher Evans, Andrew Solomon Evans, Dionne Evans, Marcus Musatto Evans, Laurie Garel, and Joseph Garel.

Untitled (1996), by Vusi Khumalo, from the Karen Baxter Collection, photographed by Robert Dillworth.

INDEX

About the Author

LEWIS R. GORDON teaches Africana philosophy and contemporary religious thought at Brown University, where he also is an affiliate of Latin American Studies, a member of the Center for the Study of Race and Ethnicity, and a Presidential Faculty Fellow of the Pembroke Center for the Study and Teaching of Women. He also has taught at Purdue University, where he was associate professor of philosophy and African American studies; Yale University, where he received his doctorate in philosophy as a Danforth-Compton fellow; and Lehman College, where he was a former Lehman Scholar. His books include *Bad Faith and Antiblack Racism* (Humanities Press), *Fanon and the Crisis of European Man: An Essay on Philosophy and the Human Sciences* (Routledge), and the edited volumes *Existence in Black: An Anthology of Black Existential Philosophy* (Routledge) and, with T. Denean Sharpley-Whiting and Renée T. White, *Fanon: A Critical Reader* (Blackwell). He is executive editor of *Radical Philosophy Review* and *The Newsletter of the Fanon Group*, and associate editor of *The C.L.R. James Journal*, *The Journal of Africana Philosophy*, and *Sophia* (in the Philippines). He is a fellow of the Society for Values in Higher Education.

RENÉE T. WHITE (author of the foreword) teaches sociology and urban studies at Central Connecticut State University. She is author of *Putting Risk in Perspective: Black Teenage Lives in the Era of AIDS* (Rowman & Littlefield) and co-editor of *Fanon: A Critical Reader* and *Spoils of War: Women, Cultures, and Revolutions* (Rowman & Littlefield). She has been a Mellon fellow and is a fellow of the Society for Values in Higher Education.